P9-AGT-939

A COMPLETE GUIDE

LAKE TAHOE & RENO

FIRST EDITION

LAKE TAHOE & RENO

Includes California Gold Country
& the Northern Sierra Nevada

Jim Moore

The Countryman Press
Woodstock, Vermont

I would like to dedicate this book in memory of my mother, Jeanne F. Moore, who nurtured my spirit of adventure. Also, to my brother, Louis E. Moore, who shares my love of the legends and lore of the Old West; and to my wife, Kathy Moore— who is both adventurous in spirit, and patient with me.

Copyright © 2009 by Jim Moore

First Edition

All rights reserved. No part of this book may be reproduced in any way by any electronic or mechanical means, including information storage and retrieval systems, without permission in writing from the publisher, except by a reviewer, who may quote brief passages.

ISBN 978-1-58157-082-3

Cover photo by Bridget Besaw/Aurora Photos
Interior photos by the author unless otherwise specified
Book design by Bodenweber Design
Page composition by Eugenie S. Delaney
Maps by Mapping Specialists Ltd., Madison, WI © The Countryman Press

Published by The Countryman Press, P.O. Box 748, Woodstock, Vermont 05091

Distributed by W. W. Norton & Company, Inc., 500 Fifth Avenue, New York, NY 10110

Manufactured in the United States of America

10 9 8 7 6 5 4 3 2 1

GREAT DESTINATIONS TRAVEL GUIDEBOOK SERIES

Recommended by *National Geographic Traveler* and *Travel + Leisure* magazines

[A] CRISP AND CRITICAL APPROACH, FOR TRAVELERS WHO WANT TO LIVE LIKE LOCALS.
—*USA Today*

Great Destinations™ guidebooks are known for their comprehensive, critical coverage of regions of extraordinary cultural interest and natural beauty. The authors in this series are professional travel writers who have lived for many years in the regions they describe. Each title in this series is continuously updated with each printing to ensure accurate and timely information. All the books contain more than one hundred photographs and maps.

Current titles available:

THE ADIRONDACK BOOK

ATLANTA

AUSTIN, SAN ANTONIO
  & THE TEXAS HILL COUNTRY

THE BERKSHIRE BOOK

BERMUDA

BIG SUR, MONTEREY BAY & GOLD COAST WINE
  COUNTRY

CAPE CANAVERAL, COCOA BEACH
  & FLORIDA'S SPACE COAST

THE CHARLESTON, SAVANNAH
  & COASTAL ISLANDS BOOK

THE CHESAPEAKE BAY BOOK

THE COAST OF MAINE BOOK

COLORADO'S CLASSIC MOUNTAIN TOWNS

COSTA RICA: GREAT DESTINATIONS CENTRAL
  AMERICA

THE FINGER LAKES BOOK

THE FOUR CORNERS REGION

GALVESTON, SOUTH PADRE ISLAND
  & THE TEXAS GULF COAST

THE HAMPTONS BOOK

HAWAII'S BIG ISLAND

HONOLULU & OAHU: GREAT DESTINATIONS
  HAWAII

THE JERSEY SHORE: ATLANTIC CITY TO CAPE MAY

KAUAI: GREAT DESTINATIONS HAWAII

LAKE TAHOE & RENO

LOS CABOS & BAJA CALIFORNIA SUR:
  GREAT DESTINATIONS MEXICO

MAUI: GREAT DESTINATIONS HAWAII

MICHIGAN'S UPPER PENINSULA

MONTREAL & QUEBEC CITY:
  GREAT DESTINATIONS CANADA

THE NANTUCKET BOOK

THE NAPA & SONOMA BOOK

NORTH CAROLINA'S OUTER BANKS
  & THE CRYSTAL COAST

PALM BEACH, FORT LAUDERDALE, MIAMI & THE
  FLORIDA KEYS

PALM SPRINGS & DESERT RESORTS

PHOENIX, SCOTTSDALE, SEDONA
  & CENTRAL ARIZONA

PLAYA DEL CARMEN, TULUM & THE RIVIERA MAYA:
  GREAT DESTINATIONS MEXICO

SALT LAKE CITY, PARK CITY, PROVO
  & UTAH'S HIGH COUNTRY RESORTS

SAN DIEGO & TIJUANA

SAN JUAN, VIEQUES & CULEBRA:
  GREAT DESTINATIONS PUERTO RICO

SAN MIGUEL DE ALLENDE & GUANAJUATO:
  GREAT DESTINATIONS MEXICO

THE SANTA FE & TAOS BOOK

THE SARASOTA, SANIBEL ISLAND & NAPLES BOOK

THE SEATTLE & VANCOUVER BOOK

THE SHENANDOAH VALLEY BOOK

TOURING EAST COAST WINE COUNTRY

WASHINGTON, D.C., AND NORTHERN VIRGINIA

YELLOWSTONE & GRAND TETON NATIONAL PARKS AND
  JACKSON HOLE

YOSEMITE & THE SOUTHERN SIERRA NEVADA

If you are traveling to, moving to, residing in, or just interested in any (or all!) of these enchanting regions, a Great Destinations guidebook is a superior companion. Honest and painstakingly critical, full of information only a local can provide, Great Destinations guidebooks give you all the practical knowledge you need to enjoy the best of each region. Why not own them all?

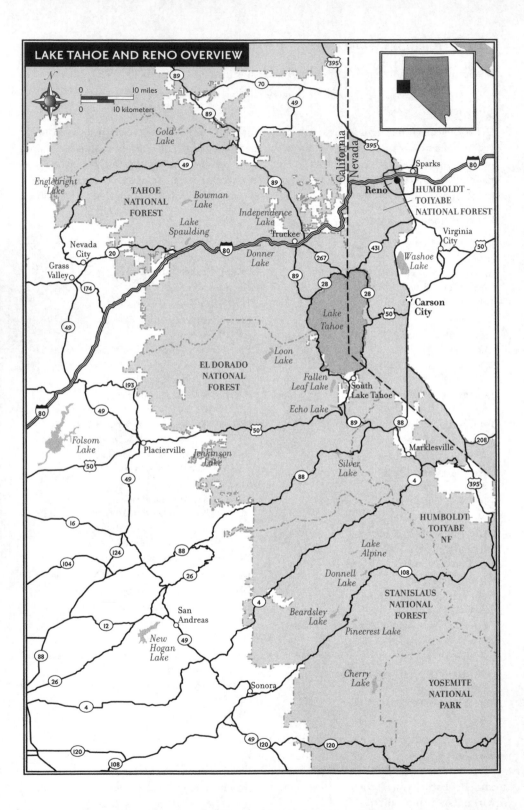

LAKE TAHOE AND RENO OVERVIEW

Contents

INTRODUCTION

This works. That was the feeling running through my bones back in 1980 as I drove up US 50 out of Placerville heading east toward South Lake Tahoe where a newspaper reporter job awaited. I had visited the area a couple of times with my family as a kid, but like most kids, I didn't pay much attention to scenery.

The anxiety of starting a new job was forgotten as I motored up the highway early that August morning, lapping up the sights of the American River cascading down the mountain, and the stark granite cliffs towering before me. This works.

Soon the highway narrowed as I crested Echo Summit and started down the mountain into the Tahoe Basin . . . and damn near drove off the road. Fortunately the builders of the highway understood the exhilaration the sight provides, and built a number of small turnouts—easily accessible from this side of the road—where people like me can park, and feast their eyes on the basin and the magnificence of Lake Tahoe in the distance below. A fresh cup of steaming coffee in hand and a deep breath of brisk, clean, mountain air forced me to recall a quote from Mark Twain: "The air up there in the clouds is very pure and fine . . . it is the same the angels breathe."

How true it is. Driving down the mountain and into the valley floor, no thoughts of the new job crossed my mind. My focus centered on the fact that I was about to begin actually living amid all this beauty and adventure. Yes, I thought, this really works.

A decade or so later, the fortunes of a writing career found me residing in a San Joaquin Valley farming town and not really thrilled about my new digs. Locals in the area joked that while the town might not be much, at least you are close to plenty of outdoor recreation. Right they were. Nobody in their right mind spent weekends and holidays in town, and so began a several-year romp up and

A statue of Mark Twain greets visitors to Utica Park in Angels Camp.

down Highway 49 through the Gold Country and into northern High Sierra. That worked too.

Today, for reasons I really can't explain, I find myself living in the San Fernando Valley, a suburb of the sprawling metropolis called Los Angeles. It's a bit farther from my treasured northern Sierra Nevada than I'd like to be. I thought that writing this book would assuage my longing for The Lake, The Biggest Little City on Earth, and the Clamper doin's in the foothills. It hasn't. That doesn't work, and will have to be remedied soon.

Jim Moore
Granada Hills, California

THE WAY THIS BOOK WORKS

This book is divided into six chapters. The three geographically based chapters cover the following regions: Lake Tahoe; Reno, and Virginia City, the Carson Valley; and the California Gold County also known as the Mother Lode. Although all three areas are located in the same basic region, each has its own historical value, personality and special attractions. For that reason, each of these chapters has its own introduction, to orient the reader as to what to look for in this area. These chapters are organized for the ideal trip through the entire region. Starting in Lake Tahoe, the book then takes the reader through the Carson Valley, Reno, and Virginia City. Finally, the book covers the Gold Country starting in the north and working its way south.

The remaining three chapters, History, Transportation, and Information, are thematic and include information on all three areas.

Travelers touring the region can turn to a specific section and find cool places to stay, great dining spots, and interesting places to shop. At the same time, the reader will learn about historical sites to visit and adventurous activities offered in the area. This information is designed to enhance the visitor's experience.

Many entries include specific information (Web site, e-mail, telephone numbers, addresses, business hours, etc.) organized for quick and easy reference in blocks at the top of each entry. All this information was rechecked as close to deadline as possible, but since these details sometimes change, often unexpectedly, it's usually a good idea to call ahead.

Lodging Prices

Within each regional chapter, lodging prices are noted in information blocks and are based on double occupancy per room. The cost is the lowest available, and that price may not be available during certain times of year. Lodging prices do vary, so be sure to call ahead for reservations and specific pricing information.

1

History

Golden Dreams with Silver Lining

The Sierra Nevada mountain range is really a new kid on the geologic block. Although geologists argue the details, it is generally accepted that the range is about five million years old, placing it among the youngest mountain ranges on the North American continent. But the geologic forces that created the Sierra Nevada started long before that.

About 250 million years ago, during the Mesozoic Era, dinosaurs ruled the earth and if they visited the eastern shores of the Pacific Ocean, they would be somewhere in eastern Nevada. During this time, the North American plate was slowly moving in a westerly direction, on a collision course with the Pacific plate approaching from the east. The collision pushed the Pacific plate under the North American plate and led to the creation of an arc-shaped chain of volcanoes. Eruptions from the volcanoes forced molten rock to the surface as lava, but most solidified deep inside the earth, forming the gray, granitic rocks that make up the backbone of the Sierra Nevada.

While volcanic action continued, the process of erosion wore away the newly formed material until about 70 million years ago when the granitic rock, once buried deep beneath the earth, began to rise to the surface. Later, about 20 million years ago, the area east of the Sierra Nevada spread in an east-to-west direction forming the Great Basin. Reno and the Carson Valley lay at the western edge of the vast Great Basin that encompasses most of the state of Nevada.

As for the Sierra Nevada mountain range, about five million years ago, the east side of the mountains experienced a violent uplifting period of what is known as the Sierran block and a sinking of the area to the east. Today, if you approach the mountains from the east, you will find they rise very sharply, but once over the crest, they gradually descend on the western slope into California's Central Valley. The same rising and sinking action in combination with enormous seismic activity also created the Tahoe Basin.

The granitic building blocks of the Sierra Nevada were now in place and it was time for a little touch-up work. Soon after the uplift process, the Earth entered the Pleistocene Epoch, otherwise known as the Ice Age. At least four periods of glacial advance coated the mountains in massive, very slow-moving ice sheets. The combination of massive glaciation and the erosion-resistant nature of the granite rocks worked together to create the

LEFT: *A statue of a pony express rider, outside of Harrah's Tahoe, Stateline, NV, pays tribute to that short-lived era.*

awesome landscape of hanging valleys, towering waterfalls, craggy peaks, alpine lakes, and huge glacial canyons. Remnants of the glaciers still exist in the higher reaches of the southern Sierra Nevada.

As the ice retreated, a massive river flowed into the basin from the south—forming Lake Tahoe—with an outlet on the north. When the glaciers returned, blocking the outlet, the lake filled to an estimated 800 feet above its current level. Again, the ice retreated and the lake found its present-day outlet, the Truckee River, on the north shore at Tahoe City. The Truckee flows out of Lake Tahoe, through the city of Reno, and into Pyramid Lake in northern Nevada.

SOCIAL HISTORY

Blazing Trails

On February 14, 1844, Lt. John C. Fremont found himself atop Red Lake Peak. Far in the distance, he and Charles Preuss, the expedition's German topographer, saw the pristine mountain lake they had been told about by their Native American allies in western Nevada. Neither Fremont nor Preuss were very impressed. Only Fremont made mention of the large lake in his daily journal and that was about it. They had bigger problems to overcome. Problems like getting themselves and the other 25 men who accompanied them over the Sierra Nevada and into the safety of the valley far below.

For reasons never explained, several weeks earlier Fremont elected to lead his men on a winter crossing of the Sierra Nevada. They had spent the previous summer and fall exploring and mapping Oregon and western Nevada, and were now attempting to reach Sutter's Fort in present-day Sacramento. Their Native American allies in Nevada told them about a very large alpine lake considered sacred by many. They were also told the Sierra crossing took "six sleeps to the land of the white people." It was six sleeps during the summer because nobody attempted such a crossing in the winter.

Following the lake sighting, it took another two weeks struggling through rugged canyons and deep snow before Fremont's chief scout, Christopher "Kit" Carson, led them to the safety of Sutter's Fort. Incredibly, not a man was lost.

In a subsequent report, Fremont named the lake Mountain Lake. Preuss, on an 1848 map, identified it as Lake Bonpland, in honor of a French botanist. However, by the 1860s, the largest alpine lake in North America was commonly referred to as Tahoe, a rough bastardization of the Washoe tribal name *Dao w a go,* meaning "edge of the lake." Other names would be proposed and even adopted, including Lake Bigler. Finally, in 1945, California and Nevada officially agreed upon Lake Tahoe.

It's Gold

Four years after Fremont's winter crossing, James Marshall, the foreman of a crew commissioned by John Sutter to build a lumber mill in the nearby Sierra foothills, inspected a new drainage system when, early on that January morning, something glittering in the water caught his eye. Marshall swore his men to secrecy and hightailed it down the mountain to share his find with his boss. Together, Sutter and Marshall tested the samples. When they proved to be the real deal, Sutter swore Marshall to secrecy and proceeded to

RIGHT: *James Marshall points to the spot where he found gold near Coloma, CA.*

brag about the find all over the streets of San Francisco. Of course, what Marshall had found was gold, and the word was soon upon the land.

In 1848, the nonnative population of the entire state numbered about 14,000. The native population—whose ancestors had migrated from Asia about 20,000 years earlier—stood at roughly 150,000.

Prior to the discovery, California was an idyllic region with a few Mexican citizens and even fewer Europeans, most of whom considered themselves Americans, living in the coastal villages of Monterey, Sonoma, Los Angeles, and the seaport at San Francisco. In 1810, Mexico successfully declared its independence from Spain, which had first colonized California in the late 1700s, erecting 20 missions along the coast from San Diego to San Francisco.

On June 14, 1846, a group of 33 Americans, acting on Fremont's advice, staged the Bear Flag Revolt. Marching on the Mexican capitol of California at Sonoma, they staged a bloodless coup, hoisted the famous flag depicting a grizzly bear, and declared California a republic, independent of Mexican rule. Fremont took control of the American forces, and a few skirmishes were fought, but it wasn't until several weeks later that Fremont and his men learned that the United States and Mexico were already at war. They quickly scrapped the notion of being a republic, replaced the bear flag with the Stars and Stripes, and fought to make California part of the United States.

Oddly enough, less than two weeks after Marshall's discovery, the Mexican-American War came to an end with the signing of the Treaty of Guadalupe Hidalgo ceding the vast American Southwest—including all of California—to the United States of America.

When Marshall told his crew on that fateful January day, "Men, I believe we've found gold," he unleashed an international torrent of humanity bound to seek their fortunes on the western slopes of the majestic Sierra Nevada. In addition to Americans, the fortune hunters—most with more heart than brains—flocked to California from Mexico, South America, Europe, and even China in such numbers that by 1860 the state's population was pegged at 380,000, with the Native American population falling to about 30,000.

Getting There

There was no easy way to get to California in the mid-1800s, and certainly no direct route to the Sierra Nevada foothills. Trails west included routes to Oregon blazed by Lewis and Clark, and the Old Spanish Trail, which terminated in Los Angeles several hundred miles to the south.

The gold seekers coming from the east had two choices: an overland crossing or travel by sea. Many early settlers arrived in San Francisco by ship, having spent at least three months on board sailing around the southern tip of South America or disembarking at Panama, trekking through the jungle, and catching another ship heading north. Only a few years after the discovery of gold, a rail line was built across the Isthmus of Panama, cutting travel time there from four days to four hours. Not only was traveling by ship relatively slow, it was also very expensive.

Most who came west during that time made the crossing by land, and those seeking a direct route to California had to deal with the Sierra Nevada. Legendary mountain man and trapper Jedediah Smith made the first recorded Sierra crossing by a nonnative in 1828. The first successful Sierra crossing by a wagon train was accomplished by the Stephens-Murphy-Townsend Party who, following the instructions of a friendly Paiute named Chief Truckee, crested the summit near Donner Lake. Members of the party were also the first

Donner Park at Donner Lake near Truckee, CA.

nonnatives to visit the shores of Lake Tahoe. The crossing was arduous. Wagons had to be dismantled and hoisted with heavy chains over the summit. It took every man, woman, and ox to accomplish the task. Although the crossing was made in November 1844, one member of the party, who remained behind to look after their belongings and supplies, wasn't retrieved until the following March. And one of the women in the party gave birth shortly after descending the western slope.

Several books and numerous newspaper articles appeared in Eastern publications extolling the quality of life in California, many of them authored by Fremont. Often these articles included trail information, which seemed to provide all one needed to know to make the crossing. Emigrant societies quickly emerged for people seeking to go to California. Independence, Missouri was the major hub for starting the trek of roughly 2,000 miles. Ideally, the oxen and horses could make 15 miles a day, which means the crossing would take about five months.

According to one account, about 2,700 people, broken up in small parties led by elected captains, set out on the trail west to California and Oregon in 1846. One of the groups was the tragic Donner Party who, roughly following the route of the Stephens-Murphy-Townsend Party two years before, became snowbound near the Sierra Nevada summit, and 42 of the original party of 91 died. Literally volumes have been written about their ordeal,

Even today, Donner Lake in the winter is both beautiful and forbidding.

and the subject of cannibalism remains a hotly debated issue to this day. A few years later, Truckee Lake and Truckee Summit were renamed Donner in commemoration of the tragedy.

While the migration had already begun, Marshall's discovery of gold the following year further fueled the magnetism of the California Dream, attracting people from around the world.

By 1850, the nation's business and political leaders understood the massive wealth gen-erated in the gold fields of California. They were also constantly being made aware of the state of lawlessness due the lack of strong leadership. A series of military officials governed the state following the signing of the Treaty of Guadalupe Hidalgo, each demanding that a civilian government take charge as quickly as possible. A cry for statehood—free of slavery—

followed a September 1849 constitutional convention in Monterey. Indeed, civil war threatened the nation until a Kentucky senator named Henry Clay formulated a compromise, part of which included California's admission to the union. California officially became a free state on September 9, 1850, and civil war was postponed—for the time being.

Transportation and Communication

Statehood may have allowed the nation to achieve Manifest Destiny, massaging the egos of the expansionists, but it only exacerbated the need for faster modes of transportation and communication. And they were not long in coming.

Until the completion of the Panama Canal a full 60 years later, ocean travelers had two choices. They could either take the voyage all the way around Cape Horn—the southern tip of South America—or they could disembark at Panama, make a treacherous, four-day jungle crossing, and wait for a northbound vessel that would carry them to San Francisco. In 1854, the *Flying Cloud* set a world record by sailing from New York to San Francisco in 88 days. However, the 15,000-mile voyage usually took in excess of 120 days. Three to four months at sea is a long time, but it was faster—and probably safer—than an overland trek of 2,800 miles in four to five months.

In the early days of the Gold Rush, ship captains were often surprised by the number of California-bound passengers boarding at ports of call in South America and Panama. And, on more than one occasion, upon reaching San Francisco, most of the crew disembarked along with the gold-seeking passengers.

By the time California achieved statehood, stagecoach routes were established within the state, but it wasn't until 1857 that the first stage line connecting the Carson Valley in Nevada to Sacramento went into operation. Only a year later, the first transcontinental stagecoach line connecting the Missouri River to the Pacific Coast opened for business. In September 1858, the Butterfield Overland Stage rolled out of San Francisco, and the Overland Stage headed west from Tipton, Missouri. The stagecoaches carried passengers, but more important from a financial standpoint, they carried mail under contract with the US government. They guaranteed transcontinental crossing in 25 days. Still, many demanded a faster means of communication.

WANTED
YOUNG SKINNY, WIRY FELLOWS
Not over eighteen. Must be expert
Riders, willing to risk death daily
Orphans preferred

The above ad never appeared in any newspaper, but utilizing the 1860s equivalent of Craigslist, such posters lured adventuresome riders from all over the country. A private company under contract with the US Postal Service sought riders for its Pony Express mail service from St. Joseph, Missouri to San Francisco, California, giving birth to one of the most colorful periods in American history.

The vision of these insanely brave young men riding through parching heat and blinding blizzards, and dodging hostile natives and highwaymen at every turn in their quest to deliver the mail overshadows the fact that the Pony Express existed for only 17 months and was a colossal financial failure for its investors.

Each horseman rode from 5 to 20 miles along a route containing 190 relay stations, where he either took a fresh mount or handed off the *mochila*—a type of saddlebag specially designed for carrying mail—to a fresh horse and rider. To keep weight to a minimum, each rider carried only the mochila, a water sack, and a revolver. A one-way crossing took roughly 10 days. The Pony Express provided a valuable service in that it not only brought letters from home, but more important, the riders delivered relatively current news as the nation prepared for the Civil War. The Pony Express probably was doomed from the beginning, because less than a year after it disbanded, the telegraph reached the West Coast and the nation was officially "wired".

A number of statues and historical markers trace the path of the Pony Express as it entered Carson City from the east and followed the Carson Valley-to-Sacramento stage route through Lake Tahoe, over Echo Summit, and down the mountain through Kyburz, Placerville, and on to Sacramento.

The Mother Lode

When the first miners, the 49ers, arrived, placer mining—that is, panning for surface (placer) gold in the numerous rivers and streams that flow out of the Sierra Nevada—dominated the search for gold. Within a few years, the placer gold gave out and more sophisticated mining techniques, including hydraulic and tunnel digging, were adopted. Over time, the region was divided between the Northern Mines, those located north of the Auburn, and those to the south were the Southern Mines. In general, the Northern Mines provided placer gold and when that ran out, hydraulic hoses powered by massive pumps were directed at entire hillsides of soft gravel. Once the gold was separated, the remains, called "slickens," ran downstream. The thick mud and silt ruined farmland and eventually caused navigation problems in the Sacramento River and San Francisco Bay. Though the practice was eventually outlawed, the era of hydraulic mining left behind a great deal of environmental degradation.

In the Southern Mines, hardrock—sometimes called quartz—mining involved sinking a shaft deep into the ground where a gold vein or pocket had been found and digging tunnels outward at various levels. This was an expensive method of mining that sometimes proved very profitable. As a matter of fact, among the deepest mines on the North American continent, the Kennedy and Argonaut mines near Jackson, produced more than half the gold mined in the Mother Lode. Mining continued at these sites until 1958.

In general, life in the mines—or the diggings, as they were called—wasn't anything like what is often depicted in movies and television shows. In the summer it was hot, at times over 100 degrees, and the winter brought rain and cold. Initially, ramshackle tent cities sprang up, and proper sanitation was nowhere to be found. Disease plagued many miners. Most of the wooden buildings erected to replace the tents and house taverns, general stores, and other commercial ventures burned to the ground—often more than once.

By 1850, the miners segregated themselves, with the Anglos working the Northern Mines and the Latinos—mostly from Mexico—the Southern Mines. That year, the state legislature passed a Foreign Miners License Tax, requiring those who were not citizens to pay a monthly fee of $20. In the town of Sonora, an estimated 15,000 Mexicans banded together and announced their refusal to pay. Hundreds of Anglos gathered to assist the tax collectors, many sporting their old Mexican War uniforms.

With all the able-bodied men off working the diggings, nobody was left to establish any semblance of social order, and lawlessness prevailed. Life at Mokelumne Hill is a good example. At one point during the early 1850s, at least one man was shot between Saturday

Virginia City looks much as it did in its heyday in the 1860s.

night and Sunday morning for 17 consecutive weeks. At one point, five men were killed in one week. The town formed a vigilance committee, and when gongs sounded, men came running, rounding up miscreants and jailing them in a dungeon beneath the Leger Hotel. Throughout the Gold Rush, country justice during this time was meted out by such committees, usually resulting in whipping, hanging, or both.

It is easy to see where Hangtown (Placerville) got its original name.

Nevada Cashes In

As early as the mid-1850s, the placer gold was pretty well mined out and, even as wave upon wave of new arrivals showed up at the diggings, most of the original 49ers left the area, looking for new riches in Australia, New Zealand, British Columbia, and nearby Nevada.

In the late 1850s, two miners working the Mt. Davidson area in Nevada found gold. Henry Comstock, a shepherd and miner, laid claim to the find but sold the claims shortly thereafter. The biggest problem was the sticky, blue-gray mud that clung to the picks and shovels. When assayed, the muck proved to be silver ore worth more than $2,000 a ton (in 1859 dollars). Almost overnight, a new tent city arose dubbed Old Virginy Town by a miner who hailed from Virginia. The Comstock Lode, sometimes called the Rush to Washoe, drew fortune hunters almost as fast as the discovery at Sutter's Mill 10 years earlier.

Old Virginy Town became Virginia City, and a few individuals made immense fortunes, wealth so vast that in 1864 President Abraham Lincoln, desperately in need of cash to keep the Union solvent during the Civil War, took notice and made Nevada a state, even though it didn't have enough people to constitutionally authorize statehood. Carson City became the state's capital thanks to Adam Curry's adept advance planning and lobbying efforts. Not only did the wealth from the Comstock Lode finance the Civil War, it is also said that investments in Comstock mining over the next 20 years raised enough money to build the city of San Francisco.

During its heyday, Virginia City was a boisterous, rancorous human beehive of 30,000 residents. The wealthy built opulent mansions and imported the finest furnishings and fashions from Europe and the Orient. The city was abuzz 24 hours a day with visiting celebrities, opera, and Shakespearian performances. And of course, along with the news-papers, fraternal organizations, and competing police precincts, were a thriving red-light district, opium dens, and music blaring out of the numerous bars and gambling houses that lined the main business thoroughfare.

By 1880, Virginia City's mines approached depths of 2,000 feet. They would never have gone that deep had it not been for the invention of square-set timbering. However, this method of reinforcement utilized vast amounts of wood, a commodity not found in any quantity near Virginia City. Wood for construction of city buildings and homes and for the mines came from the Lake Tahoe region, where it was hauled by narrow-gauge rail to Spooner Summit and floated downhill to the valley floor through a V-flume. Once on the valley floor, it was loaded and hauled via the Virginia and Truckee Railway.

Blazing the Iron Trail

Some described the undertaking as "preposterous," while one newspaper likened the notion of building a transcontinental railroad to building bridges to the planets in our solar system. But, in spite of all the detractors and the fact that the nation was mired in the bloody Civil War, construction began in 1863 on a rail line across the country. In a race to see who could lay the most track, the Union Pacific started in Omaha and the Central Pacific began in Sacramento. The route over the Sierra Nevada followed the California Trail, crossing the mountains almost exactly where the Donner Party had met its tragic fate 15 years before.

The Central Pacific could not find enough American laborers, so Chinese were brought in to do the work. The Chinese were paid less, worked longer hours, and lived in condi-tions no American would tolerate. At the height of construction, some 10,000 Coolies (the then-current name for the Chinese railroad workers) were employed by the Central Pacific.

The job took five years and cost scores of lives. During the winter of 1866–1867, some 44 blizzards howled through the Sierra as the workers attempted to blast through solid rock. At times an average of only 8 inches of track was laid in a day. Protecting the track and trains from snowdrifts called for the construction of 37 miles of snow sheds and 6,213 feet of tunnels.

In the end, the Union Pacific easily won the race to lay the most track (1,086 miles vs. 690), but the Central Pacific gets the credit for setting a record by laying 10 miles of track in a single, 12-hour day. Golden spikes were driven, completing the construction on May 10, 1869 at Promontory Summit near Ogden, Utah. On that day, a nation spanning sea to sea, yet still recovering from the vicious Civil War, knit its delicate fabric a little closer together with 3,500 miles of iron track.

TAHOE TODAY

At the dawn of the 20th century, most of the miners had abandoned the Mother Lode and the Comstock, the din of the stamp mills no longer echoed through the canyons 24 hours a day, and Lake Tahoe's forests were virtually gone. It's a fortunate accident of history that the Comstock ore ran out when it did, or the Tahoe Basin would have suffered further degradation. In spite of the Tahoe Basin's disheveled appearance, public appreciation grew, and during the 1912, 1913, and 1918 congressional sessions, unsuccessful attempts were made to designate the basin a national park.

Also about this time, the word was out among the wealthy in San Francisco, and many seeking a new getaway flocked to the beautiful alpine lake. Erected in 1902, the Tahoe Tavern near Tahoe City became one of the lake's first resort-style motels, and the Lake Tahoe Wagon Road—today, US 50—became California's first state highway. Lumber baron D.L. Bliss built a narrow-gauge railroad from Truckee to Tahoe City. The area became so popular that steamboats soon plied the lake's waters, bringing visitors and supplies to the new resorts. The ultra-wealthy built summer homes, some taking on palatial proportions in size and decoration. In 1931, engineers blasted two tunnels through Cave Rock, completing the road around the lake.

Shortly after World War II, Harvey Gross, a successful meat retailer from Sacramento, and his wife Llewellyn opened Harvey's Wagon Wheel Saloon & Gambling Hall on seven acres of land in Stateline. The single-room log cabin "resort" boasted three slot machines, two blackjack tables, a six-stool lunch counter, and the only 24-hour gas pump between Placerville, California and Carson City, Nevada. Harvey's was an instant success, and competition soon followed. The popularity of the area swelled in the 1950s to the point where roads were plowed, allowing year-round access to the alpine playground.

While all the gambling action focused the spotlight on Lake Tahoe's south shore, across the lake a major page in the basin's history unfolded. Ski resort owner Alexander C. Cushing gave the international sporting community a real shock when he bid for and received the 1960 Winter Olympics. At the time, Squaw Valley was a fledgling resort, virtually unknown outside of California.

The VIII Olympic Winter Games were the largest ever held, with 34 nations in competition. The games boasted a number of firsts, including housing athletes in their own Olympic Village, the use of artificial refrigeration for speed skating events, and computers to tally results. But the most important first involved the media. CBS paid $50,000, and the games were the first to be nationally televised, exposing millions of TV viewers, not only to the athletic competition, but to the beauty and grandeur of Lake Tahoe as a destination resort.

By 1968, many believed that development and degradation of the lake and surrounding basin was out of control, rivaling the pillage of the land for timber a century before.

California and Nevada formed the Tahoe Regional Planning Agency to oversee environmental responsibility of the Tahoe basin. The agency has limited new construction and devised a redevelopment plan to bolster the economy, allow tourist access, and protect the environment.

Today, Lake Tahoe is permanent home to more than 70,000 residents and a destination for millions of visitors seeking adventure, recreation, and relaxation.

Reno and Virginia City Today

Since the 1850s, a small group of pioneers had lived in a fertile valley along the Truckee River known as River Crossing and later Lake's Crossing. Mostly the group farmed and did some trading with travelers headed west along the California Trail. When word got out that a railroad would pass through the valley, Myron Lake made a deal with the Central Pacific Railroad. He traded land for a river crossing in exchange for a train depot. Before the line was completely finished the area incorporated as a city, taking the name Reno, in honor of Maj. Gen. Jesse L. Reno, a Union commander who had lost his life in the Civil War. In 1872, a link added Reno to the Virginia City–Truckee line, and the community prospered as an agriculture center and trading outpost.

The beginning of the 20th century was not kind to Nevada boomtowns like Virginia City. When the ore was gone, the people left. While California continued to grow and expand, Nevada's population shrank to the point where a Chicago newspaper speculated about whether Nevada should retain its statehood. Unlike other mining boomtowns like Rawhide (which once boasted 90 bars and but a single church) and Bodie, Virginia City didn't become a virtual ghost town, but it spent nearly 50 years on its deathbed.

Meanwhile, only a few miles to the northwest, the Lincoln Highway—later US 40, and today Interstate 80—attracted adventuresome motorcar travelers as they made their way to and from California. The famous arch, erected in the 1920s, greeted travelers to Reno, "The Biggest Little City In The World."

Nevada has always considered itself something of a maverick state, allowing practices such as gambling, prostitution, and quickie marriages and divorces, which are looked down upon by most of the rest of the country. Prohibition laws were not openly disobeyed, but tacitly ignored. The passage of liberal divorce laws and the legalization of casino gambling in 1931—creatively termed "legislative sin solutions"—ignited another boom for the state. While the divorce business eventually dried up as other states liberalized their laws, gaming and entertainment continue to lure visitors to this day.

Until about 1960, Reno was the gambling capital of the United States. Since that time, Las Vegas has seen a very rapid rise, and Indian gaming in California has also served to reduce business to some degree.

But Reno remains undaunted, and a major revitalization program reshapes the city, especially along Virginia Street. Gone are most of the small, often seedy casinos including Mapes, Nevada Club, Harold's Club, Money Tree, and the Comstock. These have either been torn down or converted into upscale condominiums. Most of the major resort casinos are no longer concentrated on Virginia Street, but scattered in various locations around town. The city also hosts annual events that sell out every room in town, including Hot August Nights, Street Vibrations, Best in the West Nugget Rib Cook-off, the Great Reno Balloon Race, and the Reno Air Races.

And Virginia City has found new life, living the Western image of a town too tough to die. In the 1950s, Lucius Beebe, a well-heeled New York society columnist, bought the

Restoration of beautiful old Victorian houses such as this one in Sonora helps retain the Gold Rush theme.

Territorial Enterprise and with its revival and the popularity of the TV series *Bonanza* in the 1960s, suddenly Virginia City found itself a tourist attraction.

Since then, mining has started up and closed down several times, but the tourists keep on coming, and most of the town has been rebuilt to its original look.

While Reno keeps reinventing itself to keep up with each new generation of tourists, Virginia City is doing just fine, retaining the style and culture of the late 1800s.

The Mother Lode Today

Unlike the near ghost town status of Virginia City, many of the Mother Lode communities survived and even thrived once the rush ended. As California's population swelled during the 20th century, the surviving communities became centers of ranching, agriculture, lumber, commerce, and local government, while proudly preserving their history.

Named in honor of the original fortune-seeking 49ers, California's SR 49 runs 325 miles from Vinton near the California-Nevada border south to Oakhurst in Fresno County. About 250 miles of it winds through the heart of the Mother Lode.

Most of the original mining camps are long gone, deserted as soon as the gold ran out and left to suffer the ravages of time. In the surviving communities, original buildings

Built in 1889, the A. Brosemer Building in Angels Camp is a classic example of Gold Country architecture.

erected during the Gold Rush are rare, because most burned down and were rebuilt, some-times three or four times. In some cases, such as at Marshall Gold Discovery Park in Coloma, the entire mill where gold was first discovered and other facilities are replicas, rebuilt by the California Park Service in commemoration of their historic value. The same is true in Columbia near Sonora, where the entire town is a state park, authentically recon-structed, down to the docents' 1850s-style clothing.

Private enterprise, however, is responsible for the vast majority of the reconstruction and preservation of the region. The post–World War II boom brought sportsmen, adventure seekers, and history buffs to the Sierra foothills, and soon sleepy little communities like Nevada City, Placerville, Sonora, and Angels Camp found themselves mining a Mother Lode of tourists. Throughout the 1960s, historic old buildings and many with marginal historic value became hot properties, as entrepreneurs transformed them into antique shops, theaters, eateries, and boutiques. Many of the old Victorian houses were in a pretty sorry state until the bed and breakfast craze came into vogue. Today, dozens of classy B&Bs dot the Gold Country landscape, attracting visitors from all over the world.

A good example of the breadth of the international appeal of the Mother Lode is Hangtown's Gold Bug Mine in Placerville. Here visitors take self-guided tours equipped with audio sticks (just like those used in the Louvre Museum) that tell the story of hard-rock mining in English, Spanish, French, German, and Japanese.

It is possible to drive Highway 49 in a single day, but most people allow anywhere from three to seven days. Most visitors enjoy taking time to savor the beautiful foothills scenery, take adventurous side trips to pristine Sierra lakes, do some shopping, and, of course, let their imagination run wild, with the sights and historical embellishment of a truly unique California phenomenon—the Gold Rush.

An old building is about all that's left of Chinese Camp on SR 49.

2

TRANSPORTATION

Scenic Highways and Byways

Lake Tahoe and Reno are easily accessible by all forms of transportation, while Virginia City in Nevada and California's Mother Lode require some extra planning. In order to savor all the beauty, adventure, and history this region has to offer, it is probably best, though not mandatory, to have access to some form of motorized transportation.

For the bicycle enthusiast, yes, the entire region is accessible by pedal power, but you'll need plenty of time and you had better be in great physical condition to negotiate the 8,000-foot passes through the Sierra Nevada.

And speaking of mountain passes, Lake Tahoe and the northern Sierra Nevada are beautiful, but during the winter months, the two major routes traversing the mountains are subject to heavy snowfall. Both US 50 and Interstate 80 are designed and maintained to be kept open year-round, but they can become difficult to negotiate during inclement weather. Also during the winter, all cars, trucks (except four-wheel-drive) and motorhomes traveling mountain roads are required to carry tire chains. Rental car companies do not provide chains, but they are readily available at service stations and grocery stores. Chains cost $30–50 depending on tire size.

For those traveling during non-winter months, the region offers numerous highways and byways through the mountains. They offer a lot of history as well. SR 88, south of Lake Tahoe, roughly follows the route blazed by Kit Carson and John Fremont during their misguided winter crossing of the Sierra—and "discovery" of Lake Tahoe—in 1846. US 50, the most direct route to South Lake Tahoe, follows routes opened by the Pony Express and the first stage coaches to routinely cross the Sierra. Just north of Lake Tahoe, the Amtrak railroad lies on the route blasted through the mountains to complete the nation's first transcontinental railroad as well as nearby Interstate 80 which follows much of the same route blazed by the early pioneers, including the Donner Party, and later the Lincoln Highway. A fun day can be filled anywhere in this region just driving around and stopping to read all the historical markers.

Factoid

Want to win a bar bet? Which city is located further west: Reno, or Los Angeles? Although Los Angeles is located on the Pacific Ocean, Reno is geographically farther west.

LEFT: *A steep climb leads travelers to a beautiful broad vista of Bear Valley along CA 49, the Mother Lode Highway.*

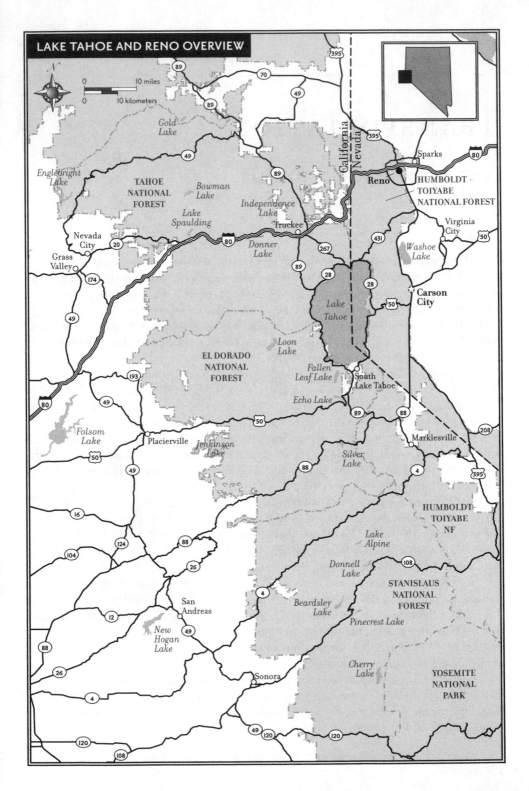

LAKE TAHOE AND RENO OVERVIEW

GETTING TO LAKE TAHOE, RENO & THE MOTHER LODE

By Car

Unless you enter the region from within the state of California, all roads lead to Reno. The city is located at the confluence of two major highways, Interstate 80 running east and west, and US 395, a major north-south highway. The majority of the travelers entering the region from the east will take I-80 directly into Reno.

Once in Reno, Lake Tahoe is 58 miles to the southwest. The most direct route to South Lake Tahoe is accessed by taking US 395 south through Carson City where you catch US 50 heading west, over Spooner Summit.

Since the Gold Country stretches roughly 300 miles along the western foothills, there are several routes that can be taken to cross the Sierra Nevada into this region. One way is to take the US 50 route, and continue through Lake Tahoe, cross Echo Summit and drive down the western face of the Sierra Nevada, linking up with SR 49 in Placerville. The most direct route to the Gold Country is to continue heading west on I-80 over Donner Summit. Continue on I-80 to its intersection of SR 49 at Auburn, or take the cutoff at SR 89 or SR 20 and enjoy a very scenic cruise into the Grass Valley–Nevada City area.

Finally, to really enjoy the entirety of the Gold Country, go north from Reno on US 395 to Hallelujah Junction. Take SR 70 only a few miles to the small community of Vinton, where SR 49 heads south beginning your journey through the Gold Country.

FROM SACRAMENTO

Getting to the region from anywhere in California isn't difficult, and allows for more choices as to which area to visit first. Entering from the west, all roads pass through the Gold Country, before crossing the Sierra Nevada. From Sacramento, there are two choices. One is to take I-80 due east, crossing SR 49 at Auburn. Here you can turn off on to SR 49 and travel north or south to visit the Gold County. If you decide to continue on I-80, it will take you directly to Reno, unless you decide to go visit Lake Tahoe's north shore, cutting off at SR 89.

The alternative is to take US 50 out of Sacramento east to its crossing with SR 49 at Placerville. Here you have the same option of getting off at SR 49 and touring the gold country, or continuing east on US 50 to Lake Tahoe and Reno.

FROM SAN FRANCISCO AND OAKLAND

This is almost too easy. Get on US 80 east to Sacramento. Once in the state capital, review your options listed above.

FROM SAN JOSÉ AND THE SOUTH BAY AREA

This is almost as easy. Take US 680 north to US 80, head east to Sacramento and review options listed above.

FROM FRESNO

Entering the region from the south via Fresno in the heart of the San Joaquin Valley, you have two basic options. Take SR 99 north through the heart of the valley to Sacramento where you pick up either US 50 or I-80 going east. Another option is to head northeast on SR 41. This highway will take you to Sequoia and Yosemite national parks, but you don't go that far. It intersects with the southern terminus of SR 49. Take a left and you are on the Mother Lode highway.

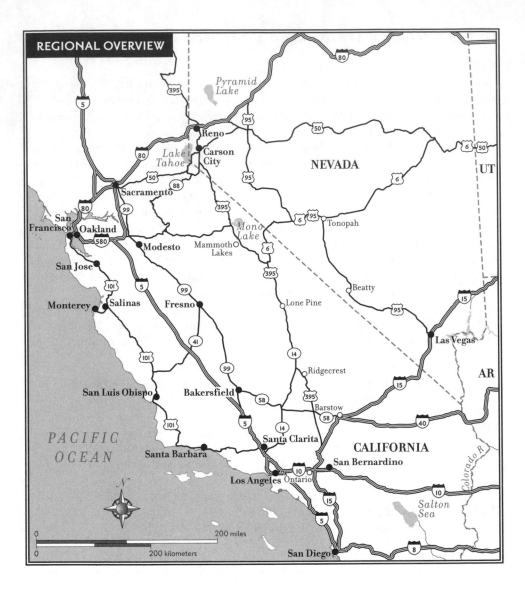

FROM LOS ANGELES AND SAN DIEGO

First, leave at 3 AM when the traffic has cleared off some and Cal Trans has had time to remove the wreckage from the previous night's rush hour. The morning commute will only be just beginning, so freeway travel shouldn't be too bad. Get on Interstate 5, and once you get over the Grapevine, you have to make a decision. You can stay on I-5 all the way to Sacramento, but that is arguably one of the most boring drives in the world. Be sure to have plenty of gas, water, and food, because services are fairly limited along this five- to six-hour haul to Sacramento.

Another option is to take US 99, which links up with I-5 south of Bakersfield. This highway parallels the Interstate, passing through Fresno and other valley communities, all the way to Sacramento, and beyond. It's a little less boring, and offers more services along the way.

If you want to avoid the San Joaquin Valley, take I-5 to SR 14 just north of Los Angeles, and stay on SR 14 until it connects with US 395 north. This will bring you up the eastern side of the Sierra Nevada, into the Carson Valley and Reno.

By Bus

Bus travelers have a couple of options. Greyhound (www.greyhound.com) has a station in Reno with connections from many locations in the United States. In addition to Reno, Greyhound also services Truckee, CA, giving travelers access to Lake Tahoe's north shore.

The South Tahoe Express provides 11 daily departures each way between Reno-Tahoe International airport and South Lake Tahoe resort casinos. An adult ticket is $24 one way. The shuttle stops at Mont Bleu Resort Casino, Embassy Suites, Harrah's Lake Tahoe, Harveys, Horizon, and the Lakeside Inn. Call 1-866-89-TAHOE or go online at: www.southtahoeexpress.com.

From the Bay Area, the Capitol Corridor train/bus system operates one bus a day departing from its Sacramento station serving South Lake Tahoe. The fair for a one-way ticket from San Francisco is $43. For more information, call 1-877-974-3322, or go online at: www.capitolcorridor.org.

Junked silver mining equipment on a hillside outside Virginia City.

By Plane

The Reno/Tahoe International Airport (RNO)—located in Reno—offers direct flights to and from many major cities as well as numerous connecting flights from metro airports in Sacramento, San Francisco, Oakland, San Jose, and Los Angeles.

In addition to commercial flights, South Lake Tahoe, Reno, and the Carson Valley all have smaller airports to accommodate private aircraft.

AIRLINES SERVING RENO-TAHOE AIRPORT

Alaska Airlines	800-426-0333	www.alaska-air.com
Allegiant Air	702-505-8888	www.allegiantair.com
Aloha Airlines	800-367-5250	www.alohaairlines.com
American Airlines	800-433-7300	www.aa.com
Continental Airlines	800-525-0280	www.continental.com
Delta	800-221-1212	www.delta.com
Delta Connection	800-221-1212	www.delta.com
Express Jet	888-958-9538	www.xjet.com
Horizon Air	800-547-9308	www.horizonair.com
Southwest	800-345-9792	www.southwest.com
United	800-241-6522	www.united.com
Ted	800-225-5833	www.flyted.com
US Airways	800-428-4322	www.USairways.com

By Rail

The California Zephyr offers one of the most scenic train rides anywhere in America and it cuts right through the heart of the northern High Sierra and the Gold Country on its daily trek from Chicago to San Francisco. The Zephyr stops in Reno and Sparks, then winds its way through the Sierra Nevada with stops in Truckee, Colfax and Sacramento.

Amtrak's Coast Starlight services the north-south corridor from Seattle to Los Angeles with stops in Oakland and San Jose. Contact Amtrak at: www.amtrak.com or 1-800-872-7245.

GETTING AROUND LAKE TAHOE, RENO & THE MOTHER LODE

By Bus

In Reno, the Regional Transportation Commission www.rtcwashoe.com operates 29 bus routes serving the entire city and some outlaying areas via the RTC Intercity and the RTC Sierra Sprint. Feel free to crack open your laptop because most buses are Wi-Fi hot spots.

As a resort community, Lake Tahoe is not lacking for public transportation. Here's a rundown of what's available and where.

NORTH SHORE

TART, 1-800-736-6365, The Tahoe Area Regional Transit operated by Placer County serves the northern and western shores of the lake from 6:10 AM to 6:30 PM, seven days a week.

An excellent way to tour the Gold Country is by motorcycle.

Tahoe Trolley, 530-581-6365, During the summer, the trolley also provides service along the lake's north and west shores serving Crystal Bay, Tahoe City, Squaw Valley, and Emerald Bay.

Truckee Trolley, 530-587-7457, This Trolley operates between the towns of Truckee and Donner Lake. Additional routes are added during the winter to Northstar, Kings Beach, and Donner Summit.

SOUTH SHORE

BlueGo, www.bluego.org, 530-541-7149, Primary routes run between Stateline and the South Y, seven days a week from 6 AM to midnight. Fixed route ski shuttles are added during the winter.

BlueGo Door to Door, www.bluego.org, 530-541-7149, Offers convenient door-to-door service along the South Shore from Meyers to Zephyr Cove.

BlueGo Casino Service, www.bluego.org, 530-541-7149, Provides 24-7 service between the South Shore and the Stateline casinos.

Heavy timbers were used to reinforce mines that sometimes wove their way hundreds of feet underground.

Nifty "50" Trolley, www.bluego.org, 530-541-7149, During the summer, this trolley offers narrated trips through the South Shore serving casinos, campgrounds, beaches, the Heavenly Tram, shopping centers, recreation sites, restaurants, and the paddlewheelers. Travel all day for just $3.

By Rental Car

To really experience all this region has to offer, a car is necessary. If you didn't drive here in the first place, renting one is necessary. Please be a cautious and courteous driver.

RENO-TAHOE AIRPORT RENTAL CAR AGENCIES

Advantage Rent-A-Car	800-777-5500	www.advantage.com
Alamo	800-GOALAMO	www.goalamo.com
Avis	800-984-8840	www.goalamo.com
Budget	800-527-0700	www.avis.com
Dollar Rent A Car	800-800-4000	www.dollarcar.com
Enterprise	800-736-8222	www.enterprise.com
Hertz	800-654-3131	www.hertz.com
National	800-CAR RENT	www.nationalcar.com
Thrifty	800-FOR CARS	www.thrifty.com

SOUTH LAKE TAHOE RENTAL CAR AGENCIES

Enterprise Inside Horizon Casino	775-586-1077
Hertz Inside Harvey's Casino	775-586-0041
Avis Inside Embassy Suites	530-544-5289

ROAD CONDITIONS

To get the latest information on road conditions in California: 1-800-427-7623. From outside California: 916-445-7623 or visit them on the Web at: www.dot.ca.gov/dist3/. For Nevada road conditions, call 1-877-687-6237 or go online at: www.nevadadot.com/traveler/roads/.

By Water

South Shore Water Shuttle 530-541-9800, Lakeside Marina, and 530-542-6570 Camp Richardson Resort & Marina. Beat the traffic and take the boat. Bicycles welcome. Operates June through Sept. 15 serving Lakeside Marina and Camp Richardson with stops at Timber Cove Marina.

A renovated Victorian house marks the intersection of SR 49 and SR 4.

3

LAKE TAHOE

Jewel of the Sierra Nevada

Locals like to call Lake Tahoe their "blue world." The sky is blue, the lake is deep blue, and nobody's singing the blues except headline entertainers. This is a special place where one can find solitude hiking in aptly named Desolation Wilderness, or party hearty with friends and family in any one of the dozens of establishments surrounding the lake.

Lake Tahoe as a year-round destination resort didn't really get rolling until the 1950s. From the time gold and silver were found in nearby Virginia City in 1860, until after the turn of the century when the mines played out, the region served as a source of fuel and timber to build the boomtowns and mines that tunneled thousands of feet into the earth. Around 1900, Lake Tahoe's pristine natural beauty lured wealthy San Franciscans, who built palatial hotels, summer homes, and cabins. The games came to town with the opening of Harvey's Wagon Wheel Saloon and Gambling Hall in 1944, and competition soon followed. New highways were constructed to provide year-round access, and the lake's communities continued to grow. The 1960 Winter Olympic Games were held at Squaw Valley, putting the entire Tahoe region on the map as a destination for tourists from around the world.

As the region continued to grow, California and Nevada formed the Tahoe Regional Planning Agency in 1968 to oversee environmental responsibility within the basin. Today all development—commercial and residential—must adhere to strict standards designed to safeguard the quality of the air, water, and environment for future generations.

Today, Lake Tahoe is a land of sheer beauty, vibrant activity, its own culture, and has also become a mecca for outdoor enthusiasts. Skiing and snowboarding rule during the winter months, and when the warm summer rolls around, water sports such as kayaking, sailing, and water skiing are popular activities. During most of the year, hiking, mountain climbing, and wilderness exploration are great options. A day at Lake Tahoe might include skiing, river rafting, or taking a nature hike in the morning, shopping the quaint boutiques or exploring the cultural attractions in the afternoon, enjoying a dinner-dance cruise on the lake in the evening, and perhaps capping the day off with a late-night headline show.

There really is no "best time of year" to visit Lake Tahoe. While the summer and winter seasons are the most popular for tourists, many locals will tell you they favor the spring and fall, when the area is less crowded and the natural scenery around the lake is at its finest.

LEFT: *The Blues Bros greet shoppers entering a Lake Tahoe boutique.*

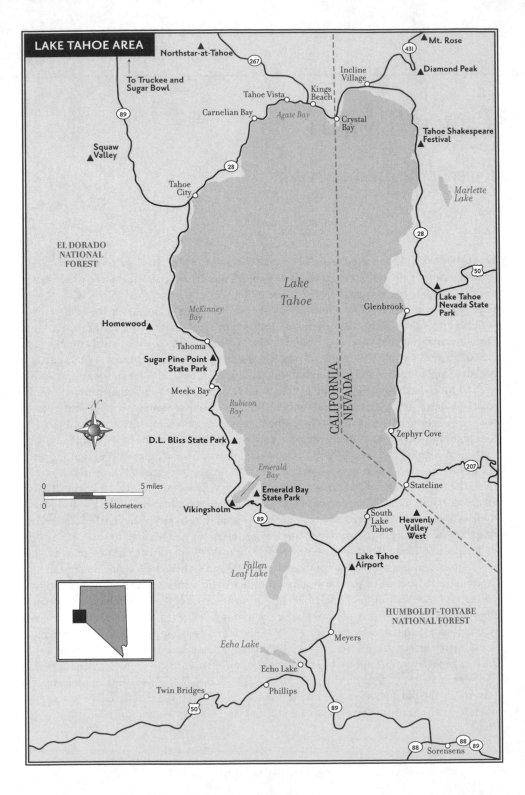

LAKE TAHOE AREA

Mt. Rose

431

Northstar-at-Tahoe

267

To Truckee and
Sugar Bowl

Incline
Village

Diamond Peak

89

Tahoe Vista

Kings
Beach

Carnelian Bay

Agate Bay

Crystal
Bay

Tahoe Shakespeare
Festival

Squaw
Valley

28

*Marlette
Lake*

Tahoe
City

28

EL DORADO
NATIONAL
FOREST

50

*Lake
Tahoe*

Glenbrook

Lake Tahoe
Nevada State
Park

*McKinney
Bay*

Homewood

Tahoma

Sugar Pine Point
State Park

Meeks Bay

*Rubicon
Bay*

CALIFORNIA
NEVADA

N

D.L. Bliss State Park

Zephyr Cove

207

Stateline

0   5 miles

0   5 kilometers

*Emerald
Bay*

Emerald Bay
State Park

Vikingsholm

89

South
Lake
Tahoe

Heavenly
Valley
West

Lake Tahoe
Airport

*Fallen
Leaf Lake*

HUMBOLDT-TOIYABE
NATIONAL FOREST

Eeho Lake

Meyers

Echo Lake

Twin Bridges

Phillips

50

89

88   89

88

Sorensens

LODGING

You won't find a broader range of lodging choices than at Lake Tahoe. From camping in the remote quiet of the tall pines in the Desolation Wilderness, to relaxing in a stylish B&B, or enjoying the breathtaking view of the lake and rugged mountains high in a penthouse suite, it's all possible here. One thing is constant—no matter what your lodging choices may be, there's absolutely nothing quite as exhilarating as that first deep breath of clean, mountain air in the early morning. Now that's living large.

Credit cards are abbreviated as follows:

  AE: American Express
  D: Discover
  MC: MasterCard
  V: Visa

Crystal Bay

CAL-NEVA RESORT HOTEL AND CASINO

www.calnevaresort.com
1-800-CAL-NEVA
2 Stateline Rd., Crystal Bay, NV.
Price: $109 and up
Credit cards: AE, D, MC, V
Children: Yes
Pets: Yes
Handicap access: Yes

This is a true taste of Lake Tahoe history. Originally built in 1926, the resort has been remodeled several times. Under the ownership of Frank Sinatra in the early 1960s, the famous Celebrity Showroom was added. Today, the facility offers cabins, chalets, and lake-view tower accommodations.

Once a winter resort for Frank Sinatra and his pals, the historic Cal-Neva splits the state line between California and Nevada.

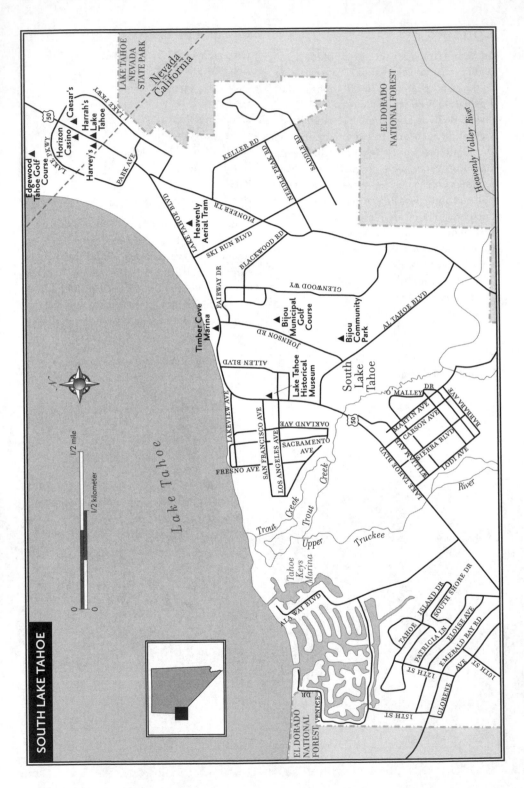

SOUTH LAKE TAHOE

Lake Tahoe

LAKE TAHOE NEVADA STATE PARK

Nevada
California

EL DORADO NATIONAL FOREST

Heavenly Valley River

▲ Edgewood Tahoe Golf Course
LAKE PKWY
Harvey's ▲
Horizon Casino ▲
Harrah's ▲ Lake Tahoe
Caesar's ▲
50
LAKE PKWY
PARK AVE

KELLER RD
NEEDLE PEAK RD
SADDLE RD

LAKE TAHOE BLVD
▲ Heavenly Aerial Tram
PIONEER TR
SKI RUN BLVD
BLACKWOOD RD

FAIRWAY DR
GLENWOOD WY

▲ Timber Cove Marina
Bijou Municipal Golf Course ▲
JOHNSON RD
Bijou Community Park ▲
AL TAHOE BLVD

ALLEN BLVD
LAKEVIEW AVE
Lake Tahoe Historical Museum

OAKLAND AVE
SAN FRANCISCO AVE
SACRAMENTO AVE
LOS ANGELES AVE
FRESNO AVE

South Lake Tahoe
50
O'MALLEY DR
MARTIN AVE
CARSON AVE
SIERRA BLVD
LODI AVE
BARBARA AVE
PATRICIA LN
LAKE TAHOE BLVD

Creek
Trout
Creek
Trout
Upper
Truckee
River

Tahoe Keys Marina
AL WAI BLVD
TAHOE ISLAND DR
SOUTH SHORE DR
EMERALD BAY RD
ELOISE AVE
12TH ST
11TH ST
10TH ST
GLORENE AVE
VENICE DR
13TH ST
15TH ST

EL DORADO NATIONAL FOREST

1/2 mile
1/2 kilometer
0
0

N

Activities include gaming, a spa, nearby golf, and fine dining. Meetings and special events are welcome.

TAHOE BILTMORE RESORT & CASINO

1-800-245-8667
No. 5 Highway 28, Crystal Bay, NV.
Price: $49 and up
Credit cards: AE, D, MC, V
Children: Yes
Pets: No
Handicap access: Yes

The Biltmore is a resort, a casino, and even a bed and breakfast. With relatively low rates and a spacious facility, the Biltmore can handle groups of up to 600 people. In addition to accommodations to suit just about every taste, the Biltmore offers plenty of casino-style gaming and nightly entertainment. The Café Biltmore is a local favorite, serving up hearty breakfasts, juicy burgers, and well-stacked sandwiches. Conrad's Grill & BBQ is a meat-eater's heaven. Ski packages available. Rates start at $49 per night.

Homewood

ROCKWOOD LODGE
BED & BREAKFAST INN

www.rockwoodlodge.com/
1-800-538-2463 or 530-525-5273
5295 West Lake Blvd., Homewood, CA
Price: $125 and up
Credit cards: AE, D, MC, V
Children: Yes
Pets: No
Handicap access: Limited

This European-style beauty nestled among the tall pines lays claim to being Lake Tahoe's first B&B. The lodge offers a variety of comfortable and tastefully appointed rooms. A good example is the Secret Harbor Room, featuring a four-poster, canopied Russian wedding bed. Enjoy breakfast in your room, sitting before a beautiful picture window soaking up the morning sun. Speaking of soaking, the deep tiled soaking tub is a perfect stop after a day of skiing or river running. In keeping with the Dutch tradition of the Rockwood, shoes are removed upon entering the facility, so bring your own slippers or use their complimentary slipper socks. Enjoy your breakfast at the antique Belgian dining table or, weather permitting, outside on the patio.

TAHOMA MEADOWS
BED & BREAKFAST COTTAGES

www.tahomameadows.com
Innkeepers: Dick and Ulli White
1-866-525-1553
6821 West Lake Blvd., Homewood, CA
Price: $95 and up
Credit cards: AE, D, MC, V
Children: Yes
Pets: Yes
Handicap access: Limited

Not everyone visits Lake Tahoe seeking fast-paced action, and for those in search of quiet and tranquility, the little red cottages at Tahoma Meadows provide a wonderful haven. Located on Tahoe's west shore, a stay at the cottages is like stepping back 50 years in time. All cottages have private entrances and many of the baths have old-fashioned, claw-footed soaking tubs. For those staying in the B&Bs, a family style breakfast is served every morning in the common room, and some late afternoons feature free wine and cheese tastings. Some of the cottages have kitchens and fireplaces. During the summer months, garden furniture and hammocks are available for total relaxation. The cottages are a place where a couple, or an entire family (the dog, too), can bask in the solitude of the Sierra Nevada, knowing that if the urge for a little casino action arises, it's only a short drive away. Will host weddings, family reunions, and special events of up to 40 people, by arrangement.

Incline Village

GABRIELLI HOUSE BED & BREAKFAST

www.gabriellihouse.com/
Innkeepers: Bill and Cindy Gabrielli
1-800-731-6222
593 N. Dyer Circle, Incline Village, NV
Price: $129 and up
Credit cards: AE, D, MC, V
Children: Yes
Pets: No
Handicap access: Limited

The Gabrielli House is located near the center of Incline Village, and only minutes from Lake Tahoe's beautiful beaches. Each of the five guest rooms has its own bath and balcony overlooking the majestic mountains and forest. Bill and Cindy go out of their way to provide guests both a touch of class in the mountains and tremendous hospitality. A full gourmet breakfast is served daily. The non-smoking environment is a great getaway for couples and family gatherings. Children 12 and older welcome. Sorry, no pets.

HYATT REGENCY LAKE TAHOE

www.laketahoe.hyatt.com
775-832-1234
111 Country Club Drive, Incline Village, NV.
Price: $200 and up
Credit cards: AE, D, MC, V
Children: Yes
Pets: No
Handicap access: Yes

Bask in the luxury of the Hyatt Regency in a private lakeside cottage, balcony room, or executive king. All accommodations come with tons of amenities, including flat-screen TVs. Enjoy pampering and relaxation in the Stillwater Spa and dine overlooking Lake Tahoe in the Lone Eagle Grille. The Hyatt has both indoor and outdoor pools. Better yet, enjoy your favorite water sport on their private beach complete with a floating pier.

Kings Beach

BROCKWAY SPRINGS

www.brockwaysprings.com
530-546-4201
9200 Brockway Springs Dr.,
Kings Beach, CA
Price: $125 and up
Credit cards: AE, D, MC, V
Children: Yes
Pets: No
Handicap access: Yes

It's time for a Lake Tahoe vacation and you want it all. A room with a stunning view of the lake, but without the traffic and noise of a downtown motel. You want the quiet solitude of the High Sierra, but prefer easy access to all the incredible activities Lake Tahoe is famous for. Brockway Springs should fit the bill. All units are privately owned condominiums, lake-view townhouses ranging from one- to three-bedrooms. Amenities include fully equipped kitchens, wireless Internet access, and cable TV with VCR/DVD players. Most units have fireplaces. On-site recreation facilities include two tennis courts, swimming pool (heated year round by natural hot springs), a fishing and boating pier, and a club house with saunas and a fitness room. Brockway Springs is centrally located so that you are only minutes away from great restaurants, casino gaming, Nordic and alpine skiing, lake cruises, golf, fishing, mountain biking, horseback riding—the list is nearly endless.

South Lake Tahoe

BLACK BEAR INN
BED AND BREAKFAST

www.tahoeblackbear.com/index.htm
1-877-232-7466 or 530-544-4451
1202 Ski Run Blvd., South Lake Tahoe, CA
Price: $200 and up, includes a full breakfast
Credit cards: AE, D, MC, V

Children: No
Pets: No
Handicap access: Yes

Whether celebrating your honeymoon, an anniversary, or just a romantic getaway, it won't take long to understand why the Black Bear Inn was recently named one of the top ten B&Bs in California. Although the inn is a rustic lodge in a beautiful mountain setting, it is also within easy walking distance of the South Shore's shopping, dining, and high-rolling nightlife. The main lodge has five comfortable guest rooms, each with private bath and gas fireplace. Or, if you would like a little more privacy, the inn also has three spacious, romantic cabins with an adjacent hot tub gazebo for a relaxing moonlight soak. The lodge prides itself on its tranquil environment, and each room accommodates only two guests. The lodge offers a large collection of complimentary DVDs, and for those who want to stay connected, the entire facility is set up with free, high-speed Internet access.

EMBASSY SUITES LAKE TAHOE HOTEL AND SKI RESORT

www.embassytahoe.com
1-800-988-9820 or 530-544-5400
4130 Lake Tahoe Blvd.,
South Lake Tahoe, CA
Price: $179 and up
Credit cards: AE, D, MC, V
Children: Yes
Pets: No
Handicap access: Yes

Walk out the door of the Embassy Suites, turn right, and you are in the heart of the Stateline casino scene; turn left, and you are at the entrance to the tram that will whisk you up the mountain to Heavenly Valley. For an elegant oasis amid all the activity and attractions Lake Tahoe has to offer, this is the place to stay. The lobby is huge, featuring three garden atriums where you can enjoy a full breakfast, including handmade omelets, or an evening cocktail with friends—all compliments of the house. The rooms are all well-appointed suites. Recline on the sundeck before going for a swim in the heated pool or kicking back in the whirlpool or sauna. The nine-story hotel offers 400 two-room suites. Every spacious suite features a living room with a sofa bed, and a well-lit table for dining or to get a little work done. A refrigerator, microwave oven, and coffeemaker are included in every suite. Wireless Internet access is available for a small fee. This is a great place for families to stay because the kids can sleep in the living room, then get up and watch cartoons, without disturbing their parents catching a little extra shut-eye in their own room. While room service is always an option for dining, the hotel also features Echo Restaurant & Lounge, where you can watch a game, enjoy a few appetizers, or dine in style. During the summer, be sure to catch some rays and listen to live music on the outdoor patio.

FANTASY INN & WEDDING CHAPEL

www.fantasy-inn.com
1-800-367-7736 or 530-541-4200
3696 Lake Tahoe Blvd.,
South Lake Tahoe, CA
Price: $139 and up
Credit cards: AE, D, MC, V
Children: No
Pets: No
Handicap access: Yes

Looking for a romantic getaway for you and your spouse, or special friend? Fantasy Inn is like having your own secret hideaway. The Inn offers 52 rooms, 15 of which are one-of-a-kind theme rooms. There is no public pool or shared Jacuzzi here, because each room has its own luxurious whirlpool spa. Let one of the theme rooms—each about 580 square feet—transport you and that special person to a historical or contemporary mood, in such rooms as Caesar's

The Heavenly Valley ski tram now extends all the way to US 50.

Indulgence, Marie Antoinette, Graceland, or Mystic Mountain. In addition to the whirlpool, all rooms come with European showers, special effects romantic mood lighting, intriguing mirror treatments, 27-inch TV, and DMX stereo system.

FIRESIDE LODGE BED & BREAKFAST

www.tahoefiresidelodge.com/
1-800-692-2246 or 530-542-1717
515 Emerald Bay Rd., South Lake Tahoe, CA
Price: $69 and up
Credit cards: AE, D, MC, V
Children: Yes
Pets: Yes
Handicap access: No

Hey *Survivor* fans—here's a great place to play amid the splendor of Lake Tahoe and the surrounding forest. Don't feel like lugging your bikes along? No problem. The lodge offers complimentary bicycles and kayaks. Just minutes from the slopes, the Fireside is a great alternative to the ski resort lodges. Suites at the Fireside Lodge are designed to make you feel at home. Each suite has a fieldstone fireplace to warm you up on a cold, snowy night. Kitchens are equipped with a refrigerator, microwave, and coffeemaker. Suites also include cable TV/VCR and computer hook-ups. Best of all, kids and the family pooch are more than welcome.

INN AT HEAVENLY BED & BREAKFAST

www.innatheavenly.com
1-800-692-2246 or 530-544-4244
1261 Ski Run Blvd., South Lake Tahoe, CA
Price: $125 and up
Credit cards: AE, D, MC, V
Children: Yes
Pets: Yes
Handicap access: No

Just down the slope from America's largest bi-state ski resort, the Inn at Heavenly offers cabin-style rooms and detached cabins nestled into a two-acre wooded park.

Each room at the Inn at Heavenly is decorated with patchwork quilts and knotty-pine log furniture. All rooms are equipped with amenities guaranteed to make you feel at home including custom-designed river-rock fireplaces, private baths, refrigerators, microwaves, makers, cable TV, and computer hook-ups. In the gathering room, an expanded continental breakfast is served all day for late risers, and tasty hors d' oeuvres are offered each evening. Kids are more than welcome, and don't leave the pooch at home because the Inn is a dog-friendly facility.

INN BY THE LAKE

www.innbythelake.com
1-800-877-1466 or 530-542-0330
3300 Lake Tahoe Blvd.,
South Lake Tahoe, CA
Price: $108 and up
Credit cards: AE, D, MC, V
Children: Yes
Pets: No
Handicap access: Yes

Set on more than six acres, the Inn is more of a retreat than your standard motel. Here you can stroll through lush lawns, take in the beauty of the numerous flower beds, and just relax. Be sure to enjoy the small pond and waterfall near the flagpoles. For adventurous activities, the Inn offers a "Tahoe a la Carte" program. Get discounts on lift passes, casino shows, dining, and much more. As for your accommodations, the Inn offers 100 rooms and suites, many with private balconies overlooking the shimmering waters of Lake Tahoe, spa tubs, and kitchens. Enjoy a complimentary deluxe continental breakfast before hitting the on-site fitness center. Free bicycles and snowshoes are available, depending on the season. And, you can stay connected via free, unlimited, wireless Internet access. All rooms are non-smoking. The Inn's Event Center provides facilities for group meetings, retreats, weddings, receptions, and family reunions.

THE BLOCK

www.blockattahoe.com
1-888-544-4055 or 530-544-2936
4143 Cedar Ave., South Lake Tahoe, CA
Price: $89 and up
Credit cards: AE, D, MC, V
Children: Yes
Pets: Yes
Handicap access: Limited

Yo, dudes and dudettes—here's an afford-ably priced motel dedicated to the board crowd. Owner Marc Frank Montoya knows what you want because he's a snowboarding pro. All rooms include important stuff like cordless phones, CD players, game con-soles, board pegs, bike hooks and, of course, free wireless Internet access. Other neat stuff includes free gift bags, microwave popcorn, waxing/tuning serv-ices in the winter, and a rooftop hot tub. Ready to hit the town? The Block is located just steps from the major casinos and the new Heavenly Gondola. As for accommoda-tions, The Block offers both top-of-the-line Signature series rooms and less expensive modern rooms. The Signature rooms are designed to the specs of the rooms sponsor. No, no Nike here—but check out the Jones Soda Room, with its queen-size lowrider bed, 33" television, boot and glove dryer, and mini fridge. Or, how about the Spy room, with its king-size bed, 27" television with kicker surround sound, dinette area, and Jacuzzi spa. Even the modern rooms are built to "not-so-standard" standards. Let's be real—no room at The Block is a cookie-cutter design; each one has its own charm.

TAHOE LAKESHORE LODGE & SPA

www.tahoelakeshorelodge.com
1-800-448-4577 or 530-541-2180
930 Bal Bijou Road, South Lake Tahoe, CA

Price: $129 and up
Credit cards: AE, D, MC, V
Children: Yes
Pets: No
Handicap access: Yes

Talk about rooms with a view! The Lakeshore Lodge & Spa is South Shore's only inn located entirely on the lake. That's right, no roads to cross, no obstructions—walk out your door, and only beach sand separates you from a romp along the shores of Lake Tahoe. The owners like to say they put the "aahhh" in Tahoe, and why not? In addition to the hotel or condominium lodg-ing, each with a cozy fireplace, you can spend the day relaxing in the full service spa or kicking back by the heated pool and hot tub. Day-spa amenities include mas-sages, facials, body scrubs, body wraps, and more. When the weather's right, go for a swim in the pool, take a dip in the lake, play volleyball, put on a BBQ, or do absolutely nothing at all. When the evening rolls around, the lodge is located only about one mile from the downtown casino action via the free casino shuttle. Group meetings welcome.

Squaw Valley

OLYMPIC VILLAGE INN AT SQUAW VALLEY

www.olympicvillageinn.com
1-800-845-5243
1909 Chamonix Place, Olympic Valley, CA
Price: $129 and up
Credit cards: AE, D, MC, V
Children: Yes
Pets: No
Handicap access: Yes

This is the North Shore's premier all-year recreational playground. Golf, raft a river, swim, hike, and fish in the summer, down-hill, cross-country ski, and snowboard in the winter. The inn is nestled at the base of Squaw Valley USA with access to all recreational activities. The facility includes five outdoor spas and a large year-round heated swimming pool. Each suite is equipped with a kitchenette and gas barbecues are located in the courtyard. A recently added clubhouse offers an exercise room, sauna, arcade, indoor lounge, and gourmet kitchen with ovens. The inn offers complimentary bicycles for cruising around in the summer, and snowshoes for tromping through the snow in the winter.

THE PLUMPJACK SQUAW VALLEY INN
www.plumpjack.com
1-800-323-ROOM or 530-583-1576
1920 Squaw Valley Rd.,
Olympic Valley, CA
Price: $169 and up
Credit cards: AE, D, MC, V
Children: Yes
Pets: No
Handicap access: Yes

The folks at The PlumpJack pride themselves on spoiling their visitors with ambiance, comfort, and excellent food and drink. The inn was built in 1959 to house for the 1960 Olympic delegation and today it remains an award winner (No. 12 of the top 50 Hotels in North America by *Condé Nast Traveler*). The elegant rooms feature down comforters, hooded terrycloth robes and slippers, and luxury amenities. Outside, go for a swim in the heated pool or splash around in the heated Jacuzzi spa. Be sure not to miss the cozy bar and beautiful restaurant, where the cuisine is a delight, and the wine list extensive.

RED WOLF INN AT SQUAW VALLEY
www.redwolfsquaw.com
530-583-7226
2000 Squaw Loop Rd., Olympic Valley, CA
Price: $110 and Up
Credit cards: AE, D, MC, V
Children: Yes

Pets: No
Handicap access: Limited

Summer or winter, outdoor sports enthusiasts have been flocking to the Red Wolf Inn for many years. The resort offers ski-in/ski-out access to Squaw Valley, and is a short walk to the High Country Tram for fine dining and great shopping. Get a good workout in the clubhouse and recline in one of two on-site hot tubs. Rooms feature queen beds, color TV with cable access, fireplaces, and fully equipped kitchens.

RESORT AT SQUAW CREEK
www.squawcreek.com
1-800-327-3353 or 530-583-6300
400 Squaw Creek Rd., Olympic Valley, CA
Price: $179 and up
Credit cards: AE, D, MC, V
Children: Yes
Pets: No
Handicap access: Yes

This four-diamond, luxury resort is ranked among the top 50 best resorts in North America by *Condé Nast Traveler* magazine. The resort offers more than 400 guest rooms, suites, and penthouses, each with a stunning view of the surrounding forests, meadows, and the Sierra Nevada. Start your day hopping on the ski-in/ski-out on-site chairlift to Squaw Valley USA and, upon your return, pamper yourself in the full-service spa. In your room, recline in the resort's famous "Deep Powder" bed, and turn on the flat screen TV. Rooms are also equipped with refrigerators and wireless Internet access. All suites and penthouses offer fireplaces and resort-style kitchens, with china, glassware, and silverware. Want a little time alone? The resort offers babysitting services, and also Mountain Buddies, a program designed just for kids. The facility also has four distinct restaurants and a shopping promenade that deserves exploration.

SQUAW VALLEY LODGE

www.squawvalleylodge.com
1-800-540-6742 or 530-583-5500
201 Squaw Peak Rd., Olympic Village, CA
Price: $139 and up
Credit cards: AE, D, MC, V
Children: Yes
Pets: No
Handicap access: Yes

Once you've visited Squaw Valley Lodge, you'll never want to go home again. This place has it all from ski-in/ski-out direct access to Squaw Valley USA to all the recreational amenities the Lake Tahoe area has to offer. The spacious condominium suites feature king and queen beds, full kitchens or kitchenettes, microwave ovens, refrigerators, and gourmet coffee. Enjoy satellite TV or surf the Web via Wi-Fi Internet access. When it's time for a workout, check out the fitness and spa center, and don't miss your opportunity for a relaxing Swedish full-body massage. In the summer, break out your tennis racquet and serve it up on one of the lodge's courts. And don't forget—world-class golfing is only minutes away.

VILLAGE AT SQUAW VALLEY USA

www.thevillageatsquaw.com
1-888-805-5022 or 530-584-6202
1750 Village East Rd., Olympic Village, CA
Price: $109 and up
Credit cards: AE, D, MC, V
Children: Yes
Pets: Yes
Handicap access: Yes

It doesn't matter what time of year you visit this recreational e-ticket, the Village at Squaw Valley offers all kinds of great things to see and do. Located at the base of Squaw Valley, world-class skiing and snowboarding is just outside your door. Exploring the European-style village is a special treat. Here you will find unique shops, excellent food, and a full-service spa. All the condo-minium-style suites have balconies and are equipped with fireplaces, full kitchens, cable TV, and Internet access. Babysitting is available for a fee. After a recreation-filled day, and a great meal, check out the billiards lounge or the fitness center

Stateline

HARRAH'S LAKE TAHOE

www.harrahs.com
1-800-427-7247
15 US 50, Stateline, NV.
Price: $69 and up
Credit cards: AE, D, MC, V
Children: Yes
Pets: Yes
Handicap access: Yes

You would have to be dead if you didn't enjoy a stay at one of the lake's premier resort/casinos. Harrah's is 18-stories high, featuring 525 guestrooms, eight restaurants, a gigantic swimming pool, luxurious spa, shopping, headline entertainment, and all the gaming one could ask for. Accommodations range from comfortable rooms to their incredible penthouse suites overlooking the lake's deep-blue waters and the rugged Sierra Nevada. Be sure to visit the South Shore Room where all the top stars in music and comedy go on stage nightly.

HARVEY'S RESORT & CASINO

www.harveys.com
1-800-427-8397
US 50, Stateline, NV
Price: $69 and up
Credit cards: AE, D, MC, V
Children: Yes
Pets: No
Handicap access: Yes

As the first hotel/casino built in South Lake Tahoe, Harvey's—like fine wine—just gets better with age. The hotel/casino features state-of-the-art guestrooms, eight dining

Harvey's has come a long way since its humble beginnings in the 1940s.

facilities, exciting gaming including a race and sports book, a fitness center, gift shops, and entertaining nightlife. The resort has two towers. For a room with a view of the lake, stay in the Lake Tower; for a mountain view, head for the Mountain Tower. During your stay, be sure to take a cruise on the *Ship of the Stars*, the private yacht once owned by gaming legend William Harrah. Excursions to scenic Emerald Bay are booked daily at either Harveys or Harrah's.

HORIZON CASINO RESORT

www.horizoncasino.com
1-800-648-3222
US 50, Stateline, NV.
Price: $59 and up
Credit cards: AE, D, MC, V
Children: Yes
Pets: No
Handicap access: Yes

Want to golf, ski, or just frolic on the shores of beautiful Lake Tahoe? These activities and much more greet the visitor to Horizon Casino Resort. Horizon features 539 guest-rooms, free live entertainment, eight movie theaters, and great dining—and there's always plenty of action at the gaming tables. Horizon also boasts the largest outdoor pool in Lake Tahoe. Relax by the pool and warm up from a day on the slopes in one of the huge hot tubs.

LAKESIDE INN AND CASINO

www.lakesideinn.com
1-800-624-7980
168 US 50, Stateline, NV.
Price: $59 and up
Credit cards: AE, D, MC, V
Children: Yes
Pets: No
Handicap access: Yes

Here you can stay in contemporary mountain lodge-style accommodations, with beautiful views of the lake. Lakeside Inn

was voted "Best of Tahoe" in 10 categories. The facility has 124 rooms, and the casino boasts the largest craps table in the state of Nevada, along with other gaming activities. Great meals can be found in either of the two restaurants, and relaxation is a joy in one of the three casino bars.

MONTBLEU RESORT CASINO & SPA

www.montbleuresort.com
1-800-648-3353
55 US 50, Stateline, NV.
Price: $75.95 and up
Credit cards: AE, D, MC, V
Children: Yes
Pets: Yes
Handicap access: Yes

MontBleu's 440 luxurious rooms and suites—many with breathtaking views of Lake Tahoe and the Sierra Nevada—entice visitors from around the world. Built around a cosmopolitan theme, the facility offers nightly Vegas-style entertainment, gaming, shopping, a relaxing spa, and a lagoon-style pool. Dining is a special experience here at any one of the casual restaurants or, for something special, check out the Ciera Steak and Chophouse. Convention and ski packages available. Pets welcome.

RIDGE TAHOE

www.ridgetahoeresort.com
1-800-334-1600 or 775-588-3553
400 Ridge Club Drive, Stateline, NV
Price: $121 and up
Credit cards: AE, D, MC, V
Children: Yes
Pets: Yes
Handicap access: Yes

Ridge Tahoe is a deluxe, 11-acre condominium/hotel resort and spa featuring 302 units on 11 acres overlooking Nevada's Carson Valley. The Ridge offers year-round vacation rentals, many with expansive

Horizon Resort and Casino is popular for gaming, dining, and relaxation.

views, a health club, an indoor sports complex, indoor/outdoor swimming pools and Jacuzzis, a restaurant, market, and much more. A shuttle service allows guests easy access to casino central, in nearby Stateline. The Ridge is located on Heavenly Ski Resort's Nevada slope, adjacent to the Stagecoach Lodge and chair lift. A conference center is available to handle corporate meetings, retreats, family reunions, and weddings.

Tahoe City

CHANEY HOUSE
A LAKEFRONT GUESTHOUSE

www.chaneyhouse.com
Innkeeper: Gary and Lori Chaney
530-525-7333
4725 West Lake Blvd., Tahoe City, CA
Price: $165 and up

Credit cards: D, MC, V
Children: Yes
Pets: By arrangement
Handicap access: Limited

Snuggle up in the old-world charm of this beautiful old home nestled among native pines, with a beautiful view of Lake Tahoe. The house was built in 1923 by Italian stone mason Umberto Sprellio, and features 18-inch walls, Gothic arches, and a massive fireplace. A gourmet breakfast is served in the formal dining room or out on the patio overlooking the lake when the weather is mild. Each of the three guest rooms in the house have private baths and king or queen beds. The Honeymoon Hideaway is a separate suite built over the garage, and features a queen feather bed, wet bar, TV, and private bath with a granite whirlpool tub.

THE COTTAGE INN OF LAKE TAHOE

www.thecottageinn.com
1-800-581-4073 or 530-581-4073
1690 W. Lake Blvd. Tahoe City, CA
Price: $158 and up
Credit cards: AE, D, MC, V
Children: 12 and older
Pets: No
Handicap access: Limited

This is the way to enjoy Lake Tahoe as it once was—a beautiful, quiet retreat away from the hustle and bustle of the everyday world. Built in 1938, the Cottage Inn retains its historic charm. The facility features accommodations from single room studios to deluxe cottages with kitchens. All rooms except one offer private entrances. Some rooms have lake views. Each cottage is decorated with its own unique theme and all have fireplaces, mini fridge, and TV. Wireless Internet access is available in the main lodge. Enjoy a stroll on the private beach before sitting down to a full breakfast, served each morning. After a day of skiing or other recreation, kick back in the sauna and enjoy homemade cookies and a glass of wine.

RIVER RANCH LODGE

www.riverranchlodge.com
1-866-991-9912 or 530-583-4264
Corner of Highway 89 and Alpine Meadows Road, Tahoe City, CA
Price: $85 and up
Credit cards: AE, D, MC, V
Children: Yes
Pets: Yes, with prior arrangement
Handicap access: Limited

Nestled on the banks of the scenic Truckee River, the River Ranch Lodge offers 19 comfortable rooms, a dining room, a bar cantilevered over the river, and a second dining room with a warm fireplace and a spacious riverside patio. This is a centrally located facility, offering access to world-class skiing and boarding in the winter.

When the weather warms, this is a great place to stay while enjoying river rafting, kayaking, or just cooling out. Every room has a private bath and cable TV. Many of the rooms have balconies overlooking the river. The original lodge was built in 1888 and was a fashionable watering spot on the railway. It fell into disrepair during the 1930s, and the site was cleared and renovated. During the 1960 Olympic Games at nearby Squaw Valley, many foreign diplomats made the lodge their headquarters.

Tahoe Vista

THE SHORE HOUSE AT LAKE TAHOE

www.shorehouselaketahoe.com
Innkeeper: Barb and Marty
1-800-207-5160
7170 North Lake Blvd., Tahoe Vista, CA
Price: $190 and up
Credit cards: AE, D, MC, V
Children: No
Pets: No
Handicap access: Yes

Planning a wedding, honeymoon, or just an intimate getaway? The Shore House at Lake Tahoe deserves a good look. The Shore House offers nine guest rooms, each with a private entrance, private balcony or deck, fireplace, knotty-pine walls, custom-built log furniture, featherbeds, and Scandia Down comforters. Your stay includes a gourmet breakfast served in the lakefront dining room or, weather permitting, outside on the lawn right at the water's edge. Here you can enjoy a day on the slopes or kayaking, and return for an afternoon massage and a soak in the hot tub, overlooking Lake Tahoe. Special packages include tasteful goodies such as flower bouquets, welcome baskets, a CD of house love songs, and chocolate-covered strawberries with champagne. And, if you are looking to tie the knot, innkeepers Barb and Marty are ministers of the Universal

Life Church and have performed more than 750 weddings. The Shore House is a non-smoking facility.

Truckee

CEDAR HOUSE SPORT HOTEL

www.cedarhousesporthotel.com
1-866-582-5655 or 530-582-5655
10918 Brockway Rd., Truckee, CA
Price: $140 and up
Credit cards: AE, D, MC, V
Children: Yes
Pets: Yes
Handicap access: Yes

Built in a hip, European design using the latest in green technologies, the Cedar House seeks to offer guests a retreat where the atmosphere sooths the mind, body, and soul. Inspired by the beauty of the surrounding Sierra Nevada, the hotel sits in a small valley only a few minutes from downtown Truckee. The hotel offers 42 rooms and suites, a full bar in the lobby, and an outdoor spa to unwind after a day of skiing, hiking, or exploring the surrounding area. Start your day at the Cedar House with a European-style continental breakfast, featuring fresh bread, pastries, yogurt, fresh fruit, cold cuts, and cheese. All rooms come with flat screen TVs, Wi-Fi Internet access, and fresh ground coffee. And yes—even the family dog is welcome, and will have his own bed and a special treat.

A classic stone building houses a board shop in downtown Truckee.

DONNER LAKE VILLAGE RESORT

www.donnerlakevillage.com
1-800-920-0994 or 530-587-6081
15695 Donner Pass Road, Truckee, CA
Price: $91 and up
Credit cards: AE, D, MC, V
Children: Yes
Pets: Yes
Handicap access: Yes

Want to get away? *Really* away, but still close enough to visit the slopes and maybe hit the gaming tables? Nestled on the shores of beautiful Donner Lake, the Village Resort boasts nice accommodations and stunning views of the lake and the surrounding Sierra Nevada. The Village Resort offers rooms for every taste ranging from small lodgette rooms with queen beds and fold-out sleepers, to studios with fully equipped kitchens. For larger groups, check out the one- and two-bedroom, condo-style units. Maybe it's time for a day off, to kick back and just relax. In the courtyard, you'll find barbecues, picnic tables, and lounge chairs all overlooking Donner Lake and the marina. If the weather is a little chilly, check out the fireplace inside the lodge.

One of many private estates that surround Lake Tahoe.

CULTURE

If Lake Tahoe is nature's crown jewel of the Sierra Nevada, then Thunderbird Lodge is the manmade jewel of the lake, and only recently has it been open for public tours. Anybody familiar with all there is to see at Lake Tahoe will tell you, Thunderbird Lodge is the No. 1 must-see attraction.

Built between 1936 and 1939 by the eccentric San Francisco real-estate magnate, animal lover, and playboy, George Whittell, the Tudor Revival summer estate on the lake's east shore includes a main lodge surrounded by three cottages, a card house, an elephant house for Mingo the elephant, a lighthouse, three garages, a gatehouse, and a boathouse that is home to one of the lake's most famous yachts, *Thunderbird*.

The beautifully landscaped grounds surrounding the estate include elaborate tree and granite boulder-filled gardens accented by fountains, waterfalls, staircases, and garden paths. A 600-foot tunnel carved through solid granite connects the main lodge with both the boathouse and the card house, which saw many a high-stakes game in its day.

Whittell owned 40,000 acres surrounding the estate, including some 27 miles of lakefront property. His initial plan was to develop the property, but after completing the estate, his love of animals, nature, and privacy outweighed anything money could buy and he retained the property until his death in 1969. Today, the estate is operated by the Thunderbird Lodge Preservation Society whose mission is to maintain the environmental, cultural, educational, and historical values associated with Lake Tahoe. Visit the lodge on the Web at: www.thunderbirdlodge.org.

There are two ways to visit the estate:

Tours by land are offered four times daily, Tuesday through Friday, from June through mid-October. Parking for shuttle pickup is located at the Incline Village/Crystal Bay Visitors Center, 969 Tahoe Blvd., Incline Village, CA. Tickets, $32 adults, $16 for children 6–11. Children under six are not permitted. Reservations, 1-800-408-2463.

Tours by water embark from Tahoe Keys Marina aboard the classic wooden boat *Tahoe*, Tuesday through Saturday, from June through September. Ticket prices included a narrated cruise along the lake's east shore, a tour of the estate, and lunch on the grounds. Tickets, $110 adults, $55 children 6–11. Children under 6 are not permitted. Reservations, 1-888-867-6394.

Historic Places

EHRMAN MANSION

www.parks.ca.gov
Sugar Pine Point State Park
530-525-7982
US 89, 10 miles south of Tahoe City
Tahoma, CA
Open Daily (July thru Labor Day) 11 AM—4 PM
Admission: $10 per car

Ehrman Mansion is a classic example of the opulence of Lake Tahoe estates at the turn of the 20th century. The three-story mansion was built in 1903, and was considered to have the best of utility systems, including electric lights and indoor plumbing. The grounds were planted with trees, expansive lawns, and gardens. As part of a state park, the facility also offers beach access and a nature center.

An old boathouse constructed of pine is still in use.

TAHOE CLASSIC YACHT

www.tahoeclassicyacht.org

530-544-2307
South Lake Tahoe, CA
Open: May–Oct. 11 AM–5 PM
Admission: Donations Appreciated

Located on the grounds of Pope and Valhalla estates, adjacent to Camp Richardson, this is both a unique maritime museum and a boatyard where the classic *Quich Cha Kiddin*, a 38-foot cruiser built in 1921, is under restoration. The vessel was one of the most luxurious yachts to ply Tahoe's deep blue waters. The museum also offers exhibits of large and small watercraft, and a variety of antique engines.

VALHALLA

www.valhalla-tallac.com
1-888-631-9153
On US 89, 2.5 miles north of South Lake Tahoe
South Lake Tahoe, CA
Open: May–Oct. 11 AM–5 PM
Admission: $10 per car

Talk about blending the natural beauty of Lake Tahoe with some serious culture, Valhalla—also known as The Heller Estate—offers theater, art, music, and special events for the entire family. Take in a play at the Boathouse Theater, or treat yourself to some serious jazz. Art exhibits feature some of the finest regional artists, and their art workshops are designed for children. Peak season runs from late June through September, but special events are offered year round. The facility is open to the public and available for private parties.

VIKINGSHOLM CASTLE

www.vikingsholm.org/
D. L. Bliss and Emerald Bay State Park
1-800-777-0369 or 540-531-3030
11001 W. Lake Blvd.
Tahoma, CA

Valhalla Estate is a popular South Shore community center.

Hours: Daily 10 AM–4 PM, May–Oct.

Admission: $10 per car

Built in 1929, Vikingsholm Castle is one of the finest examples of Scandinavian architecture in North America. Nestled on the shore of Emerald Bay, the castle offers incredible views of Lake Tahoe and the surrounding area. Designed and built as an authentic Norse fortress from around 800 A.D., the castle offers a unique blend of art and history. The home was built by Lora J. Knight after she and her architect spent time traveling and studying in Scandinavia. The surrounding area provided an abundance of timber and rock. Some sections contain no nails, pegs, or spikes. The castle is open from Memorial Day to the end of September, and tours are given every half hour.

Lake Cruises

Dream on Sailing Charters, www.dreamonsailingcharters.com, 530-659-9409, Tahoe Keys Marina, South Lake Tahoe, CA. Pack up the family and climb aboard *The Pirate* for a scenic and swashbuckling tour of the lake. This 41-foot ketch features two state rooms, each with a private head. The captain entertains with stories of buried treasure and pirate lore. Food and beverage provided. Available for private parties and weddings. Special activities for children.

Lake Tahoe Yacht Charters, www.laketahoeyachtcharters.com, 530-541-0248, 260 Beach Drive, South Lake Tahoe, CA. Enjoy a moonlight cruise aboard the elegant *Big Dream*, a 72-foot Sunseeker. Once aboard you'll be treated like royalty. Tell the captain your wishes, and leave the rest to the crew. Available for dinner cruises, sunset cruises, wedding parties, and family fun cruises. Rates: $800 per hour based on a two-hour minimum. Catering and bar service extra.

M.S. *Dixie II* Paddlewheeler, www.zephyrcove.com, 1-800-23-TAHOE, US 50, Zephyr Cove, NV. Enjoy an excellent meal aboard the M.S. *Dixie II*, voted "Best Boat Cruise" at Tahoe for 11 years in a row. What's your pleasure? How about a scenic breakfast brunch cruise for the whole family? Or, maybe a delightful champagne brunch? How about a romantic, sunset dinner/dance cruise, complete with live music? All are excellent choices aboard this historic reincarnation of the luxurious paddlewheeler that first cast off from the shores of Lake Tahoe in 1949. Several cruise destinations available including Emerald Bay and historic Glenbrook. Rates start at: $38 adults, $12 children.

North Tahoe Cruises/*Tahoe Gal,* www.tahoegal.com, 1-800-218-2464, 850 N. Lake Blvd., Tahoe City, CA. Available for breakfast, scenic shoreline, cocktail & dinner/dance cruises, this paddlewheeler is equipped with a full galley and bar. Check out the Commodore's Salon on the top deck, for more intimate parties of up to 25 guests. Rates begin at $26 adults, $16 children.

Safari Rose Cruises, www.tahoeboatcruises.com, 1-888-867-6397, 605 US 50, Zephyr Cove, NV. With two sailing and two motor vessels in its fleet, Safari Rose guarantees sailing fun for the whole family. *Woodwind I* is a 40-foot trimaran sailing from Camp Richardson, *Woodwind II* is a 55-foot catamaran sailing from Zephyr Cove, *Tahoe* is a classic 40-foot wooden powerboat departing from Tahoe Keys Marina, and *Safari Rose* is an 80-foot motor yacht also departing from Tahoe Keys Marina. The fleet is available for public cruises, private charters, and weddings. Rates start at $28 adults, $12 children (3–12).

Lake Tahoe Cruises, www.zephyrcove.com, 1-800-238-2463, 900 Ski Run Blvd., South Lake Tahoe, CA. Featuring three vessels embarking from Ski Run Marina, Lake Tahoe Cruises offers lake voyages for individuals, families, wedding parties, large groups, and corporate gatherings. The fleet includes: *Tahoe Queen*, 144-foot paddlewheeler built on the Mississippi River in 1983, with three decks and a capacity of 500 passengers; *Tahoe Paradise*, an 82-foot, two-story luxury yacht with accommodations from 25 to 120 guests; *Tahoe Princess*, a 70-foot, pontoon boat billed as the fleet's "floating ballroom." The boats are available for private charters and full-service event planners will see to it your cruise memories last a lifetime. Rates start at $33 adults, $9 children, $30 seniors.

Tahoe Thunder, www.action-watersports.com, 530-541-7245, Action Watersports at Timber Cove Marina, South Lake Tahoe, CA. Blast across Lake Tahoe to beautiful Emerald Bay on the lake's ultimate adrenaline ride. Billed as one of the fastest speedboats on the lake, *Tahoe Thunder* guarantees an unforgettable ride filled with incredible scenery. Rates: $60 adults, $30 children (12 and under).

The Party Boat, www.tahoesports.com, 1-888-542-2111, Tahoe Keys Marina, 2435 Venice Dr. E, South Lake Tahoe, CA. Want to do something special for your family reunion, wedding or reception, company retreat—whatever the reason might be—charter the Party Boat,

The Tahoe Queen *paddlewheeler is popular for sightseeing, dining, and dancing.*

a 52-foot Harbor Master available for cruises year around. Special features include spacious indoor and outdoor decks to accommodate up to 49 guests, a flybridge, and fully equipped kitchen. Rates begin at $1200 for a two-hour cruise.

Museums

EMIGRANT TRAIL MUSEUM AND THE PIONEER MONUMENT
www.parks.ca.gov/default.asp?page_id=503
Donner Memorial State Park
530-582-7892
12593 Donner Pass Road, Truckee, CA.
Open Daily 9 AM–4 PM
Admission: Free

Step into the past and learn about the people who came to this area, including Native Americans, the Donner Party, and the men who built the transcontinental railroad. The museum is also the starting point of a self-guided nature trail. Not far from the museum is the Pioneer Monument and the Donner Party's Murphy Family cabin site. Staff-led hikes, special feature shows, and campfires run from late June through Labor Day.

GATEKEEPER'S CABIN MUSEUM
www.northtahoemuseums.org/
530-583-1762
130 W. Lake Blvd.
Tahoe City, CA
Open: Daily 10 AM–4 PM, May–Oct.
Admission: Adults $3, Seniors (55 and older) $2, Children (6–12) $1; Museum members and children 5 and younger, free.

The original Gatekeeper's Cabin was built in 1909, destroyed by fire in 1978 and has since been reconstructed. The cabin originally housed the gatekeeper, whose duties included measuring and regulating the lake's water level. Located on the south bank of the Truckee River—Lake Tahoe's only outlet—the museum features the history of Lake Tahoe, natural history displays, and numerous artifacts including a delightful basket collection.

LAKE TAHOE HISTORICAL SOCIETY MUSEUM
3058 Lake Tahoe Blvd.
530-541-5458
South Lake Tahoe, CA
Open: Tues.–Sat., 10 AM–4 PM, Memorial Day–Labor Day
Admission: Free

The Lake Tahoe Historical Society Museum features the area's most extensive collections of early photographs, Native American basketry, pioneer equipment, and a beautiful replica of the historic S.S. *Tahoe*, the lake's oldest erect ship, and Osgood's Toll House from 1859.

TAHOE ENVIRONMENTAL RESEARCH CENTER
www.sierranevada.edu/admission/students/tces_home.html
Sierra Nevada College

775-881-7566
999 Tahoe Blvd., Incline Village, NV
Open Daily 8 AM—5 PM
Admission: Free

Talk about a total experience in ecology—this $24 million facility is so environmentally friendly, its walls are insulated with material made from recycled blue jeans. TERC offers demonstrations and exhibits focused on the environmental quality of the Lake Tahoe Basin. Opened in 2006, the center is home to a state-of-the-art research laboratory, hands-on public museum, and college classrooms. The center is a unique partnership between public and private institutions of higher education in two states, including Sierra Nevada College, the University of California, Davis (UC Davis), the Desert Research Institute (DRI) and the University of Nevada, Reno (UNR).

TAHOE MARITIME MUSEUM
www.tahoemaritimemuseum.org
Homewood Mountain Ski Lodge
530-525-9253
5205 West Lake Blvd., Homewood, CA
Open Thursday through Monday, May 17 to Sept. 17
Admission: Free

Check out eight historic boats, including the *Shanghai*, an 1890s launch found at the bottom of Lake Tahoe. The collection also includes a steamer room, several engines, and a quantity of other historic items. Videos are regularly shown featuring Tahoe's maritime history. Be sure to bring the kids, because the museum also offers a children activities room. Activities include line-tying, boat building, water colors, and arts and crafts.

Nightlife

Aspen Lounge, Inside Horizon Casino & Resort, www.horizoncasino.com. 775-588-6211, US 50, Stateline, NV. A locals' favorite, where the DJ cranks up the music Thursday through Sunday.

Blu Nightclub, Inside MontBleu Resort Casino & Spa, www.montbleuresort.com. 775-586-2000, Stateline, NV. The Blu's DJs preside over a dance floor ablaze with the latest technology in lights, sights, and sounds. This is a high-energy venue guaranteed not to disappoint those ready to put their rhythm in motion.

Cabo Wabo Cantina, Inside Harvey's Resort & Casino, 775-588-2411, Stateline, NV. Open well into the night, offering a wide variety of music for dancing and listening pleasure.

McP's Pub Tahoe, 530-542-4435, 4093 Lake Tahoe Blvd., South Lake Tahoe, CA. Features live music 365 nights a year and never a cover charge.

Moodys Bistro & Lounge, Inside the Truckee Hotel, 530-587-8688, 10007 Bridge St. Truckee, CA. Modeled after the jazz craze in San Francisco during the 90s, co-owner J.J. Morgan strives to reinvent Tahoe's music scene with eclectic jazz groups and DJs.

Tahoe Underground Night Club, 775-588-2333. 270 Kingsbury Grade, Stateline, NV. Open nightly at 5 PM Live music provided by local and out-of-town bands.

Vex, Inside Harrah's Hotel & Casino, www.laketahoenights.com, 775-586-6705, US 50, Stateline, NV. Ultra high energy music is accented by a state-of-the-art light and sound system. Check out the VIP booths and cabana for the ultimate night club experience.

Whiskey Dicks Saloon, 530-544-3425, 2660 Lake Tahoe Blvd., South Lake Tahoe, CA. A great place to get together. Whiskey Dicks features live music, free pinball, pool tables, and an Internet jukebox.

Theatre/Cinema

Heavenly Village Cinema, 530-544-1110, 1021 Heavenly Village Way, South Lake Tahoe, CA. A modern eight-plex popular with the skiing crowd.

Horizon Stadium Cinemas, Inside Horizon Casino & Resort, www.horizoncasino.com, 775-588-6211, US 50, Stateline, NV. Catch the latest first-run movies and Hollywood blockbusters at one of their eight state-of-the-art theaters.

Lake Tahoe Shakespeare Festival, www.laketahoeshakespeare.com, 1-800-74-SHOWS, Sand Harbor State Park, Sand Harbor, NV. What ho! 'Tis not the merry olde Globe Theatre—'tis better! Every summer the stage is lit and the curtain goes up on another season in one of the most beautiful amphitheatre settings in the world. Enjoy gourmet dining or just some wine and cheese, relax on the beautiful white sandy beach, and partake in an unforgettable summer experience. Eat your fill from numerous selections prepared in Shakespeare's Kitchen, or bring your own goodies. Small coolers and ice chests are permitted. In addition to excellent Shakespearean theatre, the facility also hosts contemporary plays and special events, including the Lake Tahoe Chautauqua, Sierra Nevada Ballet, and performances by the Reno Philharmonic Orchestra. Wheelchair and other special-needs seating is available, as are assisted listening devices.

The MontBleu Theatre, Inside the MontBleu Resort Casino & Spa, www.montbleuresort .com, 1-800-648-3353, US 50, Stateline, NV. The theatre combines theatrical stage and lighting and features some of the top names in entertainment. Terraced seating allows for 950 banquet style and up to 1,500 theatre style. Check the schedule for special kids' matinees.

South Shore Room, Located inside Harrah's Hotel & Casino. www.harrahs.com, 1-800-427-7247, US 50, Stateline, NV. Many of the hottest names in music and comedy make it a point to perform in the famous South Shore Room. The Improv features two new comics every week.

The Golden Cabaret, Inside the Horizon Casino & Resort. www.horizoncasino.com, 775-588-6211, US 50, Stateline, NV Looking for an evening of laughter, magic, or song and dance? Check the schedule at The Golden Cabaret—top-line entertainment is their forté.

SEASONAL EVENTS

JANUARY

Full Moon Snowshoe Party & Cocktail Races, 530-541-1801. Camp Richardson.

Elvis Day, 775-849-0704. Mt. Rose.

Blue Gay-la, South Lake Tahoe's Gay & Lesbian Ski Week, www.bluelaketahoe.com. 1-800-AT-TAHOE, South Lake Tahoe.

Crab Feed, www.kiwaniscluboflaketahoe.com, 530-573-4055, Stateline.

FEBRUARY
ACT Annual Winter Party, www.tahoeanimals.org, 530-400-4766, South Lake Tahoe.

President's Day Treasure Hunt, www.sierraattahoe.com. 530-659-7453, Twin Bridges.

MARCH
Annual Legislative Ski Day, www.sierraattahoe.com, 530-659-7453, Twin Bridges.

North Lake Tahoe Snow Festival, www.tahoesnowfestival.com, 530-583-7167, Various locations.

Great Race, www.thegreatskirace.com. Tahoe City.

Hope Valley Cross-Country Full Moon Tour, 530-694-2266. Hope Valley.

Hope Valley Cross-Country Snowshoe Thompson Tour, 530-694-2266. Hope Valley.

Annual St. Patrick's Wine Tasting & Corned Beef Feed, 775-588-6616. Stateline.

Easter Sunday Festivities, 530-659-7453. Twin Bridges.

JUNE
Valhalla Renaissance Faire, www.valhallafaire.com. South Lake Tahoe.

America's Most Beautiful Bike Ride, www.bikethewest.com, 1-800-565-2704, South Lake Tahoe.

DeCelle Memorial Lake Tahoe Relay, laketahoerelay.com. 530-877-9731, South Lake Tahoe.

Corvettes at Lake Tahoe, laketahoecorvetteclub.com, 530-542-0485, Stateline.

Highway 50 Wagon Train Rendezvous, www.hwy50wagontrain.com, 530-644-3761, Zephyr Cove.

JULY
Star Spangled Fourth Lights on the Lake, 530-544-5050. South Lake Tahoe.

American Century Celebrity Golf Championship, www.tahoecelebritygolf.com. 530-544-5050, Stateline.

Lake Tahoe Shakespeare Festival, www.laketahoeshakespeare.com, 1-800-747-4697, Sand Harbor.

Lake Tahoe Historical Society's Annual Garden Tour, 530-541-4654. South Lake Tahoe.

AUGUST
Brews, Jazz & Funk Fest, www.thevillageatsquaw.com/todo/events, Squaw Valley.

SEPTEMBER

Tour de Tahoe Bike Big Blue, www.bikethewest.com/tourdetahoe, 1-800-565-2704, South Lake Tahoe.

Lake Tahoe Marathon Week, www.laketahoemarathon.com,S 530-544-7095, South Lake Tahoe.

Lake Tahoe Food & Wine Festival, www.insidetahoe.net, 1-800-468-2463, Crystal Bay.

Squaw Valley Art & Wine Festival, www.thevillageatsquaw.com/todo/events. 530-583-9247, Squaw Valley.

Art Bark Fest, www.thevillageatsquaw.com/todo/events, Squaw Valley.

Village Oktoberfest, www.thevillageatsquaw.com/todo/events, Squaw Valley.

Festival of Lights/Winter Solstice, www.thevillageatsquaw.com/todo/events, Squaw Valley.

RESTAURANTS

When it's time to eat, the restaurants at Lake Tahoe provide selections to please every palate, often all under one roof. From classy French cuisine and steakhouses, to quaint international diners and Mexican-style cantinas, you're bound to find just what you wanted. All of the resort/casinos offer American and international menus as well as lavish buffets. At the same time, the area is a mecca for specialty dining establishments.

Dining Price Code

The price range below is for a single dinner that includes an entrée, appetizer, or dessert. Tax and gratuities are not included.

Inexpensive Up to $15
Moderate $15–$30
Expensive $30–$50
Very expensive $50 or more

BREWER'S BRANDING IRON BBQ & ROTISSERIE

www.brewersbrandingiron.com
530-542-1095
3600 Lake Tahoe Blvd.,
South Lake Tahoe, CA

Open: Mon.-Fri. 4 PM–11 PM; Sat, Sun, holidays 11 AM–11 PM
Price: Inexpensive to moderate
Cuisine: American BBQ
Serving: D
Reservations: No
Credit cards: AE, D, MC, V

Hankerin' for some real barbecue? Come on down to Brewer's and kick off your boots in this Western-style tavern and eatery. Bring the youngun's along, there always welcome. No bull, just great food is the order of the day here. Holdin' a family reunion or just a big get-together? No problem, there's plenty of room for everybody. The Texas Combo is the most popular selection on the menu and it includes, chicken, pork ribs, and a choice of hot or smoked sausages. The menu also includes plenty of great barbe-cue-style sandwiches and burgers, but the Texas-Style Chili Bowl with cornbread is always an excellent choice. Thirsty? Check out the saloon for a large selection of beers, wines, and spirits.

CAFÉ FIORE

www.cafefiore.com
530-541-2908
1169 Ski Run Blvd., South Lake Tahoe, CA

Open: Daily 5 PM—close
Price: Moderate to expensive
Cuisine: Italian
Serving: D
Reservations: Yes
Credit cards: AE, MC, V

Talk about the ultimate in intimacy—Café Fiore has only seven candlelit tables. No wonder it's been written up in The *Best Places to Kiss in Northern California*. Other accolades include articles in the *Sacramento Bee*, the *San Francisco Chronicle*, and an Award of Excellence from *Wine Spectator* magazine. Start your meal with an appetizer, like the scampi over cappellini, bruschetta Siciliana, or eggplant en carrozza. Selecting an entrée will be difficult, because Café Fiore offers a tremendous selection of pasta, seafood, and meat dishes. Favorites include fettuccine alla Marengo, linguine Fra diavolo, and filetto al Barolo.

CANTINA BAR & GRILL

www.cantinatahoe.com
530-544-1233
765 Emerald Bay Rd., South Lake Tahoe, CA
Open: Daily
Price: Inexpensive to Moderate
Cuisine: Mexican
Serving: L, D
Reservations: No
Credit cards: AE, D, MC, V

Dine inside or on the spacious patio, Cantina is a locals' favorite. And no wonder—it's been voted best Mexican restaurant in South Lake Tahoe on several occasions. Start your dining adventure in the bar, where you can catch a ball game on one of three big screen TVs, and sip a cold beer. Cantina features 30 different labels. If you're not up for a beer, no problem—Cantina has a full bar, and specializes in excellent margaritas. The appetizer menu is extensive, offering such treats as rock shrimp quesadilla, fiesta platter, and nachos grande. Entrées include all your southwestern cuisine favorites, including steak, chicken, or shrimp fajitas, numerous burrito combinations, and enchiladas. Smoked chicken mole enchiladas are a favorite. The menu isn't limited to Mexican food. Hearty salads include the taco salad, oriental chicken salad, and the tostada grande. The Cantina also offers a great selection of southwestern specialties including blue corn salmon, Texas crab cakes, and BBQ baby-back pork ribs.

CHRISTIANA INN RESTAURANT AND BAR

www.christianainn.com/
530-544-4777
3819 Saddle Rd., South Lake Tahoe CA
Open: Daily 5:30 PM
Price: Moderate
Cuisine: American
Serving: D
Reservations: Yes
Credit cards: AE, D, MC, V

Long a Lake Tahoe tradition, The Christiana Inn recently went through a complete restoration. None of the old charm has been lost, but the new dining house offers patrons a modern dining experience. Live music has been added every Friday and Saturday evening on the new stage in the bar area. Large windows in the restaurant allow diners beautiful views of the tall pines. The Inn also has facilities to accommodate large parties for lunch or dinner. Order a bottle of wine from the Inn's legendary wine list and dig in. Starters include clams and andouille, squash-filled ravioli, or fig and prosciutto flatbread. The Inn's entrées feature a wide variety of selections, including grilled wild salmon, spanakopita, olive oil-poached yellowfin tuna, Spanish seafood stew, and Muscovy duck.

ECHO RESTAURANT

Inside Embassy Suites Resort
www.embassytahoe.com
530-544-5400
4130 Lake Tahoe Blvd.,
South Lake Tahoe, CA
Open: Daily
Price: Moderate
Cuisine: American
Serving: L, D
Reservations: Encouraged
Credit cards: AE, D, MC, V

Echo is a cozy spot to enjoy your favorite beverage, to watch a game and munch some appetizers in the lounge, or for an intimate meal in the dining room. Open for lunch and dinner daily, the menu features fresh cuisine. Catch a little sun during the summer by dining outside on the patio, and enjoy live music as well. Some of the featured entrées are the grilled salmon, Echo's signature filet, and the chicken saltimbocca—tenderized chicken breast, stuffed with Fontina cheese, prosciutto, fresh chives and Marsala mushroom sauce. Appetizers include coconut shrimp, steamed mussels, and the grilled portobello mushroom. Salads range from Caesar and spinach, to interesting combinations such as apple fennel. Zesty soups and salads go well with Echo's lighter fare menu or their pasta selections.

Gaming, shopping, and skiing are but a short walk from the Embassy Suites in South Lake Tahoe.

EVANS AMERICAN GOURMET CAFÉ

www.evanstahoe.com

530-542-1990

536 Emerald Bay Rd., South Lake Tahoe, CA

Open: Daily

Price: Moderate

Cuisine: American gourmet

Serving: D

Reservations: No

Credit cards: AE, D, MC, V

Enjoy an elegant meal in a tasteful yet intimate cabin setting, amidst towering pines. Evans is a family owned restaurant that prides itself on great food, professional service, and a very cool wine list. During its 17 years of service, Evans has received many accolades from restaurant aficionados. To begin your meal, suggestions include seared foie gras with pineapple and golden raisin compote and port wine reduction, or scallop quenelles with sherry-lobster cream. Topping the entrée menu are grilled tenderloin of beef with garlic whipped potatoes, portobello mushrooms, and cabernet-bleu cheese sauce; and the breast of confit leg of duck with dried cherry sauce, rice pilaf with wheat berries, edamame and roast pearl onions. Other favorites include the rack of lamb, stuffed chicken, and roast venison loin. Save room for dessert, you won't be disappointed.

FIRE + ICE

Inside Marriott's Timber Lodge

www.fire-ice.com

530-542-6650

4100 Lake Tahoe Blvd.,

South Lake Tahoe, CA.

Open: Daily

Price: Moderate

Cuisine: American improvisational grill

Serving: D

Reservations: Recommended

Credit cards: AE, D, MC, V

This is a lively dining spot, where you create your own meal but don't have to cook it.

The only limit is your imagination. Let's start with the menu. What menu? There isn't one. Your first stop is the market where the food is always changing, but you're sure to find a wide range of sirloin, chicken breast, turkey, lamb, salmon, calamari, shrimp, scallops, hamburger, and more. From there, load up on pasta, fresh veggies, and excellent sauces. Drop your bowls off with the grill chef and watch as your selections become a mouth-watering feast. Plenty of great salad combinations are available—and of course, don't forget to leave room for dessert.

GRAHAM'S AT SQUAW VALLEY

www.dinewine.com

530-581-0454

1650 Squaw Valley Rd., Squaw Valley, CA

Open: Daily

Price: Moderate to Expensive

Cuisine: California

Serving: D

Reservations: Yes

Credit cards: AE, D, MC, V

"Meals to remember," is the motto at Graham's, which serves up California cuisine influenced by Old World Mediterranean recipes from Italy, France, Spain, and the Middle East. Your waiter will help you in matching your meal selection with the perfect wine, chosen from a list of more than 800 domestic and international varieties. Intimate lighting from the river-rock fireplace and the candles at each table offers a mellow ambience to enhance the dining experience. When the weather is right, dine outside amid the scenic vistas of Squaw Valley and the towering, rugged peaks of the Sierra Nevada. For the diner with more exotic tastes, it'll be a difficult to select an entrée. Suggestions include: Moroccan lamb shanks, braised and served over couscous; eggplant Marrakesh topped with tomatoes, brown rice, and chickpeas; bouillabaisse of mussels, clams, prawns, scallops, and fresh fish stewed with white sauce, garlic and saffron; and the elk chop, a grilled New Zealand elk loin with blackberry demiglaze.

KALANI'S
www.kalanis.com
530-544-6100
1001 Heavenly Village Way No. 26, South Lake Tahoe, CA
Open: Daily
Price: Moderate to expensive
Cuisine: Hawaiian/Pacific Rim
Serving: L, D
Reservations: No
Credit cards: AE, D, MC, V

Kalani's Pacific Rim Fusion cuisine blends Hawaiian traditional cooking with flavors from Asia and Europe. Tantalize your senses with fresh fish, exotic vegetables, choice meats, and unique ingredients from Hawaii. Linger at the sushi bar, and watch the sushi chefs prepare signature rolls and exotic dishes. The Puka Lounge is a full-service bar, featuring signature cocktails as well as an extensive wine and sake list. Kalani's doesn't offer appetizers per se, but their selection of "small plates" certainly fills the bill with items like blackened Hawaiian ahi tuna, steamed island-style clams, baked escargot, and Kalani's sample platter. Popular dinner entrées include Kalbi-basted rack of lamb, filet mignon and lobster tail, open-fired island opakapaka (snapper), macadamia nut-crusted opah (moonfish), and curry-lime lobster tail.

LAKESIDE BEACH GRILL
www.lakesidebeachgrill.com
530-544-4050
4081 Lakeshore Blvd.,
South Lake Tahoe, CA
Open: Daily
Price: Moderate
Cuisine: American
Serving: L, D

Reservations: No
Credit cards: AE, D, MC, V

Here's a great place to kick back on the sandy beach of Lake Tahoe, feast your eyes on the expansive vistas of the lake and surrounding Sierra Nevada, and enjoy a casual afternoon lunch or evening meal. Enjoy a relatively inexpensive lunch or brunch from 11 AM to 5 PM. Entrées include fish tacos, seared peppered ahi, shrimp Provencal, and calamari picatta. If fish isn't your thing, try one of their burgers or sandwiches with a salad or soup du jour. Devilishly tasty desserts await those with a sweet tooth. Dinner entrées include Pacific fresh salmon, filet mignon, heavenly pasta, grilled shrimp, or seared ahi.

LEWMARNELS STEAK & SPIRITS
www.stationhouseinn.com
Best Western Station House Inn
1-800-822-5953 or 530-542-1101
901 Park Ave., South Lake Tahoe, CA
Open: Daily
Price: Moderate to expensive
Cuisine: American
Serving: L, D
Reservations: No
Credit cards: AE, MC, D, V

Great steaks and fine wine are the specialty at LewMarNels; steaks so great, that the wine and food critic at the *Tahoe Daily Tribune* awarded the restaurant "best steak on the lake." As for their wines, not only do they feature one of the largest wine cellars on the lake, *Wine Spectator* magazine has honored LewMarNels with the coveted grand award for excellence six times. The dining experience begins with generous portions of their complimentary cheese fondue and fresh baked sourdough bread, followed by soup du jour or crisp tossed green salad. Entrée choices include great steaks, seafood, and tender veal dishes. All entrées include a baked potato or twice-baked potato, or rice pilaf, and fresh sautéed vegetables. While enjoying your meal in the casual rustic ambiance of LewMarNels, be sure to take in the many limited-edition bronze statues by Fredrick Remington. The close of the meal brings the most difficult of decisions: Did you leave enough room for their homemade apple pie à la mode?

MOODY'S BISTRO & LOUNGE

www.moodysbistro.com
530-587-8688
10007 Bridge St., Truckee, CA
Open: Daily
Price: Moderate
Cuisine: California
Serving: L, D
Reservations: No
Credit cards: AE, D, MC, V

Hip and happening, Moody's is a throwback to the 1950s. A great place to eat, and a cool place to gather with friends to kick back and enjoy good music. Co-owner Mark Estee is the chief chef, and he and his staff serve up what they call Northern California Cuisine. Their credo is, "fresh, seasonal, simple and local." This means that along with regular menu staples, special dishes are served "when the time is right." Moody's prides itself on serving locally grown organic produce. Dine in the classy restaurant or take it easy outside on the patio. For starters, try the pan-seared La Belle Farms foie gras, the all-natural beef tartare, or crispy Niman Ranch Trotters. Among the entrée favorites are the seared ahi tuna and the Fulton Valley Farms organic chicken. Vegetarian entrées are also offered nightly.

NEPHELES

www.nepheles.com
530-544-8130
1169 Ski Run Blvd., South Lake Tahoe, CA
Open: Daily
Price: Moderate
Cuisine: Creative Californian
Serving: D
Reservations: Recommended
Credit cards: AE, MC, D, V

Are you game to take a walk on dining's wild side, with Chef Mark Vassau? Who knows what is brewing in the kitchen, but nightly specials might include broiled elk, wild boar chops, or sautéed venison. With such a variety, it's no wonder that Nepheles has been featured in *Bon Appetit*, *Wine Spectator*, *The New York Times* and numerous other publications. If beef is what you crave, try the medallion of filet mignon or rack of New Zealand lamb. Fish entrées include orange chili-rubbed grilled prawns, ahi tuna, baked halibut, and broiled swordfish. Yes, a full bar is available, but it might be a good idea to consult your waiter for the perfect wine to compliment your menu selection. Nepheles is all that the name implies. The name? Yes, Nephele was the Greek goddess of epicurean delights. The tradition holds true today.

PACIFIC CREST

530-587-2626
142 Donner Pass Rd., Truckee, CA
Open: Daily
Price: Moderate
Cuisine: American
Serving: L, D
Reservations: No
Credit cards: AE, D, MC, V

Adjoining Bar of America in downtown Truckee, Pacific Crest offers something to satisfy just about every taste. Patrons may dine in the restaurant or the bar. The wide-ranging menu offers salads, sandwiches, wood-fired pizzas, antipasti, and salads. For more elaborate entrées, try the lamb-shank tajine, soba noodles, or fresh seafood bouillabaisse. Match your meal with just the right wine form their extensive wine list.

RIVA GRILL ON THE LAKE

www.rivagrill.com
1-888-REGATTA or 530-542-2600
900 Ski Run Blvd., South Lake Tahoe, CA
Open: Daily
Price: Moderate to expensive
Cuisine: Californian
Serving: B, L, D
Reservations: Recommended for dinner
Credit cards: AE, D, MC, V

Lakefront dining with floor to ceiling views for two or 200 is the order of the day at Riva Grill. Named for the classic runabout class of wooden boats that bears its name, Riva is a classy, but fun, restaurant. Take in a spectacular sunset while enjoying a wet wood—the house specialty drink—inside, or out on the huge, sunny deck. Open for breakfast or brunch, lunch, and dinner, Riva's boasts a great wine list as well as a full bar. Start your evening meal with braised short ribs and potato gnocchi or beer batter coconut prawns, from the appetizer menu. Excellent dinner entrées from the Riva Grill include conchiglie, seafood tagliarini, braised lamb shank, and filet and scampi. Careful, don't overdo it. The housemade desserts include white chocolate Snickers cheesecake and toasted lemon and rosemary pound cake.

RIVER RANCH LODGE

www.riverranchlodge.com
1-800-535-8900 or 530-583-4265
Intersection of CA 89 and Alpine Meadows Rd., Tahoe City, CA
Open: Daily
Price: Inexpensive to moderate
Cuisine: California continental
Serving: L, D
Reservations: No
Credit cards: AE, D, MC, V

The cozy atmosphere at the River Ranch Lodge allows diners to select a table near the river-rock fireplace, along the curved wall cantilevered over the rushing Truckee River, or, weather permitting, out on the patio. The friendly atmosphere will have you feeling like a regular in no time, discussing skiing or hiking destinations with area locals and fellow visitors. If you aren't too hungry, make a selection from the reasonably priced café menu. But, if you've got the need for some serious food, start with one of the ranch's appetizers, like the seared sesame-coated ahi tuna or the char su pork roll. When it's time for a real main course, you can't go wrong with the pappardelle scallops, portobello mushroom Napoleon, or the roasted fresh elk loin. And be sure to save room for the fruit cobbler, triple chocolate truffle cake, or their creamy New York cheesecake.

SAGE ROOM STEAK HOUSE

Inside Harvey's Resort & Casino
www.harrahs.com
775-588-2411
US 50, Stateline, NV
Open: Daily
Price: Moderate to Expensive
Cuisine: American (Traditional)
Serving: D
Reservations: Recommended
Credit cards: AE, MC, D, V

Hankerin' for a taste of the Old West? Then this is your spot. Since 1947, the Sage Room has blended Old West ambiance and great food. Dine among the works of Russell and Remington and enjoy traditional steak house cookin'. The menu is pretty much what you would expect: juicy steaks, ribs, and chicken, highlighted by tableside flambé service. Kick back after a great meal, and top it off with the Sage Room's famous Bananas Foster.

SAMURAI RESTAURANT

www.sushitahoe.com
530-542-0300
2588 US 50, South Lake Tahoe, CA
Open: Daily
Price: Inexpensive to moderate

Cuisine: Asian/Japanese
Serving: D
Reservations: Recommended
Credit cards: AE, MC, V

Serving South Lake Tahoe since 1984, Samurai has built its reputation on traditional Japanese fine dining in an authentic atmosphere reminiscent of northern Japan. Centuries of tradition go into the creation of each dish. Appetizers include firecracker salmon, shumai, yakitori, and soft-shell crab. For your entrée, favorites include sukiyaki, tempura, or teriyaki. A local favorite is the sushi platter, a tasty array of items selected from the sushi bar. A new addition to Samurai is Helen's Asian bistro featuring recipes from around the Pacific Rim, reworked into a tasty and healthy Asian fusion. Check out the Singapore fruit salad, minty tofu salad; or, for an entrée, the dancing prawns, three-dip steak, and monk's curry are excellent selections.

SOL Y LAGO

Inside the Boatworks Mall
www.solylago.com
530-583-0358
760 N. Lake Blvd, Tahoe City, CA
Open: Daily
Price: Inexpensive to moderate
Cuisine: Latin
Serving: D
Reservations: Suggested
Credit cards: AE, MC, V

This is not your typical "Mexican" restaurant; not at all. Brain R. Reccow, owner of Sol y Lago, serves up what he calls Sierra Latino dishes focusing on the little known flavors of the mountainous regions of Spain and Latin America. The menu is flexible enough to accommodate those looking for an après-ski cocktail and something to munch, or a full-blown Latin dinner. It doesn't matter where you sit, every seat offers a truly stunning view of Lake Tahoe, in this beautifully designed restaurant and bar. The menu offers something for just about every taste. Here's one possible combination. Start your meal with tapas, of provolone griddled until bubbly brown and served with crusty bread. And for your entrée, how about the chef's daily selection of four choice cuts of meat—the mixed grill—with exotic sauces, including Argentine chimichurri? The wine list includes more than 40 selections emphasizing offerings from Chile, Argentina, and some unique California varietals.

TEP'S VILLA ROMA

www.tepsvillaroma.com
1-800-490-3066 or 530-541-8227
3450 Lake Tahoe Blvd.,
South Lake Tahoe, CA
Open: Daily
Price: Moderate to expensive
Cuisine: Italian
Serving: D
Reservations: No
Credit cards: AE, MC, V

Oh, mamma mia! For more than 25 years, Tep's has brought Italian dining in old-country fashion to the shores of Lake Tahoe. This is the spot for an intimate dinner, while traditional Italian music plays softly in the background. Enjoy a cocktail or select a bottle of wine while munching homemade Italian rolls and their famous garlic sticks. Take your time, and enjoy the minestrone soup and salad bar that comes with every meal. As for your meal, Tep's offers a large menu featuring favorite traditional pasta dishes, steaks, veal, chicken, and fresh fish and seafood. Italian vegetarian dishes, pizza, and child's portions are available.

THE SUMMIT

Inside Harrah's Lake Tahoe
www.harrahs.com
775-588-6611
US 50, Stateline, NV

Open: Wed.–Sun.
Price: Expensive
Cuisine: American (Traditional)
Serving: D
Reservations: Yes
Credit cards: AE, MC, D, V

The Summit is a Lake Tahoe dining jewel, and has been voted one of the Top 10 Restaurants in America. Located on the 16th floor of Harrah's Lake Tahoe, The Summit features exquisite cuisine, a sophisticated yet relaxed atmosphere, and absolutely stunning views of Lake Tahoe and the surrounding Sierra Nevada range. While sipping a before-dinner cocktail and taking in the beautiful views, it's fun to reflect knowing that before 1990, the restaurant was the world-famous Star Suite, and hosted numerous celebrities who performed on the Harrah's stage, including Frank Sinatra, Neil Sedaka, Sammy Davis Jr., Liza Minnelli, and Bill Cosby. Paul Anka composed some of his famous hits in this room. Dinner will not disappoint. Why not get the feast started with some appetizers like Tastings of Ahi Tuna tartare with shaved cucumber, ginger lemongrass, crostini pepper-seared carmelized walnuts, and a sweet-sour sauce; or go all out, with the Ossetra caviar on toasted brioche with crème fraiche and traditional garnish? Entrée favorites include: petit filet and king crab with parsnip puree, whole garlic, veal reduction and chive

Plugrá; pistachio-encrusted rack of lamb with braised root vegetables, veal reduction and mint; and the butter-poached Australian lobster tail with flashed prosciutto spinach, haricot verts, potatoes Anna and sherry plugra. If you are looking for something really extra special, indulge in the Chef's Selection. This is a special pairing of food and wines, guaranteed to provide the ultimate in dining pleasure.

TOMAATO'S
775-833-2200
120 Country Club Drive #61,
Incline Village, NV
Open: Daily
Price: Inexpensive to Moderate
Cuisine: Pizza
Serving: D
Reservations: No
Credit cards: AE, D, MC, V

This isn't just your regular old pizza—Tomaato's serves up gourmet pizza as well as pastas and salads. Kick back in the comfortable dining room or, during the summer, relax outside on their patio. Libations include a wide variety of international beers and wines. Pastas include the three-mushroom ravioli and shrimp scampi. When it comes to ordering your pizza, consider their famous wheat crust with a smoky vegetable, Thai chicken, or primavera pizza.

FOOD PURVEYORS

Bakeries

Brockway Bakery, 530-546-2431, 8710 N. Lake Blvd., Kings Beach, CA. Fresh donuts, cakes and pastries to satisfy every taste.

Cinnabon, 530-542-2127, US 50 at Park Ave., The Shops at Heavenly Village, South Lake Tahoe, CA. Mouth-watering fresh cinnamon rolls and other bakery treats, all made from fresh ingredients. Also offers espresso drinks, smoothies, and much more.

Earthly Delights Bakery, 530-587-7793, 10087 W. River St., Truckee, CA. A great selection of fresh pastries, hot coffee, and much more.

Rude Brothers Bagel & Coffee Haus, 530-541-8195, 3117 Harrison Ave., South Lake Tahoe, CA. Select from a myriad of coffee choices and munch a fresh bagel or other pastry.

Scraps Dog Bakery, 530-546-2725, 8675 N. Lake Blvd., Kings Beach CA. Nutritional treats for the family pet.

Coffeehouses

Alpen Sierra Coffee Co.,www.alpensierra.com, 530-544-7740, 3940 Lake Tahoe Blvd., South Lake Tahoe, CA. Check out the award-winning Euro-Alpine décor at Lake Tahoe's longest established micro-roaster of specialty coffees. Alpen serves hot and chilled coffee drinks, smoothies, teas, pastries, and great sandwiches.

Koffie, 530-542-1474, US 50 at Sierra Blvd., Swiss Chalet Village, South Lake Tahoe, CA. Sip a nice cup of organic Koffie with your breakfast or lunch, while surfing the Web on Koffie's free wireless Internet.

Truckee Book & Bean, www.truckeebookandbean.com, 530-582-8302, 10009 W. River St., B, Truckee, CA. This quaint downtown coffeehouse and bookstore boasts quality over quantity when it comes to book selections. Enjoy the cozy atmosphere, sip an organic coffee drink, read, or browse on their free wireless Internet.

Farmers' Markets

South Lake Tahoe Farmers' Market, 775-588-4105, Kahle Park, Stateline, NV. Friday 8 AM to 1 PM, June through October.

South Lake Tahoe Certified Farmers' Market, 530-622-1900, American Legion Hall parking lot, 2732 South Lake Tahoe Blvd., South Lake Tahoe, CA. Tuesday 8 AM to 1 PM, June through October.

Truckee Farmers' Market, Truckee River Regional Park, 10500 Brockway Road, Truckee, CA. Tuesday 8 AM to 1 PM, June through October.

Frozen Desserts

Cold Stone Creamery, 530-544-3000, US 50 at Park Ave., The Shops at Heavenly Village, South Lake Tahoe, CA. Plenty of options here with handmade gourmet ice cream flavors to fit every taste. Bet you can't resist trying the creative hand-chopped toppings.

Jamba Juice, 530-544-8890, US 50 and Park Ave., The Village Center, South Lake Tahoe, CA. Imagine any fruit or combination of fruits and Jamba Juice will serve up the frothy concoction.

RECREATION

Lake Tahoe is the place to stay and play. It doesn't matter what time of year, rest assured there's plenty to do. This is home to world-class skiing and boarding in the winter, all manner of water sports in the summer and some of the greatest hiking on the planet, all year long. Getting bored here just isn't possible.

Adventures

Granlibakken Ropes Course, 530-583-4242. Located at 625 Granlibakken Rd, Tahoe City. Action orientated adventure program including games and problem-solving activities. Group and organization rates, half and full-day sessions.

Tahoe Adventure Company, LLC, www.tahoeadventurecompany.com, 530-913-9212, Tahoe City, CA. Features professionally guided, fully outfitted adventure trips in the Lake Tahoe area. Trips include kayaking, biking, hiking and rock climbing. Excellent for team building, corporate outings, and customized adventures.

Tahoe Trips and Trails, www.tahoetrips.com, 530-581-4453, 700 River Road, Tahoe City, CA. Offers customized multi-sport tours. Packages include upscale lodging and meals. Excellent team-building programs.

Arcades

GameWorld, Inside Horizon Casino Resort, www.horizoncasino.com, 775-588-6211, US 50, Stateline, NV. Want to ski the slopes in virtual reality, race at Daytona, or become a jet pilot? GameWorld is a great spot for kids of all ages and considered one of the best sources of high-tech entertainment in Lake Tahoe.

The Children's Memorial on US 50 is the handy work of a Lake Tahoe artist.

Harrah's Tahoe Arcade, Inside Harrah's Lake Tahoe, www.harrahs.com, 775-588-6606, US 50, Stateline, NV. Games and guaranteed fun for the whole family. Offers everything from old-fashioned pinball machines to some of the latest seek-and-destroy video games.

Ballooning

Lake Tahoe Balloons, www.laketahoeballoons.com, 1-800-872-9294, Tahoe Keys Marina, South Lake Tahoe, CA. Ever wonder how a soaring eagle views the majesty of Lake Tahoe? Find out in a hot air balloon ride. Sunrise flights offered seven days a week, May through October, weather permitting. Children welcome. Reservations required. Rates: $250 per person.

Bicycling

BICYCLE RENTALS

Camp Richardson Mountain Sports Center, www.camprichardson.com, 530-542-6584, located in Camp Richardson Resort & Marina, 1900 Jameson Beach Rd.

Lakeview Sports, www.tahoesports.com, 530-544-0183, 3131 Lake Tahoe Blvd., South Lake Tahoe.

Porter's Ski and Sport, 775-831-3500, 885 Tahoe Blvd., Incline Village.

Powder House, www.tahoepowderhouse.com, 1-800-555-2065, 3930 Lake Tahoe Blvd., South Lake Tahoe.

Shoreline Ski & Sports, www.shorelineoftahoe.com, 1-888-877-7669, 259 Kingsbury Grade, Stateline.

Sierra Ski & Cycle Works, www.sierraskiandcycleworks.com, 530-541-7505, 3430 Lake Tahoe Blvd., South Lake Tahoe.

South Shore Bike & Skate Shop, 530-541-1549, 1132 Ski Run Blvd., South Lake Tahoe.

Spooner Lake Outdoor Company, www.theflumetrail.com, 775-749-5349, NV 28 at Spooner Lake day use area.

Tahoe Bike Shop and Tahoe Boot and Ski Works, 530-544-8060, 2277 Lake Tahoe Blvd., South Lake Tahoe.

Tahoe Sports Ltd., www.tahoesportsltd.com, 530-542-4000, The Village Center, 4008 Lake Tahoe Blvd., South Lake Tahoe.

The Village Mountain Surf & Sports, 530-541-4444, 3552 Lake Tahoe Blvd., South Lake Tahoe.

Village Ski Loft, www.villageskiloft.com, 775-831-3537, 800 Tahoe Blvd., Incline Village.

Paved Bike Trails

Pope-Baldwin Bike Path, A beautiful ride that parallels CA 89. The ride begins one mile north of the intersection with US 50, passing through Camp Richardson. Side trips include Pope and Baldwin beaches, the Tellac Historic Site, and Taylor Creek Visitors Center.

South Lake Tahoe Bike Path, A scenic tour that begins on US 50 at El Dorado Beach. The path connects to other bike trails throughout the South Shore.

Mountain Bike Trails

Angora Lakes Climb, This eight-mile run is suitable for beginners. It begins at the inter-section of Tahoe Mountain and Angora Ridge roads and offers stunning views of Fallen Leaf Lake and Lake Tahoe.

Emigrant Trail, Starting in Truckee, the trail is a 22-mile run (out and back) to Stampede Reservoir.

Northstar-at-Tahoe Mountain Bike Park, Offering more than 100 miles of trails, the facility boasts some of the best mountain biking in California.

Tahoe Rim Trail, The 150-mile trail follows the ridges and mountain tops that ring Lake Tahoe.

The Flume Trail, The trail begins at Spooner Lake and is named for the flume constructed to transport water and timber to Virginia City during the silver boom. The trail is consid-ered one of Western America's Top Ten routes.

Mr. Toad's Wild Ride, Advanced ride begins at Big Meadow Trailhead just off CA 89 near Luther Pass. Take the 1500-foot plunge down Saxon Creek trail and you'll understand how this run got its name.

Campgrounds and RV Parks

Campground by the Lake, www.recreationintahoe.com, 530-542-6096, 1150 Rufus Allen Blvd., South Lake Tahoe, CA. Open April through October, the facility is operated by the City of South Lake Tahoe and is adjacent to the city's recreation complex including the ice arena, recreation hall, and swimming pool. Camping facilities include group sites and hookups. Dogs are welcome, but must be kept on a leash

Chris Haven Mobilehome & RV Community, www.geocities.com/Eureka/Executive /9918/index.html, 530-541-1895 2030, E. Street, South Lake Tahoe, CA. Conveniently located on Lake Tahoe's south shore, Chris Haven is open all year, offering 96 full hookups, hot showers, restrooms, and laundry facilities. Cable TV and wireless Internet access are also available.

Coachland RV Park, 530-587-3071(13 miles north of Lake Tahoe) Truckee, CA. Coachland caters primarily to senior citizens spending the summer in the Tahoe-Truckee area. The park features 131 RV sites including hook ups, cable TV, showers, flush toilets, clubhouse, and craft room.

D.L. Bliss State Park, www.parks.ca.gov/pages/505/files/D.L.Bliss%20Campground.pdf 1-800-444-7275 or 530-525-7277, 17 miles south of Tahoe City, CA on US 89. This facility is operated by the California State Parks and offers 168 sites, RV dump, water faucets in the campground, but no hookups. The facility also offers paid showers and flush toilets. Pets are welcome with restrictions.

Donner Memorial State Park, www.parks.ca.gov/default.asp?page_id=503, 1-800-444-7275 or 530-582-7894, US 80, Truckee, CA. Donner features 150 campsites and a day use area along Donner Lake. The facility can accommodate campers up to 28 feet and trailers up to 24 feet. Other features include picnic tables, restrooms, beach access, and a boat ramp.

You're never too young to learn to ski, especially under the expert guidance at Northstar-at-Tahoe.

Eagle Point Campground, www.parks.ca.gov/pages/506/files/Emerald%20Bay%20 Campground.pdf, 1-800-444-7275 or 530-525-7277, US 89 at Emerald Bay, CA. This California State Parks facility offers 100 sites and faucets in the campground, but no hookups. Paid showers and flush toilets are also available. Dogs are allowed with restrictions.

Fallen Leaf, 1-877-444-6777 or 530-544-0426. Located 3 miles north of South Lake Tahoe, CA. off Fallen Leaf Road. Operated by the US Forest Service, the facility offers 206 sites, water and flush toilets. Dogs must be kept on a leash.

KOA of South Lake Tahoe, www.laketahoekoa.com/, 1-800-KOA-3477 or 530-577-3693, US 50 and Upper Truckee Rd., South Lake Tahoe, CA. KOA of South Lake Tahoe is privately owned and operated offering pull through, RV dump, water, electric, sewer, showers, flush toilets and laundry facilities. Cable TV and wireless Internet access available at select sites. Officially open April 1 to Oct. 15 with winter camping available by special arrangement.

Meeks Bay Campground, www.fs.fed.us/r5/ltbmu/recreation/camping/meeks.shtml, 530-544-5994, US 89, West Lake Tahoe, CA. Meeks Bay Campground offers 40 tent and RV campsites and can accommodate RVs up to 20 feet. No RV hook ups, but does provide showers, water, flush toilets, and BBQ rings.

Meeks Bay Resort, www.meeksbayresort.com, 530-525-6946, US 89 West Lake Tahoe, CA. The resort's campground has 20 basic campsites and 10 RV sites. It can accommodate RVs up to 30 feet and full hook ups are available at some sites. Other amenities include showers, flush toilets, store, snack bar, and marina.

Nevada Beach, 1-877-444-6777 or 775-588-5562. Located 2 miles north of Stateline on US 50 off Elk Point Rd., Zephyr Cove, NV. Run by the US Forest Service, the facility features water and flush toilets.

Sugar Pine Point, www.parks.ca.gov/pages/510/files/sugar_pine_campground.pdf, 1-800-444-7275 or 530-525-7982. Located on the west shore of Lake Tahoe, 10 miles south of Tahoe City on US 89. This California State Parks facility features 175 sites, RV dump, water faucets in the campground by no hookups. Also offers paid showers and flush toilets. Dogs permitted with restrictions.

Tahoe Pines Campground, www.tahoepinescampground.com/, 530-577-1653, US 50 at Upper Truckee Rd., South Lake Tahoe, CA. Set in the pine forest along the babbling Truckee River, Tahoe Pines is a privately owned campground featuring more than 50 campsites. The facility offers RV dump, sewer, water, electric, flush toilets, shower, and laundry.

Tahoe Valley Campground, www.campingfriend.com/TahoeValleyCampground/, 530-541-2222, 1175 Melba Dr. South Lake Tahoe, CA. Open year round and privately owned, Tahoe Valley Campground is a "luxury" resort for the camping/RV crowd. With 415 campsites, the facility offers all the usual campground necessities including full hookups, pull through, RV dump, water, electric, sewer, shower, and laundry. Additionally, Tahoe Valley offers a general store, tennis & sport courts, horseshoe pits cable TV, Internet access, heated pool (summer only), and concierge service.

Zephyr Cove Resort, www.zephyrcove.com, 1-800 238-2463 or 775-589-4910, 750 US Hwy. 50, Zephyr Cove, NV. In addition to classic Tahoe-style cabins and lodge rooms, the resort also has an RV park and camping facilities. The family-orientated complex is open all year round and features 93 RV sites, 47 "walk-in" campsites and 10 "drive-in" sites. Some of the sites offer stunning lake views. The RV sites are large and provide sewer, electric, cable TV, and telephone and Internet access. Amenities open to all include laundry, shower, outdoor patio at the new Four Seasons building, and transportation to the casinos at Stateline.

Fishing

Don Sheetz Fishing Guide, www.tahoefishingguides.com, 1-877-270-0742, Tahoe Keys Marina, South Lake Tahoe, CA. Specializing in light-tackle fishing on Lake Tahoe, for Mackinaw, kokanee salmon, and rainbow and brown trout. All equipment provided.

Four Reel Sportfishing, www.fourreelsportfishing.com, 530-543-1353, Tahoe Keys Marina, South Lake Tahoe, CA. Year-round sport fishing, specializing in downrigging, toplining, drifting, and jigging. Equipment provided.

Mickey's Big Mack Lake Tahoe, www.mickeysbigmack.com, 1-800-877-1462, CA 28 at Sierra Boat Company, Carnelian Bay, CA. Year-round fishing with master guide. Mickey Daniels has been featured on *Fishing the West,* and numerous other TV shows and in magazine articles.

Mile High Fishing Charters, www.fishtahoe.com, 1-866-752-3474, 2438 Venice Dr., South Lake Tahoe, CA. Year-round fishing charters available, equipment provided. Voted "Best of Lake Tahoe 2004."

Tahoe Fly Fishing Outfitters, www.tahoeflyfishing.com, 530-541-8208, 2705, Lake Tahoe Blvd., Suite 1, South Lake Tahoe, CA. The most complete fly-fishing store in the area. Offers classes and guided fly-fishing outings.

Tahoe Sport Fishing, www.tahoesportfishing.com, 1-800-696-7797, 900 Ski Run Blvd., Suite 102, (Ski Run Marina) South Lake Tahoe, CA and 760 Highway 50, (Zephyr Cove Marina) Zephyr Cove, NV. Lake Tahoe's largest fishing fleet, with six vessels. Individual fishermen, families, and private charters can be accommodated. Equipment available.

Golf Courses

Bijou Municipal Golf Course, www.recreationintahoe.com, 530-542-6097, 3464 Fairway Ave. South Lake Tahoe CA. Public; 9 holes. Par 32, 2002 yards. Pro shop, club rental, practice nets, snack bar, no tee times required. Open Apr–Nov. Rate $15–$18.

Coyote Moon Golf Course, www.coyotemoongolf.com, 530-587-0886, 10685 Northwoods Blvd. Truckee, CA. Public 18-hole course. Par 72, 7,117 yards, rating 73.7, slope 136. Cart rentals (with GPS), practice facility, bar and grill, dress code. Open May–Oct. Rates $95–$150.

Edgewood Tahoe Golf Course, www.edgewood-tahoe.com, 1-888-881-8659, US 50, Stateline NV. Public; 18 holes, par 72, 7445 yards, rating 75.5, slope 144. Pro shop, driving range, putting green, lessons, cart rental, and bar/restaurant. Open May–Oct. Rates $150–$200. Home of the American Century Celebrity Golf Championship.

Lake Tahoe Golf Course, www.laketahoegc.com, 530-577-0788, 2500 Emerald Bay Rd. South Lake Tahoe, CA. Located in a meadow surrounded by the beautiful High Sierra. The Truckee River comes into play on two holes. Public, 18 holes, 6741 yards, par 71, rating 70.8, slope 126. Pro shop, cart rental, club rental, driving range, putting/chipping green, lessons, bar, plus restaurant and snack bar. Open Apr–Oct. Rate $52–$75.

Magic Carpet Golf, 530-541-3787, 2455 Lake Tahoe Blvd. South Lake Tahoe, CA. Miniature golf.

Northstar-at-Tahoe Golf Course, www.northstarattahoe.com, 530-562-2490, Basque Dr. off Northstar Dr., Truckee, CA. Public 18-hole course. Par 72, 6,897 yards, rating 72.4. Cart rental, club rental, lessons, driving range, pro shop, restaurant/bar, snack bar. Open May–Oct. Rates $45–$99.

Old Brockway Golf Course, www.oldbrockway.com, 530-546-9909, Intersection of CA 28 and CA 267, Kings Beach, CA. Public 9-hole course. Par 35, 3,250 yards, rating 67.6, slope 116. Cart rental, lessons, putting green, pro shop, restaurant and bar. Home of the first Bing Crosby golf tournament. Open Apr–Nov. Rates $38–65.

Ponderosa Golf Course, www.ponderosagolfclub.com, 530-587-3501, 10040 Reynold Way, Truckee, CA. Public 9-hole course. Par 35, 3033 yards, rating 68.2, slope 119. Practice green, club rental, restaurant. Open May–Oct. Rates $32–$52.

Resort at Squaw Creek Golf Course, www.squawcreek.com, 530-583-6300, 400 Squaw Creek Road, Squaw Valley, CA. Public 18-hole course. Par 72, 6,815 yards. Cart rental, club rental, lessons, driving range, pro shop, plus restaurant and bar. Open May–Oct. Rates $45–$110.

Tahoe City Golf Course, 530-583-1516, 251 N. Lake Tahoe Blvd., Tahoe City, CA. Public 9-hole course. Par 33, 2,700 yards, rating 32.6, slope 111. Club rental, cart rental, practice area, and restaurant and bar. Built in 1917, the course was designed by May Webb Dunn, one of the first women in the golf course design business. Open Apr–Nov. Rates $36–$74.

Tahoe Donner Golf Course, www.tahoedonnergolf.com, 530-587-9443, Truckee, CA. Public 18-hole course. Par 72, 6968 yards, rating 73.5, slope 132. Driving range, putting green, club rental, restaurant. Open May–Oct. Rates $45–$120.

Tahoe Paradise Golf Course, www.tahoeparadisegc.com, 530-577-2121, 3021 Hwy. 50, Meyers, CA. Public, 18 holes, 4034 yards, par 66. Cart rental, club rental, lessons available, driving range, pro shop, snack bar. Open May–Oct. Rate $40–$58.

The Golf Courses at Incline Village–Championship, www.golfincline.com, 1-866-925-GOLF, 955 Fairway Blvd. Incline Village, NV. Public 18-hole course. Par 72, 7,106 yards, rating 74.1, slope 144. Pro shop, club rental, cart rental, driving range, putting green, restaurant and bar. Open May–Oct. Rates $99–$165.

The Golf Courses at Incline Village–Mountain Course, www.golfincline.com, 1-866-925-GOLF, 690 Wilson Way, Incline Village, NV. 18-hole target course, Par 58, 3,440 yards. Cart rental, club rental, practice facility, pro shop. Open May–Oct. Rates $35–$65.

Hiking

Angora Lakes Trail, CA 89 to Fallen Leaf Lake Rd., turn left on to Forest Service Rd. 12N14. This is a popular destination for hikers, so it's best to arrive early. This is an easy stroll, and if you bring the family dog, make sure he's on a leash.

Cascade Creek Falls, CA 89 north from South Lake Tahoe to Bayview Campground. An easy 1-mile stroll offers incredible views of the 200-foot-high falls and Cascade Lake.

Eagle Falls Trail, CA 89 north from South Lake Tahoe to Eagle Falls Picnic Area. This is a steep, strenuous trek, into the heart of Desolation Wilderness. It's worth the effort, offering fantastic views of the northern High Sierra backcountry. Mileage (one way): 1 mile to Eagle Lake, 4 miles to Dicks, Upper & Middle Velmas, 5 miles to Fontanilli's. Wilderness permit required.

Echo Lakes Trail, US 50 to Echo Summit and turn onto Johnson Pass Road, stay left to the parking area at Lower Echo Lake. This moderately difficult trail takes you to some of the most beautiful alpine lakes in the High Sierra. It's 2 miles to Upper Echo Lake, 5 miles to Lake of the Woods, 6 miles to Tamarack and Aloha Lake.

Glen Alpine Trail, CA 89 north to Fallen Leaf Lake Road and continue to the Glen Alpine trailhead. This is a moderate to strenuous hike, climbing from 6,500 feet to more than 9,700 feet. This trek offers a marvelous wilderness experience. Wilderness permit required.

Rugged and remote, the Desolation Wilderness is popular with hikers.

Mt. Tellac Trail, Located north of South Lake Tahoe on CA 89 at the Mt. Tellac trailhead sign. This hike may be only 1 mile, but it's an arduous, steep mile. The hiker is rewarded by spectacular views of Lake Tahoe, Fallen Leaf Lake and Desolation Wilderness.

Sugar Pine Point State Park, Located off CA 89 1 mile north of Meeks Bay. Hike or cross-country ski along a number of trails. Check out the spectacular views of Ehrman Mansion.

Tellac Historic Site, The trail begins at Kiva Picnic Area just of CA 89 in South Lake Tahoe. This is an easy, 0.3 mile stroll along the Lake of the Sky Trail, and is accessible to persons with disabilities. At the site, take a step back in time and explore the events, personalities and summer homes of turn-of-the-century Tahoe landowners.

Vikingsholm Trail, Take CA 89 north about 9 miles from South Lake Tahoe to Vikingsholm. The trail begins directly across from the castle. This is an ease 1-mile jaunt to Lower Eagle Falls. The parking lot fills up quickly in the summer, so plan to get an early start.

Horse and buggy is another way to get around Stateline and South Lake Tahoe.

Horseback Riding

Camp Richardson Corral, www.camprich.com, 1-877-541-3113, CA 89 at Fallen Leaf Rd., South Lake Tahoe.

Cascade Stables, 530-541-2055, 2199 Cascade Rd., South Lake Tahoe.

Kirkwood Corrals, www.kirkwood.com, 530-694-0568, CA 88 Kirkwood.

Northstar Stables, www.skinorthstar.com, 910 Northstar Dr., Truckee.

Tahoe Donner Equestrian Center, Info at: www.tahoedonner.com, 530-587-9470, 15275 Alder Creek Rd., Truckee.

Zephyr Cove Stables, www.zephyrcovestables.com, 775-588-5664, US 50 at Zephyr Cove Resort.

River Rafting

Tahoe Whitewater Tours, www.gowhitewater.com, 1-800-442-7238, (two locations) 303 Alpine Meadows Rd., (off CA 89) Tahoe City, CA and 400 Island Ave., Reno, NV. Choose from a wide variety of whitewater adventures on the Truckee River or a milder run through downtown Reno. All necessary gear provided. Rates: $68 adult, $63 kids 7 to 12 years old.

Truckee River Raft Company, www.truckeeriverraft.com, 530-583-0123, 185 River Road, Tahoe City, CA. Enjoy a great couple of hours on a self-guided float from Tahoe City to the River Ranch Bar, Restaurant and Hotel. Here, you can enjoy a drink, have a meal and catch the free shuttle back to Tahoe City. Rates: $32 adults, $27 kids, free for children under 5.

Spas

South Lake Tahoe Spa—A Body ReNEW Massage Spa, www.southlaketahoemassage.com, 530-545-3501, 2264 Lake Tahoe Blvd., #4, South Lake Tahoe, CA. Relax and rejuvenate with a massage customized for each client. Specializing in deep tissue, Swedish, sports injury, chronic pain, and prenatal. Reservations required.

Tranquility Massage and Healing Arts, www.tahoetranquility.com, 530-542-3906, 3330 Lake Tahoe Blvd., #4, South Lake Tahoe, CA. Offers a wide variety of massage services, body treatments, and pamper packages. Individual, couple, and group rates available. Reservations required.

Reflections The Spa, www.harrahs.com, 775-588-6611, Located in Harrah's Lake Tahoe, Stateline, NV. Seeking to integrate the finest health and beauty treatments, Reflections offers Roman baths, Turkish steam, Finnish saunas, and Swedish massage.

Water Sports

Action Watersports, www.action-watersports.com, 530-544-5387, 3411 Lake Tahoe Blvd., South Lake Tahoe, CA (Timber Cove Marina) and across from the Hyatt Regency Lake Tahoe Resort, Spa and Casino, 111 Country Club Drive, Incline Village, NV. Talk about having a great time on beautiful Lake Tahoe, Action Watersports has it all. Action Watersports offers lake cruises, power and sail boat rentals, jet skis, paddle boats, parasailing, and aqua cycling.

Enviro-Rents, www.tahoeecosports.com, 530-546-2780, 8612 North Lake Blvd., Kings Beach CA and 6873 North Lake Blvd., Tahoe Vista, CA. This is the North Shore's one-stop adventure shop offering kayak, sailboard, and mountain bike rentals. Here's a good tip—go kayaking in the morning when the lake is calm and glassy. Then check out a sailboard in the afternoon, when the winds usually kick up. Hourly rates: Kayaks $18 single, $30 double, sailboards $60.

Kayak Tahoe, www.kayaktahoe.com, 530-544-2011, Located on the pier at Timber Cove Marina, South Lake Tahoe, CA and on the North Shore just east of Sierra Boat Company in Carnelian Bay, CA. Great fun for expert kayakers and beginners alike. Take a guided tour and see some of the most pristine spots on the lake, or go exploring on your own. Lessons and group rates available. Hourly rates: $15 single, $28 double.

Lake Tahoe Water Trail, www.laketahoewatertrail.org, 530-542-5651, Paddle through paradise and explore Lake Tahoe's 72 miles of shoreline. Customize your own trip with the Lake Tahoe Water Trail Guide/Map. This waterproof, tear-proof guide lists access points, resting places, campgrounds, lodging, points of interest, and support facilities for kayakers and canoeists.

Recreation & Swim Pool Complex, www.recreationintahoe.com, 530-542-6056, 1180 Rufus Allen Blvd., South Lake Tahoe, CA. Operated by the city, the complex is open year-round offering a variety of activities for people of all ages. Facilities include: playground, outdoor sand volleyball, BBQ, multi-use gym, and weight room, as well as a 25-yard, six-lane pool with 1-meter diving board and a slide. Swimming lessons available. Snack bar and swim shop on site. Room rentals for parties and meetings. Pool use rates: $4.25 adult, $2.75 youth, senior and disabled $3.25.

Round Hill Pines Beach & Marina–H2o Sports, www.rhpbeach.com, 775-588-3055, Located two miles north of Stateline, off US 50 at Round Hill, NV. This is a great place for the whole family to spend a day or more. The facility offers set ski rentals, parasailing, kayak rentals, yacht tours, tennis, and heated swimming pool. The facility boasts a quarter mile of sandy beach and a bar & grill. $7 parking. Group rates and weddings available.

Tahoe Paddle and Oar, www.tahoepaddle.com, 530-546-3279, 8299 North Lake Blvd., Kings Beach, CA. Open May through September, Tahoe Paddle and Oar boasts the largest selection of canoes and kayaks on the lake. Specializes is organizing team building events for small groups and large corporations. Paddle your way into Crystal Bay, featuring a natural hot spring and gigantic boulder mazes. Guided tours and lessons available. Hourly rates: $15 kayak, $25 canoe.

Zephyr Cove Marina, www.zephyrcove.com, 775-589-4908. Located just four miles north of Stateline casinos on US 50 at Zephyr Cove, NV. The marina offers lake cruises, boat and jet ski rentals, parasailing, kayak, and pedal boat rentals. Also provides boat moorings and fuel. Kick back on the mile long stretch of beach.

WINTER RECREATION

Dog Sledding

Husky Express, www.lake-tahoe.highsierra.com, 775-782-3047. Located 30 miles south of Lake Tahoe on CA 88 at Hope Valley. No, this isn't the Iditarod, but dog sledding through beautiful Hope Valley is great family fun. Operated by 30-year mushing veteran Dottie Dennis and her dog teams, the trails run through some of the most beautiful territory in the High Sierra. Rides last about an hour, and there is a 375-pound limit per sled. Rates: $100 for adults and children over 60 pounds. $50 for children under 60 pounds. Minimum charge per sled is $185. Box trail lunch provided for $10, with advance notice. Reservations mandatory.

Ice Skating

South Tahoe Ice Arena, www.recreationtahoe.com, 530-542-6262. 1176 Rufus Allen Blvd., South Lake Tahoe. The South Tahoe Ice Arena is a full-service skating facility, complete with an NHL regulation hockey rink, snack bar, locker rooms, retail store, and arcade and party rooms. The facility offers public skating, but because of the many special events held at the arena, it is best to call ahead when planning an ice-skating outing. The facility offers hockey school, hockey camps, skating, and figure-skating lessons. Rental equipment is available. Rates: $9 adult, $8 junior and senior, $6 children under five (includes rental skates), $3 skate rental.

Ski/Snowboard Resorts

Alpine Meadows, www.skialpine.com, 1-800-441-4423. Located six miles northwest of Tahoe City off CA 89. Alpine Meadows was recently recognized as one of the country's top winter resorts by *Ski* and *Skiing* magazines. The resort is located in the Tahoe National Forest and many of its runs offer breathtaking views of Lake Tahoe. Skiers and snowboarders alike rave about Alpine Meadows. *Lifts*: One high-speed six-passenger chair, two high-speed express quads, three triple and five double chairs, two surface lifts (one for kids only). *Trails*: Situated on 2,400 patrolled acres featuring more than 100 designated runs—40 percent moderate, 25 percent easier, 35 percent difficult/expert. *Vertical drop*: 1,800 feet. *Snowmaking*: Covers a network of runs served by 11 of the 13 lifts. *Terrain parks and pipes*: One terrain park, one terrain park for kids. *Facilities*: Alpine Meadows an expansive day lodge with sun deck, a full-service restaurant, bar cafeteria, deli, and barbecue, as well as an on-mountain restaurant and snack bar. Parking lot shuttle service gets skiers from their cars to the lodge. The facility features equipment rental, a retail shop, and an equipment repair shop. *Ski school*: Ski and snowboard instruction is available for adults and children. *For kids*: The Little Mountaineers program allows children ages 4 to 6 to learn in a safe environment. The Junior Mountaineer program is offered for kids from 7 to 12 years of age. *Rates*: $46 adult, teen $39, child $15, senior $39, super senior $15. Half-day passes and season tickets are available. Rates slightly higher on holidays.

Boreal, www.rideboreal.com, 530-426-3666. From Reno, take I-80 west and exit at the Boreal/Castle Peak off ramp. From San Francisco/Sacramento, take I-80 east and exit at the Boreal/Castle Peak off ramp. Boreal prides itself for being ahead of the industry curve. It was one of the first resorts to embrace snowboarding, and is one of the first to offer a terrain park. Additionally, shredders can take part in night superpipe competition. *Lifts*: Two quads, three triple, four double, moving carpet. *Trails*: 41 trails—55 percent intermediate, 30 percent beginner, 15 percent advanced. Lanes open for sledding. *Vertical drop*: 500 feet. *Snowmaking*: 75 to 80 percent terrain coverage. *Terrain parks and pipes*: Jibassic Terrain Park. *Facilities*: Boreal has a number of restaurants, cafés, and bars to meet every skier's need. *Ski school*: Boreal offers ski equipment and snowboard rental. Individual and group lessons are available for children and adults of all abilities. *For kids*: The Moving Carpet is exclusively for Kids Club participants. It is a fun and simple way for youngsters (4 to 10) to learn to ski or snowboard. *Rates*: $38 Adult, $10 child, $25 senior, $38 parent shared, $5 over 70. Group packages and annual passes are available.

Heavenly Mountain Resort, www.skiheavenly.com, 775-586-7000. Located at the intersection of Wildwood and Saddle Road in Stateline, NV. It's been just over 50 years since Chris and Dottie Kuraisa opened Heavenly Valley, after purchasing two rope tows and Bijou Skin Run for $5,700. To say the resort has come a long way is the ultimate understatement. At 4,700 acres and 91 runs, Heavenly is now California's largest ski resort and offers trails for all levels of skier and snowboarder. *Lifts*: 30 (15 in CA and 15 in NV), one eight-passenger gondola, one aerial tramway, two high-speed six-passenger, seven high-speed quads, five triple chairs, six surface lifts, and four magic carpets, for a total hourly uphill capacity of 52,000. *Trails*: 91 trails—45 percent intermediate, 20 percent beginner, 35 percent expert. *Vertical drop*: 3,500 feet. *Snowmaking*: 70 percent of the mountain trails. *Terrain*

A snowboarder takes to the air at Heavenly Valley. Courtesy of Heavenly Valley Resorts

parks and pipes: High Roller California for advanced boarders and High Roller Superpipe. *Facilities*: Heavenly offers 11 dining facilities, eight on the California side and three on the Nevada side. A large number of boutiques and ski/board shops assure the visitor a world-class mountain experience. *Ski schools:* Heavenly offers a number of school schools for individuals and groups. *For children:* Heavenly Day Care is for children six weeks through six years (reservations required). Children ages three to four may participate in the ski/play program, and for four- and five-year-olds, Heavenly provides a Half-&Half program. Heavenly also has a Nanny for a Day Program. *Rates*: Heavenly offers a number of pricing and discount plans. List prices for two- or three-day lift tickets are: $150 adult, $124 teen, $76 children, $124 seniors.

Kirkwood, www.kirkwood.com, 1-800-967-7500. Located on CA 88 about 35 miles south of South Lake Tahoe, Kirkwood first opened to the public in 1972. The ski facilities and resort are the result of private enterprise money from Kirkwood Meadows Inc. in cooperation with the US Forest Service and the State of California. Today, Kirkwood offers winter recreation for skiers, snowboarders, cross-country skiers, and snowshoe hiking. *Lifts*: two high-speed quads, one fixed quad, six triple chairs, one double chair, two surface lifts. *Trails*: 65 trails and growing—50 percent intermediate, 15 percent beginner, 20 percent advanced, 15 percent expert. *Vertical drop*: 2,000 feet. *Snowmaking*: Top to bottom coverage on four runs. *Terrain parks and pipes*: Three terrain parks. *Facilities*: Kirkwood offers lodging for overnight visitors, rates start at $164. Eight restaurants and stations are open for anything from a quick snack to a great dining experience. *Ski School*: Kirkwood's Ski and Board School promotes accelerated learning with their "Get Good Fast" teaching

Checking out the slopes. Courtesy of Heavenly Valley Resorts

methodology. Lessons are available for adults and children. *For Children*: Kirkwood does not have programs or facilities for children under two years of age. For children ages two to six, the Mini-Mountain is a fully licensed childcare facility. For children four to 12, Kirkwood offers the Children's Ski and Snowboard School. *Rates*: Adults full day $67, Juniors $54, Children $14, Seniors $37; half-day and season passes available.

Mount Rose Ski Tahoe, www.mtrose.com, 1-800-754-7673 or 775-849-0704. Located just off NV 431 (Mt. Rose Highway) 11 miles from Lake Tahoe's north shore, and 25 miles from downtown Reno. Shortly after World War II, Sky Tavern Lodge opened to service the hardy skiers who visited the Slide Mountain and Mt. Rose ski areas. In the late 1980s the two facilities merged into one major ski resort. The facility has continued to evolve into one of the better winter retreats in the West. *Lifts*: Two 'six pack' high-speed chairs, two quad chairs, two triple chairs, two surface lifts. *Trails*: 60 trails—30 percent intermediate, 20 percent beginner, 40 percent advanced, 10 percent expert. *Vertical drop*: 1,800 feet. *Snowmaking*: 28 percent coverage top to bottom. *Terrain parks and pipes*: Two terrain parks. *Facilities*: Seven eateries serve Mount Rose, serving up just about anything from simple sandwiches to mouth-watering ribs and brats. Ski packages and shuttle services are available from many of the resort hotels in Reno. Ski equipment and snowboards are available for rent, and there is also an equipment repair shop. *Ski school*: Individual and group lessons are available for both kids and adults. *For kids*: Rosebuds Children's Camp is specifically geared for kids to learn from skilled instructors—however, Rosebuds is not a daycare facility, and parents must remain on site. *Rates*: $58 adult, $38 teen, $38 senior, $12 kids. Season passes and group rates are available.

Northstar-at-Tahoe, www.northstarattahoe.com, 1-800-466-6784. From Reno, go west on I-80; from Sacramento or the Bay Area, go east on I-80 and exit at CA 267. Travel south for about eight miles and turn right at Northstar Drive. A longtime favorite among winter sports enthusiasts, Northstar recently invested more than $10 million in facility improvements. This destination resort has it all: skiing, snowboarding, ice skating, shopping, and much, much more. Who knows, you may not be able to resist investing in one of the brand-new condos. *Lifts*: One express gondola, one six-pack express, six express quad chairlifts, one triple chairlift, one double chairlift, two surface lifts, four Magic Carpets, uphill capacity of 23,600 skiers per hour. *Trails*: 79 trails, 62 percent intermediate, 13 percent beginner, 25 percent advanced. *Vertical drop*: 2280 feet. *Snowmaking*: 50 percent. *Terrain parks and pipes*: One superpipe, one halfpipe, five terrain parks and six adventure parks. *Facilities*: The Northstar lodge has 260 units. There are a wide variety of on-mountain dining facilities offering menus to please the entire family. *Ski School*: Ski and snowboard lessons for children and adults, individual and group are available. *For children*: Minors' Camp offers state licensed child care and outdoor play for non-skiing children ages two to six. Child and toddler lessons are also available. *Rates*: $69 adult, $59 young adult, $24 child, $59 senior, $24 super senior. Group rates, season, and multi-day passes are also available.

Sierra-at-Tahoe, www.sierraattahoe.com, 530-659-7453. Located west of Lake Tahoe on US 50. A Lake Tahoe local, Vern Sprock, opened what was then called Sierra Ski Ranch in 1946. The facility was moved to its present location in 1968 to make way for the widening of US 50. The Sprock family operated the facility until 1993 when it was sold to Fiberboard Inc. who gave the facility its current name. Booth Creek Ski Holdings purchased the facility in 1996. *Lifts*: Three express family-friendly quad chairlifts, one triple lift, five double lifts, two "Magic Carpet" children's surface lifts, one tubing surface tow. *Trails*: 46 slopes and trails—50 percent intermediate, 25 percent beginner, 25 percent "most difficult." *Vertical drop*: 2,212 feet. *Terrain parks and pipes*: Six terrain parks. *Facilities*: Sierra-at-Tahoe is dedicated to family entertainment. The facility is laid out so that most of the ski runs end near the lodge. Sierra also offers preferred parking for families, and value meals for children. *Ski school*: The facility offers equipment rental and lessons for adults and children focusing on downhill skiing, snowboarding, and telemarking. *For children*: Wild Mountain Daycare Center is located at the base of the mountain. Half- and full-day childcare is available for children 18-months to five years of age, and this is a licensed daycare center. *Rates*: $61 adult, $51 young adult, $15 child, $36 senior, $17 super senior, half-day rates and three-day packages also available.

Squaw Valley USA, www.squaw.com, 1-800-403-0206. From Sacramento and the Bay Area go east on I-80, from Reno, go west on I-80. Exit at Truckee and take CA 89 south for eight miles to the Squaw Valley Road exit. Turn right, and follow the road to the base of the mountain. Squaw Valley opened in 1949 with one chair lift, a rope tow, and a lodge. Talk about growth—Squaw Valley hosted the 1960 Olympic Winter Games. Today it remains a premier destination stop for the global skiing community. *Lifts*: One cable car, one funitel, one pulse gondola, three express six-packs, four express quads, one fixed-grip quad, eight triple chairs, ten double chairs, three surface lifts, two magic carpets. Uphill capacity of 49,000 skiers per hour. Trails: 170 trails, 16 bowls—45 percent intermediate, 25 percent beginner, 30 percent advanced. *Vertical drop*: 2840 feet. *Snowmaking*: 600 acres, seven miles. *Terrain parks and pipes*: Three terrain parks, one superpipe, one halfpipe, 12 tabletops, and more than 30 rails and boxes. *Facilities*: Olympic Ice Pavilion for ice skating, 1960 Olympic Museum, many restaurants, bars, and cafés. *Ski school*: Squaw Valley offers a wide variety of ski and snowboard instruction programs, for groups and individuals. *For children*: Squaw Valley has a 12,000 square foot facility dedicated for children. It offers ski and snow play program for children from three to twelve. *Rates*: $69 adult, $52 youth, $42 senior, free for super seniors, $5 children under twelve. These rates may change during peak and non-peak times. Group discounts, season, and multi-day passes are also available.

Sugar Bowl, www.sugarbowl.com, 530-426-9000. From Sacramento and the Bay Area, take I-80 east to the Norden/Soda Springs exit and go three miles south to the village. Often considered the Grand Dame of Sierra ski resorts, Sugar Bowl was founded in the late 1930s by an investment group headed up by Walt Disney. Today, the resort is in the midst of a major facelift, bringing new facilities and equipment to add to the skiing experience. *Lifts*: 10 lifts, five high-speed express quads. *Trails*: 84 trails—45 percent intermediate, 17 percent beginner, 38 percent advanced. *Vertical drop*: 1500 feet. *Snowmaking*: 25 percent of the terrain. *Terrain parks and pipes*: Two terrain parks, one family park, and one superpipe. *Facilities*: Sugar Bowl features three restaurants, a formal dining room in the lodge, three bar/lounges, and four sundecks. *Ski school*: The Sugar Bowl Mountain Learning Center offers private and group lessons for kids and adults. *For children:* Sugar Bowl offers child care for kids ages three to five, and skiing programs for children ages five to twelve. *Rates*: $50 adult, $50 young adult, $15 children, $50 senior, $5 seniors 70-plus. Rates do vary depending on the season. Half-day, multi-day, and season passes and group rates are also available.

Sledding/Tubing

Heavenly's Adventure Peak, www.skiheavenly.com, 775-586-7000. Located at the intersection of Wildwood and Saddle Road, Stateline, NV. Just getting to Adventure Peak is an adventure requiring a gondola ride and featuring some of the most beautiful scenery anywhere in the Sierra. Upon reaching the park, visitors can take part in sledding, tubing, cross-country skiing, snowshoeing, and snow biking. Equipment is available for rent, but is not included in the gondola ride fee. The park is open from 10 AM to 3 PM daily, from late November through April. The Adventure Peak Grill serves up a wide variety of burgers and sandwiches, and has a full-service bar. Rates: gondola rides $24 adults, $22 teens, $15 children, $22 seniors, free for kids four and under. Slightly higher during holidays.

Sleigh Rides

Borges Family Sleigh and Carriage Rides, www.sleighride.com, 1-800-726-RIDE. Located at the intersection of US 50 and Lake Parkway, Stateline, NV. Your sleigh ride in one of several antique European sleighs will take you over the meadow and through the woods. Be sure to take your camera, as the driver will gladly take pictures of you and your friends with beautiful Lake Tahoe in the background. Dinner sleigh rides and even wedding events are available. Rates: $20 adult, $10 children.

Snowmobiling

Lake Tahoe Adventures, www.laketahoeadventures.com, 1-800-865-4679. The tour center is located on US 50 just south of South Lake Tahoe in Meyers, CA. Tours are offered for

Lake Tahoe Facts

• Lake Tahoe is the largest alpine lake in North America, and the highest lake of its size in the United States.

• At 1,645 feet, Lake Tahoe is the second deepest lake in the United States. The deepest is Crater Lake in Oregon, at 1,949 feet.

• If all the water in Lake Tahoe were released at once, it would cover the entire state of California to a depth of 14.5 inches.

• On average, about 1,400,000 tons of water evaporates off the lake's surface every 24 hours, dropping its levels a whopping one-tenth of an inch. If all that water could be recovered, it would meet the daily requirements of 3.5 million people.

• There are 63 rivers and streams feeding into Lake Tahoe, and only one outlet, the Truckee River.

• Lake Tahoe's water is 99.9 percent pure. The water is so clear, that a 10-inch white plate is visible 75 feet below the surface.

• Lake Tahoe never freezes, due to its depth and the constant movement of water from the bottom to the surface. In February 1989, Emerald Bay froze over for the first time since 1952.

Lake Tahoe by the Numbers

Maximum Elevation: 6,229 feet

Length: 22 miles

Width: 12 miles

Maximum depth: 1,645 feet

Average depth: 989 feet

Shoreline: 72 miles

Surface area: 193 square miles or 122,200 acres

Volume: 39 trillion gallons, or 122 million acre feet of water

Surface water temperature: Maximum 68 degrees F; minimum 41 degrees F

Temperatures at 200 feet: Maximum 47 degrees F; minimum 41 degrees F

* Source: United States Geological Survey

A little repair work will be needed before setting sail on the lake.

snowmobilers of all skill levels, from beginners through expert riders. Tours are offered in several scenic locations. First-time riders are encouraged to stop by the tour center and take a ride. Snowmobiles are set at moderate speeds so kids eight through adult can take a spin. No reservations required. Rates: $50 per half-hour at the tour center. $102 and up for scenic tours.

Zephyr Cove Snowmobile Center, www.zephyrcove.com, 775-589-4908. Located about four miles north of Stateline on US 50 at Zephyr Cove Resort. The tours feature miles of beautiful trails with fantastic views of Lake Tahoe. All skill levels welcome. Family tours available led by experienced guides. Rates: $109 single rider, $149 double rider Lakeview tour. $179 single rider, $239 double rider Sierra Summit tour.

SHOPPING

Arts & Crafts

Art for the Home Gallery, artforthehomegallery.com. 530-541-1658, 900 Ski Run Blvd., South Lake Tahoe, CA. Specializing in nature, landscape, and wildlife art, glass, pottery, and bronze sculpture. Considered one of Lake Tahoe's finest regional galleries.

Fire and Rain Gallery, www.fireandraingalleries.com, 530-541-9300, The Village Center, 4000 Lake Tahoe Blvd., #30, South Lake Tahoe, CA. Check out the handcrafted furnishings, original art works, custom jewelry plus a large collection of blown glass. Definitely not your traditional gallery.

Gaia Licious, www.gaialicious.com, 530-542-4244, 987 Tellac Ave., South Lake Tahoe, CA. An eclectic little gift shop and gallery, featuring global gifts, local art, incense, music, books, clothing, and body-care products.

Jon Paul Gallery, www.jonpaulgallery.com, 530-544-4269, The Village Center, 4000 Lake Tahoe Blvd., C-18, South Lake Tahoe, CA. The gallery features the nature photography of Jon Paul. Photographic seminars and outings by appointment. Check out his coffee table book, *Visions of Lake Tahoe.*

Justin Bailie Photography, www.justinbailie.com, 530-545-0694, 1245A O'Malley St., South Lake Tahoe, CA. Bailie's studio features his work, including scenic, landscape, nature, adventure, and lifestyle photographs.

Marcus Ashley Galleries, www.marcusashley.com, 530-544-4278, 4000 Lake Tahoe Blvd., Suite 29, South Lake Tahoe, CA. A treasure trove of oil and acrylic paintings, limited edition prints, sculpture, art glass, and jewelry.

Tahoe Country, 530-544-6600, The Shops at Heavenly Village, 1001 Heavenly Village Way, Suite 27, South Lake Tahoe, CA. The theme here is Celebrating the High Sierra. The shop carries everything from coffee mugs to books, cards, gifts and fine art celebrating the beauty of Lake Tahoe and the High Sierra.

Wyland Galleries, www.wylandgalleries.com, 530-541-8865, 900 Ski Run Blvd., South Lake Tahoe, CA. Here's a collecting paradise of marine art, located in the mountains of Lake Tahoe. The gallery features ocean paintings, dolphin art, whale art, sculptures, and tons of other marine-themed pieces.

Books

Bookshelf, www.bookshelfstores.com, 1-800-959-5083, 530-582-0515, 11310 Donner Pass Road, Truckee, CA; and inside The Boatworks Mall, 760 N. Lake Blvd., Tahoe City, CA. Owner Deborah Lane guarantees her staff to be knowledgeable, committed, and well-read. Offerings include, but are not limited to, publications on westward immigration and the Donner Party and recreation and nature guides for the Lake Tahoe/Sierra Nevada region.

Fashion

1000 Bathing Suits, 530-543-3333, 3564 Lake Tahoe Blvd., South Lake Tahoe, CA. The name says it all.

Atlas–Squaw Valley, www.atlasshops.com, 530-584-6055, 1850 Village South Road, Squaw Valley, CA. Great stop for the latest in men's clothing and shoes. Specializing in jeans, and casual and dress wear, as well as accessories.

Cache, www.cache.com, 530-543-3463, The Shops at Heavenly Village, South Lake Tahoe, CA. A must-stop place for the latest in women's fashions. Check out the leather and suede salon, and the accessories section.

Fine 'N Funky, www.finenfunky.com, 530-583-1400, Boatworks Mall, 760 N. Lake Blvd., Tahoe City, CA. Very hip, specializing in high-fashion clothing, and shoes for men and women.

First Street Leather Squaw Valley USA, www.firststreetleather.com, 1750 Village East Rd., Olympic Valley, CA. First Street Leather offers a full line of leather clothing and accessories for men and women. Everything from gloves and belts to handbags will be found here. Also features a wide variety of fur garments and accessories.

Gary Angelica, www.garyangelica.com, 530-543-3400, The Shops at Heavenly Village, 1001 Heavenly Village Way, #9, South Lake Tahoe, CA. Get hooked on the latest premium denim, sexy T-shirts, and hoodies. Great place to find all the latest in casual California couture, and don't miss the handbag and jewelry sections.

Rain Urbana, www.rainurbana.com, 530-544-1700, The Shops at Heavenly Village, South Lake Tahoe, CA. This is a thoroughly modern concept store offering premium clothing for men and women, modern household accessories, music, books, and more. Brands include Diesel, Juicy Couture, 7 for All Mankind, and Da-Nang.

Ruffles & Ruffnecks, 530-583-1128, Cobblestone Center, 472 North Lake Blvd., Tahoe City, CA. This is a children's store bursting with clothing, toys, books, and accessories. Take your time, browsing encouraged.

Sidestreet Boutique, www.sidestreetboutique.com, 1-800-626-1889, The Village Center, 4000 Lake Tahoe Blvd., #19, South Lake Tahoe, CA. This is one of the largest and hottest fashion stores in the area, offering all the latest styles for men and women. Sidestreet also is an excellent stop for all your formal needs, including tuxedos, dinner jackets, furs, and the latest in premium denim.

LEFT: *Wood art is popular all around the Tahoe Basin.*

Something Bleu, Inside MontBleu Resort Casino & Spa, www.montbleuresort.com, 1-800-648-3353, Stateline, NV. This boutique offers a complete line of men's and women's active wear, as well as great gifts and accessories.

Styles for Less, www.stylesforless.com, Factory Outlets at the Y, 2028 Lake Tahoe Blvd., South Lake Tahoe, CA. Offering a full line of women's apparel at prices that won't break the bank. Caters to women of all ages featuring the right look for every season.

Tees'N Things, 1-800-590-9847, 4079 Lake Tahoe Blvd., South Lake Tahoe, CA. This fun stop features T-shirts with the best one-liners, pirate memorabilia, hoodies, and tank tops.

Truckee River Llama Ranch, 530-587-4320, 10052 Donner Pass Road, Truckee, CA. This is a must stop on any Tahoe tour because the history of the Ranch's building is as colorful as the inventory. Parts of the building date back to the 1800s, and some old inscriptions can still be seen. Name-brand apparel for men and women, including Hot Chillys, Tuskany, Wahmaker, and much more. Don't forget to check out their fine jewelry.

Specialty

Gundy of Scandinavia, 530-583-4533, Cobblestone Center, 475 N. Lake Tahoe Blvd., Suite 151, Tahoe City, CA. This shop features a veritable treasure trove of goodies from all over the world. Here you will find watches, pewter knickknacks, jewelry, sweaters, and Scandinavian linens. The Christmas ornament center is open year-round.

Simpson's Jewelers, 1-800-541-5361, 4097 Lake Tahoe Blvd., South Lake Tahoe, CA. From diamonds that dazzle to simple watch repair, Simpson's is a full-service jeweler. Custom design services available. Walking distance to Stateline casinos.

Rainbow Bridge, www.therainbowbridge.com, 530-583-4323, Cobblestone Center, 475 N. Lake Blvd., Tahoe City, CA. This is a wild store, with all kinds of interesting stuff, including one of the best gemstone jewelry collections in the area. Also, lots of candles, aromatherapy, crystals, and body and bath products. The store bills itself as "an eclectic store for the soul."

Runes & Jewels, www.runesandjewels.com, 530-581-1644, Boatworks Mall, 760 N. Lake Blvd., Tahoe City, CA. Designer Iva Winton creates jewelry of wearable beauty that evokes emotion and meaning. Among her specialties are rings, hoop earrings, and bangle bracelets.

Sporting Goods

House of Ski, www.houseofski.com, 1-800-475-4432, 209 Kingsbury Grade, Stateline, NV. Since 1979 this shop has provided locals and visitors top-of-the-line ski and snowboard gear, featuring the latest equipment apparel and premium rental equipment. Pick up rental equipment a day early, at no extra charge.

Olympic Bike Shop, www.olympicbikeshop.com, 530-581-2500, 620 N. Lake Blvd., Tahoe City, CA. Whether you are looking for a lazy pedal around the lake or some serious trail blasting, this is the shop for the bicycling enthusiast. For more than 30 years, Olympic has provided sales and service for locals and visitors alike.

Sierra Ski and Cycle Works, www.sierraskiandcycleworks.com, 530-541-7505, 430 Lake Tahoe Blvd., South Lake Tahoe, CA. This is the store for outdoor enthusiasts. Whether you need a mountain bike, backpack or ski gear, Sierra Ski and Cycle has it all. The staff prides itself on their knowledge of the gear they sell, and for excellent advice on the really cool places to visit.

Tahoe Dave's, www.tahoedaves.com, 1-800-398-8915, Four locations including Tahoe City, Truckee, Squaw Valley and Kings Beach. Dave's is an award-winning ski and snowboard outfitter. Stocks all the name-brand equipment, and the latest in ski and board fashion. Boasts the largest selection of rental/demo equipment on the North Shore. Also rents snowshoes and cross-country ski gear.

Tahoe Sports Ltd, www.tahoesportsltd.com, 530-542-4000, Village Center, 4000 Lake Tahoe Blvd., Suite 7, South Lake Tahoe, CA. In addition to stocking all the latest equipment for skiing and bike riding, Tahoe Sports also boasts the best line of climbing gear in the Tahoe Basin. A knowledgeable staff will help get you outfitted for whatever sporting adventure you undertake.

Village Ski Loft, www.villageskiloft.com, 775-831-3537, 800 Tahoe Blvd., Incline Village, NV. Rental and retail shop featuring the latest in ski and snowboard equipment. Also has a large selection of specialty equipment for the backcountry and Nordic winter recreation. Ski tuning and boot fitting services on site.

4

RENO, VIRGINIA CITY, AND THE CARSON VALLEY

Where History is Still Alive

Against the backdrop of the snow-capped Sierra Nevada lies the vacation wonderland of western Nevada. This region has a rich tradition of providing sustenance and shelter. Long before westward expansion brought nonnatives into the area, the banks of the Truckee River—near Reno—served as winter home to Native Americans, including the Washoe and Paiute peoples.

The discovery of gold—and more notably, silver—in 1859 spawned a new era, launching the region into an economic, industrial, and social transformation. Virginia City and the surrounding boomtowns sprang up almost as fast as the ore was hauled out of the ground. At one time, Virginia City boasted a population of 25,000, making it one of the larger communities in the entire country. This mineral wealth attracted people from all over the world, giving rise to its rancorous and bawdy Wild West way of life. During this same time period, Nevada culture took root, as many of the people who were fortunate enough to garner great wealth from the mines built magnificent Victorian-style homes and mansions, decorating them with furnishings and artwork from around the world. It was also in Virginia City that a young Samuel Clemens began his writing career at the *Territorial Enterprise,* and took the pen name Mark Twain.

What visitors to northwestern Nevada will find today is a charming blend of historic preservation and high-tech attractions. Virginia City retains the architecture and atmosphere of the late 1800s. The community devotes itself to preserving its rich history and sharing this with visitors from home and abroad. Here you can tour a silver mine, take a ride on the Virginia & Truckee Railroad, poke around in Mark Twain's newspaper office, and visit many other historic sites and attractions.

Culture and entertainment are alive in nearby Carson City and the surrounding communities, especially when the legislature is in session. As the state capital, the city is overflowing with museums, art galleries, historic buildings, and numerous special events. Not far to the south lies Genoa, Nevada's oldest community. Between checking out the stores and museum, stop by the Genoa Saloon and hoist a cold brew in the state's oldest—and still operating—saloon. But to get a real feel for the vastness of the state and what it was like

LEFT: *Is the dome really made of silver? State Capitol building, Carson City, NV.*

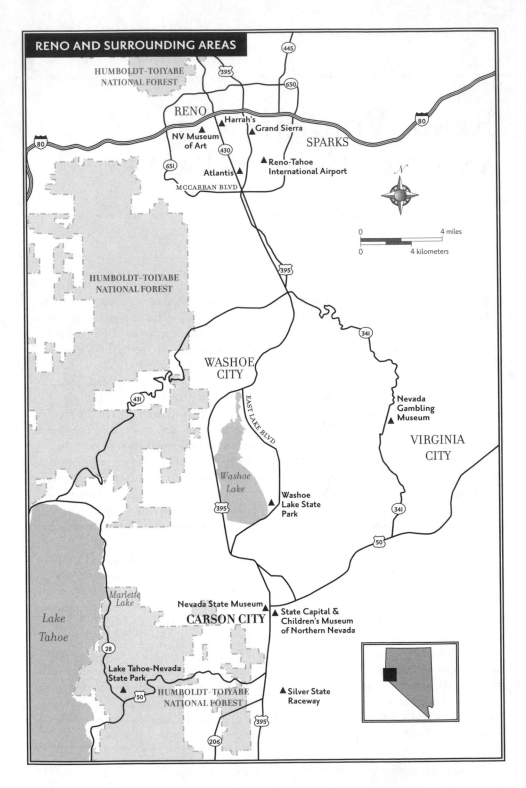

RENO AND SURROUNDING AREAS

HUMBOLDT–TOIYABE
NATIONAL FOREST

RENO

Harrah's
Grand Sierra

NV Museum
of Art

SPARKS

Reno-Tahoe
International Airport

Atlantis

MCCARRAN BLVD

HUMBOLDT–TOIYABE
NATIONAL FOREST

WASHOE
CITY

Nevada
Gambling
Museum

VIRGINIA
CITY

EAST LAKE BLVD

Washoe
Lake

Washoe
Lake State
Park

Marlette
Lake

Lake
Tahoe

Nevada State Museum

CARSON CITY

State Capital &
Children's Museum
of Northern Nevada

Lake Tahoe-Nevada
State Park

HUMBOLDT–TOIYABE
NATIONAL FOREST

Silver State
Raceway

N

0   4 miles

0   4 kilometers

A Hollywood portrait of Butch Cassidy and the Sundance Kid greets visitors to a Virginia City tavern.

only 150 years ago, take a drive or bicycle ride into the Great Basin just east of the Sierra Nevada. Here one might kick back on a cool night and peer into a sky glistening with stars, and possibly hear the mournful cry of a coyote off in the distance. The area offers plenty of quaint B&Bs and guest ranches that will make such an experience memorable.

And then there's Reno, where the gaming action and headline entertainment never cease. The large resort-casinos stand as testaments to all the luxury and entertainment available to today's traveler. But away from the obvious tourist attractions, Reno possesses a business and social culture all its own. Spend an afternoon exploring the wonders of outer space at the Fleischmann Planetarium on the University of Nevada campus, or take a stroll through the arts district along the Truckee River, where local artisans work in their studios and, only a few feet away, kayakers ply the river rapids.

Reno is such a vibrant community, with activities and attractions to suit every taste, that it's no wonder it's called "The Biggest Little City in the World."

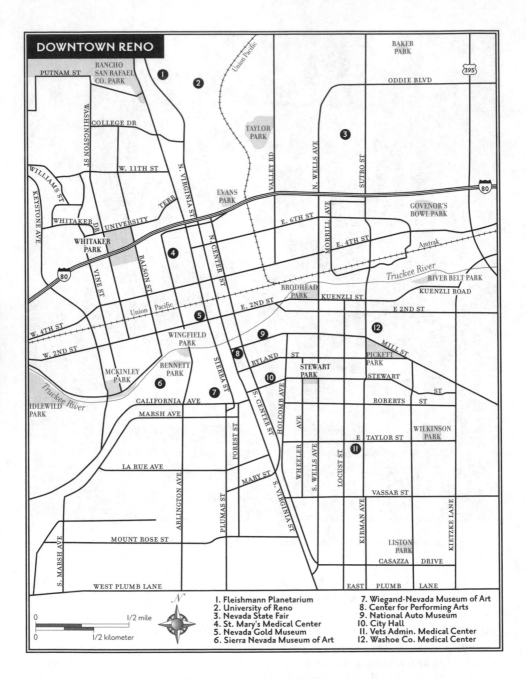

DOWNTOWN RENO

1. Fleishmann Planetarium
2. University of Reno
3. Nevada State Fair
4. St. Mary's Medical Center
5. Nevada Gold Museum
6. Sierra Nevada Museum of Art
7. Wiegand-Nevada Museum of Art
8. Center for Performing Arts
9. National Auto Museum
10. City Hall
11. Vets Admin. Medical Center
12. Washoe Co. Medical Center

LODGING

Since the discovery of the Comstock Lode, this region has accommodated guests from all over the world. Today, it's all here, from lavish, ultramodern, high-rise resorts to historically quaint B&Bs, and restored, period-themed grand hotels. A word of caution is appropriate. Room rates change frequently—especially at the casino-resorts—depending on the time of year and during special events. Similarly, rates also vary greatly for weekend and weekday visits. It is for that reason that only the lowest rate available is listed. Many of the facilities host moderate-to-large conventions and business meetings, while almost all will cater to special events such as weddings and reunions. The listings that follow are by no means comprehensive, but each one offers a special charm of its own. Enjoy your stay. **Credit cards** are abbreviated as follows:

AE: American Express
D: Discover Card
MC: MasterCard
V: Visa

Carson City

BLISS BUNGALOW . . . AN INN
www.blissbungalow.com
1-800-887-3501 or 775-883-6129
408 W. Robinson St., Carson City, NV
Price: $115 and up
Credit cards: AE, D, MC, V
Children: Yes
Pets: No
Handicap access: Yes

Originally built in 1914, the Bliss Bungalow was fully restored in 2005 in an Arts and Crafts motif. The Inn retains its original fir

Mark Twain's desk and chair on display in the Territorial Enterprise *building, Virginia City, NV.*

floors, bay windows, and pine molding. All rooms are adorned with large Indian /Pakistani/Turkish rugs with distinctive colors and designs. Each of the five guest rooms has a private bath with shower, refrigerator, and television. A special treat is sitting on the large front porch and simply letting the world go by in the historic district of Carson City. Self-serve continental breakfast is available 24-hours in the kitchen. Wi-Fi is available throughout the house. A great stop for the discerning traveler or business person desiring to avoid casinos and franchise motels.

CARSON NUGGET

www.ccnugget.com
1-800-426-5239 or 775-882-1626
507 N. Carson St., Carson City, NV
Price: $49 and up
Credit cards: AE, D, MC, V
Children: Yes
Pets: Yes
Handicap access: Yes

A warm and friendly atmosphere greets gamers when they arrive at the Carson Nugget, which features all the standard casino games. The slots and video poker machines, where you can gamble pennies

Bliss Bungalow is a favorite Victorian style B&Bs in Carson City.

or dollars, are the latest and most high-tech. Try your hand at blackjack, roulette, or 3-card poker. Speaking of poker, be sure to pull up a chair in their poker room, or try your luck in the bingo and keno parlors. Dining in the steak house is always a pleasure. Portions are generous and the red-brick walls, burgundy and white tablecloths, and silk roses make for a quaint setting. Catch live entertainment in the casino's Show Lounge, where there is no cover or minimum charge. The adjacent motel, owned by the same company, is simple, clean, and comparatively inexpensive.

DEER RUN RANCH BED & BREAKFAST
www.bbonline.com/nv/deerrun
Innkeepers: David and Muffy Vhay
1-800-378-5440 or 775-882-3643
5440 Eastlake Blvd., Carson City NV
Price: $99 and up
Credit cards: AE, D, MC, V
Children: Yes
Pets: No with some exceptions
Handicap access: Limited

Secluded, but not isolated, Deer Run Ranch is a cozy country getaway. Surrounded by alfalfa fields and offering beautiful vistas of Washoe Lake and the Sierra Nevada to the west, this is true country living. The ranch is an Audubon Bird Count site and many large birds including hawks, herons, ducks, geese, and barn owls are often spotted. Look closely out in the fields and you might get a glimpse of a coyote, deer, bobcat, or badger taking a drink from one of the ponds. When it's warm, take a dip in the pool; or enjoy a chilly winter night by the fire and peruse the extensive library collection. Modern amenities, including satellite TV and high-speed internet access, are available. A full ranch breakfast is served each morning, including homemade breads and muffins. The menu is seasonal, depending on what's ripe in the garden. The meal is served on pottery plates made

in the ranch studio. Accommodations in either the Navajo Room or the Old Ranch Room are comfy and ranch casual. You'll find a welcome basket of fruit, wine, and snacks upon arrival.

GOLD DUST WEST
www.gdwcasino.com
1-877-519-5567 or 775-885-9000
2171 Highway 50 E. Carson City, NV
Price: $80 and up
Credit cards: AE, D, MC, V
Children: Yes
Pets: Yes
Handicap access: Yes

Whether you stay in the motel or the RV park with full hook-ups, Carson City's Gold Dust West is centrally located with Lake Tahoe, Reno and historic Virginia City just a few miles away. While here, try your luck on the slots, video poker, blackjack, craps, 3-card poker and more. Enjoy good old home cookin' in the Coffee Shoppe where signature favorites include the chicken-fried steak, homemade soups, homemade cinnamon rolls and other baked goods. Gold Dust West also features a 32-lane bowling center

THE PLAZA HOTEL
AND CONFERENCE CENTER
www.carsoncityplaza.com
1-888-227-1499 or 775-883-9500
801 S. Carson St., Carson City, NV
Price: $59 and up
Credit cards: AE, D, MC, V
Children: Yes
Pets: Yes
Handicap access: Yes

The Plaza Hotel is a great place to make base camp for exploring the entire area. It's right downtown and within walking distance of the state capitol, the Nevada State Museum, the historic walking tour and the downtown casinos. Also, it's only minutes by car from Lake Tahoe, Reno, and Virginia

City. The 168 rooms are comfortably furnished with queen- and king-sized beds, Wi-Fi Internet access, refrigerators, and microwave ovens. A free continental breakfast is served daily. The 3,300 square foot conference center is equipped to handle all your convention, banquet, and business needs.

Gardnerville

COTTONWOOD CREEK FARM BED & BREAKFAST

www.ccarabians.com

775-782-3057

1702 Sanchez Rd., Gardnerville, NV

Price: $125 and up

Credit cards: MC, V

Children: Under 12 by arrangement

Pets: No

Handicap access: Limited

Dust, dirt, and miles of scrub brush are often the first things that come to mind when one thinks of a Nevada horse ranch, but when it comes to Cottonwood Creek you can forget those images. Yes, it is a working horse ranch, but the grounds around the ranch house are something to behold. It's no wonder it was chosen for a recent pond and garden tour. The pond has an island and is surrounded by fountains and water lilies. A small birch forest invites investigation. A day here might be spent investigating the gardens, watching horses being trained and cared for, and within a mile of

The Genoa Saloon is Nevada's oldest thirst parlor.

Workers perform a little maintenance on the Virginia & Truckee locomotive.

the property, a herd of wild horses often makes a visit. Also nearby, an alpaca farm, llama farm, and Arabian horse farm welcome visitors. The ranch house is decorated with original paintings and antiques from around the world. Two of the guest rooms are located upstairs, the third downstairs. Each room is decorated in its own distinctive style. A full breakfast is offered, but a discount is provided if you opt for the continental breakfast. Cottonwood Creek Farm is a non-smoking facility and accepts bed and breakfast guests from May through October.

Genoa

GENOA HOUSE 1872 INN
A Bed & Breakfast Establishment
www.genoahouseinn.com
Innkeepers: Keith and Suzanne Corban
775-782-7075

180 Nixon St., Genoa, NV
Price: $99 and up
Credit cards: D, MC, V
Children: 12 and older
Pets: Yes
Handicap access: Limited

Genoa is considered to be Nevada's oldest recorded settlement and is nestled in the foothills of the Sierra Nevada. Built in 1872 by A.C. Pratt, publisher of the first newspaper in the Carson Valley, the Genoa House is an authentic Victorian dwelling. It is tastefully decorated to reflect the tranquility of the 1870s. Each of the three guest rooms is distinctive but all are adorned with Victorian antiques. The Rose Room has a large private balcony and beautiful stained glass windows. The Blue Room has a Jacuzzi in its private bath, while the Garden Room has a private entry via the garden, and a faux fireplace.

WILD ROSE INN BED & BREAKFAST

www.wildrose-inn.com
Innkeeper: Sue Knight
1-877-819-4225 or 775-782-5697
2332 Main St., Genoa, NV
Price: $140 and up
Credit cards: AE, MC, V
Children: 12 and older
Pets: No
Handicap access: Limited

Queen Anne Victorian is the theme throughout the Wild Rose Inn. Nestled in the foothills of the eastern Sierra Nevada, the three-story inn offers five guest rooms, each with its own private bath. The Sierra View Suite is a large "honeymoon" suite with a large bathroom, Jacuzzi tub, and a private deck with a beautiful view of the Sierra Nevada. The Gables occupies the third floor, and is a great place for a family or small group. This suite includes a large bathroom, wet bar, and a dining area. Wedgwood wallpaper with pink roses accents the Cameo Rose suite. A large bay window offers beautiful valley views. Lots of sun graces the Garden Gate room which features beautiful valley and mountain views. A full breakfast and afternoon tea are included in the price. The inn is a non-smoking establishment.

The Wild Rose Inn in Genoa is one of the quaint B&B's to be found in Nevada.

Minden

CARSON VALLEY INN HOTEL CASINO RV RESORT

www.cvinn.com
1-800-321-6983 or 775-782-9711
1627 US 395 N., Minden, NV
Price: $62 and up
Credit cards: AE, D, MC, V
Children: Yes
Pets: No
Handicap access: Yes

Away from the hustle and bustle of Lake Tahoe and Reno, the Carson Valley Inn has built its reputation based on its popularity with locals and a faithful following of vacationers. CVI is not overly glitzy or garish, it's clean, casual and fun. For gaming, the inn features more than 650 slots, ten table games, keno, a poker room and a sports book. Comfortable accommodations can be found in the 230 rooms and suites, or park your own rig in the 59-site RV resort. Nightly entertainment can be found in the cabaret lounge, and the inn features three dining facilities. It's proximity to Reno and Lake Tahoe make it a great base camp for golfing, skiing, birding, bike riding, and many other activities. After a day of having too much fun, relax in the pool, spa and fitness facility before heading out again to enjoy the inn's festive nightlife.

DAVID WALLEY'S RESORT, HOT SPRINGS & SPA

www.davidwalleys.com
775-782-8155, ext. 8100
2001 Foothill Rd., Genoa, NV
Price: $145 and up
Credit cards: AE, D, MC, V
Children: Yes
Pets: No
Handicap access: Yes

Want to get away? I mean *really* away. No loud music, no casino hustle and bustle, no flashing neon lights. At David Walley's, a day might be spent playing tennis in the morning, before indulging yourself to a luxurious body treatment, followed by a long soak in a natural mineral hot-spring tub, gazing at the majesty of the snow-capped High Sierra. And then maybe a nap, followed by a gourmet meal in the award-winning DW's Restaurant or a light meal or snack on the patio at the Sierra Deli Café. Well-appointed accommodations include charming cabin rentals, hotel rooms, and luxury suites with fully equipped kitchens, private balcony, and a fireplace. The spa offers a full range of body treatments to soothe not only your body, but your mind and spirit as well. Catch a head-banging show in the cabaret lounge? Not here. That world is about 20 minutes away.

Reno

ATLANTIS CASINO RESORT SPA

www.atlantiscasino.com/reno
1-800-723-6500 or 775-825-4700
3800 S. Virginia St., Reno, NV
Price: $48–very expensive
Credit cards: AE, D, MC, V
Children: Yes
Pets: Yes
Handicap access: Yes

Atlantis combines luxury and the casual atmosphere of a European-style spa and salon with accommodations to meet every budget. Amenities abound. Of course there's nonstop gaming as well as fine dining, with restaurants offering menus from around the world, and it is conveniently located in downtown Reno (the convention center is just across the street). Atlantis is the only hotel offering both indoor and outdoor pools. Rooms range from the luxury of the concierge tower to the super-value motor lodge, with plenty of choices in between, including the Luxury Tower, Atrium Tower, or Royal Dolphin. Of course there are the Grand Penthouse suites. Once settled in, head for the spa and salon where

David Walley's Resort Hot Springs & Spa is a historic landmark on the road to Carson City.

experienced massage therapists, and estheticians demonstrate their knowledge of human physiology with a nurturing healing touch. With eight restaurants to choose from, nobody goes hungry.

BOOMTOWN CASINO HOTEL

www.boomtownreno.com
1-800-648-3790 or 775-345-6000
I-80, Exit 4, Reno, NV
Price: From $99
Credit cards: AE, D, MC, V
Children: Yes
Pets: Yes
Handicap access: Yes

What Boomtown lacks in the elegance of downtown resorts, it makes up for in its wide variety of offerings for the entire family. There's an RV park adjacent to the facility for those who bring their bedroom with them and the rooms in the hotel section are clean and well appointed. Each of the 318 guest rooms and suites have easy access to the huge indoor swimming pool and fitness center. As for gaming, there are plenty of slots, keno, poker tournaments, and a great sports book. And, while you try your luck at the tables, let the kids run wild in the 30,000 square foot family fun center, where they'll find a 3-D motion theater, climbing wall, flight simulator, antique carousel, covered wagon Ferris wheel, and more than 200 video and redemption games. The four restaurants feature mostly standard American favorites, and on Friday and Saturday nights kick up your heels and dance the night away in the Can Can Cabaret Lounge where you'll listen to top live entertainment.

BORDERTOWN CASINO AND RV RESORT
www.bordertowncasinorv.com
1-800-218-9339 (resort) or 1-800-443-4383 (casino)
19575 US Highway 395 N, Reno, NV
Price: $29.99
Credit cards: AE, D, MC, V
Children: Yes
Pets: Yes
Handicap access: Yes

Okay, so you've been driving that self-contained RV or hauling that fifth wheel for hours on the road, and Reno's up ahead. After all that driving, the last thing you want to do is negotiate city streets and the hassles of finding a parking space. Guess what—you don't have to. Just 15 miles north of Reno lies a gambling oasis for RVers: Bordertown. This is a full-service RV resort with 50 large pull-through spaces, with room for slide-outs and hook ups. Each space is paved and has a picnic table. At the Winner's Corner fuel station you'll find gas, diesel, and propane—and very competitive prices. Inside the casino, you'll find a live sports book and more than 200 of the latest slot machines, including penny slots and video poker. When it's time to chow down, relax in The Kafana at the Border, and dine on American and Mexican American cuisine; or check out the Border Deli for all your favorites, including soups, salads, sandwiches, and hot dogs. And don't miss the gift shop, where you can choose from a wide assortment of beer, wine, and liquor, and also pick up a neat trinkets for the folks back home.

CIRCUS CIRCUS RENO HOTEL & CASINO
www.circusreno.com
1-800-648-5010 or 775-329-0711
500 N. Sierra St., Reno, NV
Price: $50 and up
Credit cards: AE, D, MC, V
Children: Yes
Pets: Kennel on the property
Handicap access: Yes

The heavy emphasis on the circus theme can be a bit overwhelming, but it sets the stage for fun for the whole family. Out on the Midway of Fun, you'll find an expansive collection of carnival-style games and free circus shows on the midway stage. Acts from all over the world perform ten daily shows. Additionally, there are always nightly headliner acts and cabaret shows. As for gaming, there are 1,200 slots and video poker machines, all the standard table games, poker rooms, and the exciting race and sports book. Accommodations at Circus Circus range from double queen bedrooms to mini suites, VIP suites, and executive suites. The dining options are many, with restaurants specializing in steaks and seafood, American cuisine, sushi, pizza, deli-style meals, and a great buffet.

ELDORADO HOTEL CASINO, RENO
www.eldoradoreno.com
1-800-879-8879 or 775-786-5700
345 N. Virginia St., Reno, NV
Price: $59 and up
Credit cards: AE, E, MC, V
Children: Yes
Pets: No
Handicap access: Yes

Gourmet dining, nightlife, and exciting gaming action are all at your fingertips at the Eldorado. Hotel accommodations run the gamut from standard rooms; to e-suites for business professionals; to player spa suites, which include California king beds, Jacuzzi tubs, and a pop-up television at the foot of the bed. When it comes to dining, the only problem is making up your mind. Eldorado offers four fine dining restaurants specializing in steaks and seafood, Italian, Chinese, and prime rib. They also offer six casual dining restaurants guaranteed to please just about any taste. Out on the casino floor, play as little as a penny or up to $100 a pull, on one of the 1,200 slot and video poker machines. Try your hand at poker, toss the dice, and spin the roulette wheel on the table games, and get a bet down on your favorite team in the sports book.

FITZGERALDS CASINO & HOTEL

www.fitzgeraldsreno.com
1-800-535-5825
255 N. Virginia St., Reno, NV
Price: $38 and up
Credit cards: AE, D, MC, V
Children: Yes
Pets: No
Handicap access: Yes

A festive Irish theme is the order of the day at Fitzgeralds, and every day seems like a grand celebration of St. Patrick's Day. Although the establishment offers little in the way of live entertainment, its 350 rooms, mini-, and full suites—of course decorated with an Irish flair—are among the least expensive of any of the major resort casinos. Many of the rooms have views of the famous Reno Arch. Food and gaming rule the day here, featuring 800 slots ranging from the popular penny machines to the "certified loose" dollar and five dollar machines. You'll also find plenty of action at the popular table games including black-jack, craps, and roulette. Good food at reasonable prices is available in Limericks Pub & Grille featuring steaks, prime rib, fresh seafood, and pasta dishes. If you are looking to feed a major hunger, head for Lord Fitzgeralds Feast and Merriment, for the All You Can Eat, Drink & Be Merry Buffet.

GRAND SIERRA RESORT AND CASINO

www.grandsierraresort.com
1-800-501-2651 or 775-789-2000
2500 E. Second St., Reno, NV
Price: $59 and up
Credit cards: AE, D, MC, C
Children: Yes
Pets: No with limited exceptions
Handicap access: Yes

The Grand Sierra Resort is just that—it's grand. with a capital "G." Built on a 145-acre property, it includes accommodations and activities for everyone. Amenities include branded retail shopping, headliner entertainment, a 50-lane championship bowling center, a cinema, outdoor thrill rides, golf driving range, and a massive casino. Grand Sierra boasts nearly 2,000 guest rooms and suites and 16 restaurants, bars, and lounges. But, what makes Grand Sierra unique are the outdoor attractions. The top thrill is what they call The Ultimate Rush, a combination of skydiving, hang-gliding, and bungee jumping. Climb to the top of the 185-foot tower where as many as three people are tethered to the same elastic wire and . . . and . . . JUMP! And you thought filling an inside straight at the poker table was the ultimate adrenaline rush. Other outdoor events include the Sling-Shot, a sort of bungee in reverse, cart racing on the oval or road course, and a standard family favorite—bumper cars. And if all that isn't enough, the ultimate water park is set to open in early 2009. After an afternoon of outdoor fun and thrills you'll be ready to hit the spa and health club or go for a relaxing swim in the heated pool or enjoy a soothing massage.

HARRAH'S RENO
www.harrahsreno.com
1-800-427-7247 or 775-786-3232
210 N. Center St., Reno, NV
Price: $55 and up
Credit cards: AE, D, MC, V
Children: Yes
Pets: Yes with restrictions
Handicap access: Yes

It's hard to go wrong at Harrah's Reno. Clean and comfortable rooms at affordable prices, great dining variety, plenty of live entertainment, and, of course, a wide variety of gaming opportunities. Harrah's is steeped in Nevada gaming and entertainment history. Sammy Davis Jr., arguably one of the greatest entertainers to go on stage, had a long-term contract with Harrah's Reno, and following his death, the showroom was renamed Sammy's Showroom. Harrah's also offers nightly entertainment in the Sapphire Lounge. Sip your favorite cocktail and enjoy entertainment from guest DJ's and karaoke divas. As for dining, pick your feast from any one of the eight restaurants. The Steak House is renowned for its meat and seafood cuisine, and Andreotti's serves up Italian favorites and tasty desserts. At Ichiban—Japanese Steakhouse and Sushi Bar—colorful chefs prepare your meal right at your table. Did somebody say sushi? By all means, step up to the all-you-can-eat sushi and tempura bar. To keep in shape or just for relaxation, step into the spa, health club and pool. You can also sip on your favorite Starbucks coffee while playing the slots, poker, blackjack, roulette, or getting a bet down on your favorite team in the race and sports book.

JOHN ASCUAGA'S NUGGET CASINO RESORT
www.janugget.com
1-800-648-1177 or 775-356-3300
1100 Nugget Ave., Sparks, NV
Price: $59.99 and up
Credit cards: AE, D, MC, V
Children: Yes
Pets: No
Handicap access: Yes

Not far from downtown Reno, John Ascuaga's Nugget recently completed an entire renovation of their east tower. Here you'll find 600 rooms boasting the ultimate in comfort and style, including 42-inch plasma TVs in each room, rich wood décor, and chic lighting. Many of the rooms offer beautiful views of the Sierra Nevada mountains and the high desert. Headline entertainment can always be found in the 700-seat Celebrity Showroom and the 2,000-seat Rose Ballroom. Entertainment can also be found in a more intimate setting in the Casino Cabaret, Orozko Lounge, and Trader Dick's. Nine restaurants—featuring everything from steaks and seafood to oysters and noodles—are located in the complex, and the indoor atrium pool, salon, and health club, are always inviting. Of course, the gaming never stops, and the Nugget offers plenty of slot machine and table game action. Put a bet down on your favorite horse in Leroy's Race & Sportsbook, or try your hand in the bingo parlor. The Nugget also hosts many gaming tournaments.

PEPPERMILL HOTEL CASINO
www.peppermillreno.com
1-800-648-6992, 1-866-821-9996 or 775-826-2121
2707 S. Virginia St., Reno, NV
Price: $59 and up
Credit cards: AC, D, MC, V
Children: Yes
Pets: Yes
Handicap access: Yes

What was already one of Reno's top destination resorts just got a whole lot better with the addition of their $400 million Tuscany Tower and Convention Center. Now boasting more than a thousand luxurious rooms and suites it's no wonder that the Peppermill hits the list for "Top 10" casinos by MSN and Citysearch. Also, having won the most "best of" awards in town, the Peppermill ranks as a favorite for locals and vacationers alike. The resort offers 14 themed bars and lounges, world-class gaming, and a full-service salon for relaxation. Talk about variety, enjoy a cocktail in the Casino Cabaret offering free live entertainment nightly, or venture into the Fish Bar, order a tiki drink and take in the tropical aquariums, or just kick back in the Fireside Lounge on a comfortable sofa with surround sound. Dining options include the elegant and upscale White Orchid, for award-winning American cuisine; or dine in Mediterranean splendor in Romanza Ristorante Italiano. Thinking seafood and sushi? Head for Oceano for the seafood, sushi and oyster bar. When it's time to get some sleep or a little work done, head for your custom-decorated room in the tower and enjoy 24-hour room service as you flick on a movie on the 42-inch, high-def plasma television, or cruise the Internet at your computer desk with Wi-Fi access. When it's time to call it a night, relax in a comfortable bed featuring triple sheeting and goose down pillows. If it's the little things that matter, check out the luxurious towels and linens with 310-thread count. Go ahead—count them.

SILVER LEGACY RESORT CASINO

www.silverlegacy.com
1-800-687-8733 or 775-325-7401
407 N. Virginia St., Reno, NV
Price: $59.99 and up
Credit cards: AE, D, MC, V
Children: Yes
Pets: No with limited exceptions
Handicap access: Yes

Headline entertainment and more than 1,700 rooms and suites make Silver Legacy Resort Casino one of Reno's most popular downtown destinations. The theme here is Victorian, and all of the rooms and suites are decorated in turn-of-the-century elegance. All rooms feature a beautiful wood armoire and 20-inch televisions. The action is nonstop and guests can casino-hop via sykwalks connecting Silver Legacy to Eldorado Hotel Casino, Reno and Circus Circus Reno. Enjoy a cocktail in Rum Bullions Island Bar—Reno's only rum bar— and check out the world's largest composite dome and its encased silver mining rig. Dining is robust at Sterling's Seafood Steakhouse and also Fairchild's Oyster Bar. Kids and grown-up kids will have a ball in the arcade, playing Daytona 500, air hockey, pinball, NBA Jam, and many others. Of course, the real gaming is on the casino floor, where Silver Legacy features slots, blackjack, pai gow, Caribbean stud poker, and roulette. Be sure to check out the keno lounge and the race and sports book.

SIENA HOTEL SPA CASINO

www.sienareno.com/casino
1-877-743-6233 or 776-327-4362
One S. Lake St., Reno, NV
Price: $99 and up
Credit cards: AE, D, MC, V
Children: Yes
Pets: No, with limited exceptions
Handicap access: Yes

Built along the banks of the Truckee River and modeled after its Italian namesake, Siena has an international allure that attracts travelers from all over the world. The goal here is to offer 24-hour gaming action, distinctive food and wine, and a full-service day spa amidst surroundings reminiscent of the Tuscan countryside. Hotel accommodations range from standard rooms to palatial suites. If you really want to treat yourself, check out the penthouse suite overlooking the city skyline, complete with king-size bed, plush down

The Silver Legacy is one of Reno's classier downtown resort casinos. Sebastian Diaz/RSCVA

comforter, and an oversized bathroom with a spa-style tub and many other amenities. For a light dining treat, check out Enoteca (Italian for "wine cellar"), where more than 35 wines are served by the glass, and a special appetizer menu serves as a guide matching items to accentuate the flavor of each wine. The day spa is the place to go to really pamper yourself. Expert massage therapists perform their magic on your body. A number of spa packages are offered, each designed to be a soothing and relaxing experience.

WILDFLOWER VILLAGE BED & BREAKFAST
www.wildflowervillage.com
775-827-5250

4275-4395 W. Fourth St., Reno, NV
Price: $100
Credit cards: MC, V
Children: Yes
Pets: No
Handicap access: Yes

The B&B is part of a village, housing two galleries featuring the work of many established and emerging glass artists. The B&B rooms are appointed with designer linens and French lace, where Tiffany-style lamps cast a soothing light. Most of the rooms at this cozy retreat have views of the Truckee River. Wake up to a delicious gourmet champagne breakfast delivered to your door. Numerous art shows, events, and art classes are scheduled throughout the year.

Smith Valley

WALKER RIVER RESORT

www.wrresort.com
1-800-446-2573 or 775-465-2573
No. 1 Hudson Way, Smith, NV
Price: $94 and up
Credit cards: AE, D, MC, V
Children: Yes
Pets: Yes
Handicap access: Limited

Hey, outdoor enthusiast—this is the place you've been looking for. Go bird hunting or fly fishing, target practice, ride ATVs and explore old ghost towns and mining camps, or just kick back and go for a swim. It's all here, at Walker River Resort. You can also wheel your RV into a nice spot, or even tent camp if you feel like just "roughing it." A big draw is their 15-station, sporting clays target course. The Walker River winds through the property, luring abundant wildlife. Try your hand at chukar or pheasant hunting. The facility abuts thousands of acres of land owned by the Bureau of Land Management, containing hundreds of miles of established trails and dirt roads for spectacular ATV riding. Each of the cottages features vaulted ceilings, air conditioning, and full kitchens.

Virginia City

CHOLLAR MANSION

www.chollarmansion.com
Innkeepers: Gena and Jeff Wood
1-877-246-5527 or 775-847-9777
565 South D St., Virginia City, NV
Price: $135
Credit cards: MC, V
Children: Yes
Pets: No
Handicap access: Limited

Chollar Mansion is an historic site originally commissioned in 1860, and used as a business office during the boom times of the Nevada Comstock. Its colorful history includes visits by such literary figures as Mark Twain, a newspaper writer for the *Territorial Enterprise*, and many years later in the 1940s and 50s, the house was the residence of novelist Walter Van Tilburg Clark, author of *The Ox-Bow Incident*. The mansion is built in a modified Federalist style, and boasts 16-inch-thick brick walls, 14-foot-high ceilings, and a three-story cantilevered staircase with banister made of Honduran rosewood. The two guest rooms within the mansion are decorated with Eastlake furnishings from the late 1800s, and each has a private bath. Another option is the O'Connell Cottage. Located on the property, it was built in 1870 as a playhouse for the children of former owners. Today it is furnished with Art Deco antiques from the 1930s. A hearty breakfast is included in the price and guests are encouraged to eat dessert first, and enjoy the freshly baked pastries.

EDITH PALMER'S COUNTRY INN

www.edithpalmers.com
Innkeepers: Pat and Leisa Findley
775-847-7070
416 South B St., Virginia City, NV
Price: $85 and up
Credit cards: MC, V
Children: Yes
Pets: No
Handicap access: No

The inn was officially established in 1947, but its two buildings date back to 1860s—and the height of the region's silver boom. Today, the gardens are well maintained, and make for a great stroll any time of day. The current owners have restored the property, but retained its Victorian charm. The Edith Palmer House contains four guest rooms. Edith's Room honors the renowned cook and innkeeper who first started the inn and Marilyn's Room is named in honor of the famous actress Marilyn Monroe who stayed at the inn during the filming of *The Misfits*. The Story

House contains two suites, both with private bath, beautiful views of the Sugarloaf Mountains, and plenty of morning and afternoon sunshine.

SEVEN MILE CANYON GUEST RANCH

www.nevadaduderanch.com

775-847-7223

SR 341, Virginia City, NV

Price: $125 and up

Credit cards: MC, V

Children: Yes

Pets: Yes

Handicap access: No

This is a secluded, western-style B&B out on the range, that welcomes horse owners and casual tourists looking for a laid-back setting. The wine bar is a popular evening gathering spot. Out on the patio, live music is often the entertainment—but don't be surprised if you are treated to an evening of cowboy poetry under the stars. The facility offers several sleeping options, including the bunkhouse, the Longhorn Lodge, and the Carriage House. Some rooms have hot tubs so you can enjoy a long soak. All rooms have kitchen facilities and fireplaces. A light breakfast is at your door to begin the day. When summer rolls around, check out the Tepee Campground, with two 22' tepees accommodating up to four adults each, for only $75.00 per night, with linens and outdoor bathhouse provided.

The Bucket of Blood is a favorite watering hole in Virginia City.

The Gold Hill Hotel & Saloon near Virginia City is all that's left of a once bustling Comstock era community.

THE GOLD HILL HOTEL

Nevada's Oldest Hotel
www.goldhillhotel.net
775-847-0111
One mile south of Virginia City on NV 342
P.O. Box 740, Virginia City, NV
Price: $45 and up
Credit cards: AE, D, MC, V
Children: Yes
Pets: Yes
Handicap access: Limited

Local tradition has it that the original hotel was built around 1859, then fell into disrepair, but was resurrected and fully renovated in the late 1980s. The hotel is about all that is left of a once-thriving boomtown known as Gold Hill, a sister community to Virginia City. After the silver played out and the town's occupants went elsewhere, the elements—including at least one major flood—took their toll on the community as well, and all that remains today is the renovated hotel. There are five small guest rooms in the original hotel and another 19 rooms and suites contained in various additions and outbuildings. Each room has its own personality, but all are furnished and appointed in a style appropriate to retaining the theme of the late 1800s. Casual gourmet dining can be found in the hotel's Crown Point Restaurant, and an extensive collection of wine, liquor, and beer is available in the Gold Hill Saloon. Belly up to the bar and enjoy.

CULTURE

Architecture

The entire history of western Nevada can be summed up in the architecture found in Virginia City, Carson City, and Reno. When gold and silver were discovered in 1859, Virginia City was born. The wealth generated by the mines was used to build the city, much of which has been restored and can still be seen today. Carson City, on the other hand, is the state capital, and while retaining much of its rich architectural history, it has also evolved into a modern center of government and commerce. Reno is a testament to 21st century bling-bling, as far as the high-rise resort casinos are concerned, while the downtown is also home to great urban renewal projects, including a tasteful arts district and river walk.

Cinema

Century Parklane 16, www.cinemark.com, 775-824-3300, 210 E. Plumb Ln., Reno, NV. Large complex, first-run movies. Buy tickets online.

Century Riverside 12, www.cinemark.com 1-800-326-3264, 11 N. Sierra St., Reno, NV. Enjoy a first-run film in the theatre's comfy stadium seating.

Century Summit Sierra, www.cinemark.com, 1-800-326-3264, 13965 S. Virginia St., Reno, NV. Located in the Summit Sierra Shopping Center, this facility was recently remodeled for maximum viewing pleasure.

The River Walk in downtown sports galleries, restaurants, and quaint shops.

Grand Sierra Cinema, Inside the Grand Sierra Resort. 775-789-2093, 2500 E. Second St., Reno, NV.. Great spot to catch second-run movies and art films at very affordable prices.

Ironwood Cinema 8, www.cinemasonline.com, 775-782-7469, 1760 US Highway 395 North, Minden, NV. Modern theatre complex with eight screens. Matinees daily, and Thursday night is family night. Gift certificates available at the box office or by mail.

Northgate Movies 10, 775-883-5427, 2751 N Carson St., Carson City, NV. Home to first-run films in Nevada's state capitol. Comfortable seating and large snack bar.

El Rancho 4 Drive-In & Public Market, www.westwindpublicmarkets.com, 775-358-6920, 555 El Rancho Dr., Sparks, NV. What's this? Well, take me back to the 1950s. (Quick—somebody call Joe Bob Briggs!) Enjoy a little Americana, with a night out at the drive-in. This is the real deal—four screens to choose from, plus double features and a monstrous snack bar boasting some of the best junk food on the planet. Yes mom, there's healthy stuff here, too.

Gardens

RANCHO SAN RAFAEL REGIONAL PARK AND WILBUR D. MAY CENTER
www.maycenter.com
775-785-5961
1595 N. Sierra, Reno, NV
Open Daily
Admission Free

The park itself is a large, multi-use facility featuring fun and recreation for the whole family. One of the primary highlights is the Wilbur D. May Arboretum and Labyrinth Garden. The 12-acre living museum contains groves of trees, wetlands habitats, outdoor courtyards and secluded gardens. In the museum, visitors are greeted by a cascading waterfall and indoor garden. The museum features a great collection of artifacts from Wilbur D. May, a Nevada rancher and businessman, as well as world traveler and philanthropist. And for the kids, there's the Great Basin Adventure, featuring animals who loved to be petted, pony rides, the Great Flume Ride, and panning for gold. Don't miss the Discovery Room where the kids are encouraged to touch everything, and even climb on dinosaurs—or at least kid-friendly replicas of these impressive creatures—that once roamed the earth right here.

Historic Places

KIT CARSON TRAIL AND TALKING HOUSES
www.carson-city.org/attractions/kitcarson_talkinghouses.php
1-800-638-3321 or 775-687-7410
Carson City, NV

Put on your hiking shoes, grab your iPod and take a narrated walk through an authentic Old West community. The Kit Carson Trail is a 2.5 mile stroll through Carson City's historical residential district. A painted blue line and bronze medallions mark the route. The tour features more than 60 landmarks including museums, churches and Victorian-style homes. Sixteen of the featured stops are designated "Talking Houses" where you can listen to historical narrations of frontier life on iTunes. These downloadable podcasts include the voice of John Wayne (J.B. Brooks) at the Krebs-Peterson house, where he filmed his last

The Krebs-Petersen house in Carson City is where John Wayne filmed his last movie, The Shootist.

movie, *The Shootist.* In addition, hear celebrated Carson City locals of yesteryear tell their tales including Mark Twain, Carson City founder Abe Curry, and Hannah Clapp, the town's original feminist.

THE CAPITOL BUILDING

www.visitcarsoncity.com/attractions/capitol.php
775-687-4810 (for tour arrangements)
Capitol Complex, 101 N. Carson St, Carson City, NV
Self-guided tours available. Guided tours upon advance notice

Built in 1870 out of native sandstone, this stands as the second oldest state capitol building located west of the Mississippi River. For many years it housed all three branches of state government, but the legislature and judiciary have since moved into their own buildings in the Capitol Complex. The building's second floor, which once housed the legislature, is now home to rotating historical exhibits, which are open to the public. Nevada is known as the Silver State and, according to local lore, the Capitol dome's cupola is made of silver. In reality, it was originally made of tin. Following the building's most recent retrofit, silver-colored fiberglass replaced the tin.

The Governor's Mansion in Carson City is decked out for both Halloween and Nevada Statehood Day.

MORMON STATION STATE PARK
parks.nv.gov/ms.htm
775-782-2590
2295 Main St, Genoa, NV
Open: Daily 9 AM–4:30 PM
Admission: Free
No pets

Mormon Station is Nevada's first nonnative settlement. Today, there is a museum inside a replica of the original trading post, which was built in 1851. Numerous artifacts from the early days of settling Nevada are on display. Periodic talks and other events are scheduled throughout the year. Outside the park has plenty of room for a nice picnic.

THE RENO ARCH—DOWNTOWN RENO
Driving or walking down Reno's main drag, Virginia Street, you can't miss the famous arch proclaiming Reno as, "The Biggest Little City In The World." With a population in excess of 210,000, Reno isn't so "little" anymore. In fact, it is Nevada's second largest city. In spite of the city's growth, city officials retain the catchy motto. The arch seen today, complete with its "disco" type ball and twin gold towers, is the third reconstruction. The first arch—which did carry the motto—was built in 1926, to celebrate the completion of the Lincoln Highway (now I-80), the first transcontinental highway across America, as well as being the first major thoroughfare to carry auto travelers over the northern Sierra Nevada. In spite of modifications and complete reconstructions, today's arch remains one of the most well-known welcoming arches of any city.

VIRGINIA CITY

www.virginiacity-nv.org
Visitor Center
1-800-718-7587 or 775-847-4836
86 South C St, Virginia City, NV

If modern-day Nevada has a soul, it must live in Virginia City. For a state nicknamed "The Silver State," this is where it all began back in the 1860s. The precious ores, especially silver, brought wealth beyond imagination to those who seized the opportunity. Altogether, more than $400 million in gold and silver came up from the mines of the Comstock Lode. Those who struck it rich built opulent mansions, imported the finest furniture and fashions from Europe and the Orient, and, by some accounts, are responsible for financing the Civil War and building the city of San Francisco. Virginia City today isn't a city; preservation and restoration have created a living museum. Walking its streets is like taking a step back into the 19th century, to a time when Virginia City was a center for arts and culture—including opera and Shakespearean theater—as well as a center for mining labor and wealth. On your walking tour, be sure not to miss:

The Crystal Bar, This is the best place to start your walking tour because it is an historic building and it's now also the city's Visitor Information Center. As the name implies, it was once famous as a raucous tavern. Of historical significance here are the beautiful chandeliers that were originally gas, but are now converted to electricity. Also, don't miss the Mystery Clock. What's so mysterious about the clock? You'll just have to come on in and find out.

Now in its third re-creation, the famous Reno Arch greets visitors to the city.

The Fourth Ward School is one of Virginia City's many historic landmarks.

Comstock Firemen's Museum, Displays 19th century firefighting equipment.

Fourth Ward School Museum, Built in 1876 for the area's one thousand school-aged children. Today it hosts art exhibitions, oral history lectures, and scholar-in-residence programs.

The Mackay Mansion, Built in 1860 and later purchased by John Mackay, one of the area's "silver kings." Today it houses mining artifacts, original furnishings, and Tiffany silver.

The Nevada Gambling Museum, It's rich displays include gaming memorabilia, more than 100 antique slot machines, cheating devise and gamblers' weapons.

Piper's Opera House, No wonder it is said ghosts live here. Built in 1885 and still in use today, the stage once welcomed President Ulysses S. Grant, Buffalo Bill, Harry Houdini, and Mark Twain.

Radio Museum, This is a must for all old radio buffs. Home to numerous antique and vintage radios. Displays include descriptions of their significance in radio history. Be sure not to miss the display of photographs and signed posters of radio personalities.

St. Mary's Art Center, Built in 1876 as a 36-room hospital, today it is utilized for art instruction.

St. Mary's in the Mountains Catholic Church, Built in 1875 and reflective of the numerous beautiful churches built during the era, St. Mary's is considered one of the most prominent historical structures in Virginia City. The church still holds weekly Mass.

Story County Courthouse, Justice isn't blind here—the courthouse is home to one of very few statues of Lady of Justice where she is not blindfolded. After fire destroyed the original courthouse in 1875, the present structure was erected the following year.

The Way It Was Museum, The museum houses one of the most extensive collections of Comstock mining artifacts in the world. Check out the rare photos, lithographs, and maps of the "Bonanza" period.

Virginia and Truckee (V&T) Railroad, All 'board! Be sure not to miss this 35-minute train ride through the heart of the Comstock mining region.

Kids' Stuff

THE CHILDREN'S MUSEUM OF NORTHERN NEVADA
www.cmnn.org
775-884-2226
813 N. Carson St, Carson City, NV
Open: Daily 10 AM–4:30 PM
Admission: Children 2–13, $3; adults 14 and older, $5; seniors 55 and older, $4. Toddlers are free.

Built in 1885, and still in use today, Piper's Opera House has welcomed numerous dignitaries, including President Ulysses S. Grant, Buffalo Bill, Harry Houdini, and Mark Twain.

Why is there a Radio Museum in downtown Virginia City? Good question.
RIGHT: *St. Mary's Catholic Church also doubles as a Virginia City museum.*

This nonprofit educational center offers unique and innovative learning adventures in the arts, sciences, and humanities for children and families of economically and culturally diverse backgrounds. Among the exhibits are Sally's Playhouse, Jacob's Ladder, and dress-up costumes. Be sure to visit the cool collections center, including HO trains and the antique rocking horses. Facilities and planetarium are available for private parties.

Museums

CARSON VALLEY MUSEUM & CULTURAL CENTER
http://www.historicnevada.org/
775-782-2555
1477 US Hwy. 395 N., Gardnerville, NV
Admission: Adults $3; youths 6–18, $2; under 6, free
Hours: Mon.-Sat. 10 AM–4 PM year round

A doll collection is one of the features at the Children's Museum of Northern Nevada in Carson City.

Built in 1915, the facility served as the Douglas County High School until the school board leased it to the local historical society in 1988. The museum is home to a collection of animals hunted in the area, as well as Native American murals and artifacts created by the Washoe people. Don't miss the early-American furniture and the great exhibit featuring items from the early years of the Carson Valley medical profession.

GENOA COURTHOUSE MUSEUM
http://www.historicnevada.org/
775-782-4325
2304 Main Street, Genoa, NV
Admission: Adults $3; youths 6–18, $2; under 6, free
Hours: May–Oct., Daily 10 AM–4:30 PM

Located in the heart of Genoa, Nevada's first permanent town, settled in 1851, the courthouse was built in 1856. The county seat was later moved to nearby Minden and the old courthouse served as a school from 1916 until 1956. Today, visitors can get a real taste of the Old West through the exhibits and displays. Of particular interest is the Snowshoe Thompson exhibit which commemorates John A. "Snowshoe" Thompson (1827–76) who acquired his nickname by skiing over the Sierra Nevada to carry mail to Placerville, CA and back to Genoa.

NATIONAL AUTOMOBILE MUSEUM

www.automuseum.org

775-333-9300

10 South Lake St., Reno, NV

Open Mon.–Sat. 9:30 AM–5:30 PM, Sun. 10 AM–4 PM (Closed Thanksgiving and Christmas Day)

Admission: Adults, $9; seniors (over 62), $7; youths 6–18, $3; under 6, free.

Whether you are a full-fledged car buff or just have a passing interest in the history of the world of motorized wheels, the National Automobile Museum is a must-stop. Here you will find more than 200 cars and motorcycles dating from 1892 to the present. The majority of the displays and in-depth interpretations came to the museum from the world-famous Harrah Collection, amassed by gaming pioneer Bill Harrah. The museum includes four period street scenes complete with autos and artifacts reflecting the era's styles and modes. For the technical and/or more scholarly inclined car enthusiast, the museum is home to the Automotive Research Library, spanning more than 100 years of auto history from the age of the horseless carriage, to the latest issues of *Autoweek*. The library's holdings include technical books, sales literature, restoration, shop, and owner's manuals.

The famous Thomas Flyer is one of scores of vintage autos on display in the National Automobile Museum in Reno.

FLEISCHMANN PLANETARIUM & SCIENCE CENTER
planetarium.unr.nevada.edu
775-784-4812 (business office)
775-784-4811 (showtime hotline)
1650 N. Virginia St., University of Nevada, Reno
Open: Sun.–Thurs. 10:30 AM–7 PM, Fri.–Sat. 10:30 AM–9 PM (closed Thanksgiving,
Christmas, and New Year's Day)
Admission: Free and paid exhibits and programs

Welcome to stargazer's paradise. In addition to public star observing, the planetarium is
open daily offering star shows and large-format films in the theater. Fantastic 3-D images
are created with the Spritz SciDome digital projector. The planetarium is one of the first in
the world to utilize this high-tech visualization tool. Additionally, rotating exhibits featuring astronomy-themed art work from regional and national artists are offered free of
change in the center's lower level.

NEVADA MUSEUM OF ART
www.nevadaart.org
775-329-3333
160 W. Liberty St., Reno, NV
Open Tues.–Sun. 10 AM–5 PM, Thurs 10 AM–8 PM; closed Mondays and all national holidays.
Admission: $10 adult; $8 for students, and seniors 60 and older; $1 for children 6–12;
children under 6 are free.

The Nevada Museum of Art is a four level, 55,000 square foot complex designed by internationally renowned architect Will Bruder. The main exhibition gallery houses the
museum's permanent collection. The Donald W. Reynolds Center for the Visual Arts offers
video and experimental exhibits as part of the gallery's regular offerings. Permanent collections are divided into five groups and include more than 1,900 works. The facility also
houses an extensive research library, lecture hall, sculpture garden, and expanded
museum store. Group and guided tours are available.

NEVADA STATE MUSEUM
http://dmla.clan.lib.nv.us/docs/museums/cc/carson.htm
775-687-4810
600 N. Carson St. (US 395), Carson City, NV
Admission: Adults $5; seniors $3; children 17 and younger are free.
Hours: Daily 8:30 AM–4:30 PM

Built in 1866, the Nevada State Museum was home to the United States Mint for more than
20 years. Today it is rated as one of the best regional museums in the West. Inside the
museum, visitors can walk through a life-size ghost town, see the insides of a silver mine,
and check out the actual equipment used to stamp a veritable fortune—exceeding $50 mil-
lion in gold and silver coins, mined from the Comstock Lode. The anthropology gallery
and clothing and textile exhibits are enticing, but of particular interest is the Hal V. Dunn

RIGHT: *"Large, Left-handed Drummer," a bronze sculpture by Barry Flanagan, is on display on the roof at the
Nevada Museum of Art in Reno.*

collection of historic postcards, exonumia (tokens, medallions, medals, etc.), and memo-rabilia from the mint itself. Wheelchair access. Docent tours by appointment.

NEVADA STATE RAILROAD MUSEUM
www.nsrm-friends.org/
775-687-6953
2180 S. Carson St., Carson City, NV
Admission: Adults $4; seniors over 65; and children under 18 free
Hours: Daily 8:30 AM –4:30 PM

All aboard! Take a train ride celebrating the history of the Old West. The museum is home to more than 65 historic locomotives and cars, 40 of which were built before 1900. Dozens of old mining and railroad artifacts are on display year-round. Many of the exhibits were bought from Hollywood studios, where they were made famous in movies and television shows. Be sure to visit the museum store which features books on Nevada and railroad history, including the hobos of the West.

Performing Arts & Events

BREWERY ARTS CENTER
www.breweryarts.org
775-883-1976
449 West King St., Carson City, NV

The Brewery Arts Center consists of two major buildings in the historic downtown district of Carson City. It is a premier art center, hosting musical performances and theatre troops as well as art shows and exhibits. Listen to great jazz while dining on an elegant Sunday brunch or attending one of the many wine- and beer-tasting events. The center also offers featured events throughout the year. Numerous fine-arts classes are offered including pottery, sculpture, acting, singing, and dance. Special "fine arts for kids" classes are offered as well. Check the center's calendar for current activities and events.

RENO EVENTS CENTER
www.visitrenotahoe.com/facilities/reno_events
1-800-367-7366
Intersection of 4th and 5th Streets, Reno, NV.

You never know who's taking the stage at the Reno Events Center. Hosting a broad spectrum of artists from superstar headliners to internationally acclaimed dance troupes, it's even home to some tremendous boxing matches. The 7,000-seat center is located in the heart of all the action in downtown Reno.

RENO-SPARKS LIVESTOCK EVENTS CENTER
www.visitrenotahoe.com/facilities/reno_livestock
775-688-5752
1350 N. Wells Ave., Sparks, NV 89512

This is a world-class venue for rodeos, horse shows, livestock sales, auctions, and all sports involving animals—even cat shows. The facility has 35,000 square feet of exhibit space, 686 stalls, and 19 barns. The lighted arena has seating for 9,000. Keep an eye on their schedule for upcoming events and concerts.

Nightlife

210 North & Divinity Lounge, www.210north.com, 775-786-6210, 210 N. Sierra St., Reno, NV. Two facilities in one location allow visitors to choose between the Meta-Lounge and the Divinity Lounge. The Meta-Lounge caters to young professionals and the club crowd. It has two full-service bars and is decorated with European furniture and glossy fabrics. The Divinity Lounge is their over-the-top décor lounge with glittering chrome curtains, an Eva Menz-designed 5,000 piece, blown-glass chandelier, velvet loveseats, and a white marble bar. All this is set in a gaming environment where "suits and stilettos prevail."

Alturas Bar & Nightclub, www.alturasbar.com, 775-324-5050, 1044 E. 4th St., Reno, NV. Open 24 hours, Alturas is famous as Reno's blues haven. This is the place to kick up your heels on the dance floor to live music from top name R&B bands. Don't dance? No problem. Darts, pool tables, and gaming machines are always available. And, if all else fails, food is served.

BuBinga Lounge, Inside Eldorado Hotel Casino, Reno. www.eldoradoreno.com, 775-786-5700, 324 North Virginia St., Reno, NV. The BuBinga Lounge bills itself as Reno's swankiest and sexiest ultra lounge. Readers of *Nevada Magazine* voted it the best place to go dancing. The lounge features innovative cocktails, and DJ Freeze spinning today's hottest dance sounds.

Designed by Will Bruder, the Nevada Museum of Art in Reno draws visitors from all over the world.

Cabaret Lounge, Inside the Carson Valley Inn. www.cvinn.com, 1-800-321-6983 (for reservations only) or 775-782-9711, 1627 Hwy. 395 N., Minden, NV. The Lounge is open 24/7, and features live entertainment Tuesday through Sunday nights beginning at 7:30 PM. The schedule alters slightly during major sporting events, when the giant pull-down screen and four plasma screen TVs cover the action.

Chocolate Bar, www.thechocbar.com, 775-337-1122, 475 S. Arlington St, Reno, NV. This dessert and liquor bar is a swanky, urban rest stop, and a long-time locals' favorite. It features a variety of chocolate specialties, including house-made biscotti, cakes, and cookies, a cocoa amaretto martini, and the chai-tini. Enjoy watching *Charlie and the Chocolate Factory*, Charlie Chaplin films, or Betty Boop cartoons on the mini TV screens along the bar.

Club Underground, www.clubunderground-reno.com, 775-786-2582, 555 E 4th St., Reno, NV. Get down to some great rock-and-roll entertainment and partake from a wide assortment of beers, wine and liquors. The establishment also boasts a wide array of nostalgic bar scenery with mosaic tiles and other artwork. Outdoor patio seating available. Live entertainment Friday and Saturday.

Club Voo Doo, 775-333-6942, 1126 E. 4th St., Reno, NV. Here's a fun little spot where you can dance to live bands on Friday and Saturday nights and enjoy some great comedy every Sunday. Club Voo Doo also has plenty of pool tables. After-hour parties available by appointment.

Divine Ultra Lounge, www.divineultralounge.com, 775-329-8088, 95 N. Sierra St., Suite 101, Reno, NV. Unwind in the exclusive, upscale atmosphere, and let the world go by. DJ talent nightly, and unique amenities include mood lighting, VIP booths, and bottle service. Dining is a very good option.

The Garage, Inside the Grand Sierra Resort. www.grandsierraresort.com, 1-800-501-2651 or 775-789-2000, 2500 E. Second St., Reno, NV. Great music, overstuffed couches, and dual bars have made The Garage a favorite with locals and visitors. A great place to kick back and relax, or kick up your heels on the dance floor.

The Green Room, www.renogreenroom.com, 775.324.1224, 144 West St., Reno, NV. Eclectic music is the order of the day at this establishment. Don't look for slots or other gambling, because there isn't any here. The atmosphere here is "everybody is somebody." This is a place to enjoy music, art, camaraderie, and cocktails. Free Wi-Fi too.

Imperial Bar & Lounge, www.imperialbarandlounge.com, 775-324-6399, 150 N. Arlington Ave, Reno, NV. This locals favorite calls itself a "gastropub" where friends gather after work for beers and sliders, or for a glass of wine after a movie. Its stripped-down, wide-open venue features 20-foot ceilings, exposed steel beams, and natural brick. Modern amenities include widescreen TVs, custom-designed booths, and a sleek bar. The diverse menu includes thin-crust pizzas, panini sandwiches, meats, and cheeses.

Jungle Vino, www.javajunglevino.com, 775-329-4484, 248 West 1st St., Reno, NV. A sophisticated yet intimate setting greets visitors here. Fine wine, food, and a full-service bar are complemented by weekly wine tastings, and special events supporting local arts and music.

Knuckleheads Sports Bar, 775-323-6500, 405 Vine St. Reno, NV. Can't decide between live music or sports TV? No problem—Knuckleheads has both, and much more. Take your pick, enjoy your favorite libation, and play pool, darts, dance, and karaoke. Select something great to eat from the extensive menu.

Little Waldorf Saloon, 775-323-3682,1661 N. Virginia St., Reno, NV. Get down with the college crowd from the University of Nevada, Reno. This is a campus hangout featuring great (loud) bands, okay food, and plenty of spirits to keep up the spirit. Voted best of nothing by no one.

Metropolis Nightclub Complex, 775-329-1952,45 W. 2nd St., Reno, NV. This nightclub has four separate rooms, each with its own theme. Plenty of live music keeps Metropolis rockin' all night long. Also has pool tables, a juke box, and food service.

Peppermill's Fireside Lounge, Inside Peppermill Hotel Casino. www.peppermillreno .com/lounges, 1-866-821-9996, 2707 S. Virginia St., Reno, NV. Considered one of Reno's hippest casino lounges. Get warm by the fire pit or cozy up in a plush booth. Each booth features a state-of-the-art sound system, and high-resolution plasma screen playing all the latest music videos. Enjoy a specialty drink and sample free appetizers.

Rum Bullions Island Bar, Inside Silver Legacy Resort Casino. www.silverlegacyreno.com, 1-800-687-8733 or 775-325-7401, 407 N. Virginia St. Reno, NV. Down this way you can run away to Reno's only rum bar, where the rum flows and the fun never stops. Partake in exotic rum drinks—like the flaming Kava Kava—and raucous entertainment, including the outrageous dueling pianos.

Sapphire Lounge, Inside Harrah's Reno. www.harrahs.com, 1-800-427-7247 or 775 788-2953, 219 N. Center St., Reno, NV. Ready to mellow out just a bit? Step into the Sapphire Lounge and enjoy San Francisco-based diva Clairdee as she creates the ideal nighttime mood with original blues, ballads, and jazz improvisations. Smooth melodies, creative cocktails, and low lighting are the order of the evening.

Se7en Teahouse and Bar, www.seenatse7en.com, 775.348.9526, 100 N. Arlington Ave, 102, Reno, NV. This teahouse, bar, and food venue adds to the flavor, class, and culture of the downtown Reno community. By day, it provides a sanctuary for friends to gather and sip from a wide variety of organic and herbal teas from around the world. Coffee, sandwiches, pastries, and appetizers are also available. By evening, the teahouse turns into a cocktail lounge, featuring a complete wine list as well as organic alcoholic and tea-accented concoctions.

Sierra Tap House, www.sierrataphouse.com, 775-322-7678, 252 W. 1st St., Reno, NV. The patio is the place to be at this relaxed, nonsmoking tavern. Watch passersby and enjoy a great microbrew served up by the friendly staff. A full liquor menu is available as well.

The 5-Star Saloon, www.5starsaloon.net, 775.329.2878, 132 West St., Reno, NV. This is Reno's only downtown gay bar. It's a friendly, sassy place with pool tables, live shows, live DJs, and an Internet jukebox. No cover charge and free Wi-Fi to boot.

Tonic, 775-337-6868, 231 W. 2nd St., Reno, NV. Furnished in urban, hip décor, Tonic is a "downtempo" establishment. Entertainment includes DJs, dancing ,and a plasma TV

Burning Man

For more than 20 years, a dusty, dry, remote corner of northern Nevada is transformed into Black Rock City, as about 50,000 people gather for the annual Burning Man celebration.

The festival is hard to describe. Some say it's nothing more than a bunch of counterculture types—hippies, if you will—who spend a week in the desert partying and not bathing. Let's just say it's much more than that.

Here you will find what is best described as a celebration of life. The dry lake bed of La Playa comes alive with creative self-expression, surreal art, innovative sculpture, and off-the-wall theatrical performances. Attire for the festivities ranges from elaborate costumes to no clothes at all. Art-on-wheels is ubiquitous, as bicycles, golf carts, and floats are wildly decorated—you won't see this at the Rose Parade. The weather is usually scorching hot, and dust storms so fierce they cause white-outs are not uncommon. The celebration culminates with the burning of a huge effigy of a man, hence the name.

A word of caution before venturing out into the desert. Advance planning is a must. Be sure to take plenty of water, food, and camping gear. Plan to get good and dirty. Organizers provide portable toilets, but no showers or running water.

featuring cult-classic movies. Check out the draft beer, wine, and martini menus, and be sure not to miss the new Hooka Lounge.

Seasonal Events

JANUARY

Antique Show, Sale & Appraisal Clinic, www.genoaevents.com, 775-782-4951, Genoa.

Happy Days Dance, 775-265-3102, Minden.

Sheep Dip Show, 1-800-648-1177, Sparks.

Topaz Lake Fishing Derby, www.topazlodge.com, 775-266-3338, Topaz Lake.

Winter, Wine and All That Jazz, 775-883-7477, Carson City.

FEBRUARY

Chinese New Year Celebration, 775-782-9828, Minden.

Eagles and Agriculture Event, 1-800-727-7677, Carson Valley.

Minden/Douglas Elks Annual Crab Feed, 775-782-3416, Gardnerville.

Sporting Clays and Game Feed, 775-782-9711, Minden.

Super Bowl Sunday Golf Tournament, www.carsonvalleygolf.com, 775-265-3181, Carson City.

Topaz Winter Cribbage Tournament, 775-342-2532, Topaz Lake.

MARCH

Annual Cowboy Jubilee and Poetry, 775-883-1532, Carson City.

Puttin' On The Ritz, 775-782-8692, Genoa Lakes.

St. Patrick's Day Celebration, 775-785-3300, downtown Reno.

APRIL

Annual Comedy Tribute to Admin Professionals, 775-783-6216, Minden.

Annual Spring Stag Golf Invitational, 775-782-9711, Minden.

Chili Cookoff and Craft Fair, 775-266-3468, Minden.

Easter Egg Hunt, 775-782-8696, Genoa.

Fashion Show Extravaganza, 775.783.8676, Genoa Lakes.

Pops Orchestra Concert, www.carsonvalleypops.org, 775-267-5575, Minden.

Reno Jazz Festival, www.unr.edu/rjf., 775-784-4046 Reno.

Topaz Sagehens Annual Rummage Sale, 775-266-1076, Topaz Ranch Estates.

MAY

'50s Rockathon Car Show & Swap Meet, 775-265-0548, Gardnerville.

Big Mama's Show and Shine Classic Cars, 775-783-6455, Gardnerville.

Cinco de Mayo Festival, www.nhsreno.org, 775-826-1818, Reno.

Kit Carson Trail–Wild West Tour, 775-687-7410, Carson City.

Historic Carson Valley Barn Tour, 775-782-2555, Carson Valley.

Nevada Wide Open Marathon De Mayo, www.marathondemayo.com, 775-825-1727, Reno.

Pembrooke Renaissance Faire, www.pembrookefair.com, 775-315-4219, Carson City.

Stars of Tomorrow, 775-783-0875, Carson City.

Reno River Festival, www.RenoRiverFestival.com, 1-800-367-7766, Reno.

Summer Family Concert Series, 775-782-9828, Minden.

The Reno Film Festival, www.renofilmfestival.com, 775-334-6707, Reno.

JUNE

Carson Valley Trails Association Celebrates National Trails Day, www.carsonvalley trails.org, 775.782.6859, Gardnerville.

Carson Valley Days, www.carsonvalley2030.org, 775-220-7913, Carson Valley.

Carson City Rendezvous, www.carsoncityrendezvous.com, 775-687-7410, Carson City.

CVAA Art Show, 775-782-5606, Carson City.

Great Eldorado BBQ, Brews & Blues Festival, www.eldoradoreno.com, 1-800-648-5966, Reno.

Kids' Fishing Derby, 775-782-9828, Gardnerville.

Minden Ranch Rodeo, 775-969-3832, Gardnerville.

Magiko, www.magikonv.com, 775-782-8144, Carson Valley.

Minden Run4Fun, 775-782-8144, Minden.

Pony Express Re-Ride, www.visitcarsoncity.com, 1-800-638-23-21, Carson City.

Reno Rodeo, www.renorodeo.com, 775-329-3877, Reno.

Street Vibrations–Spring Rally, 775-329-7469, Sparks.

Tour de Nez, www.tourdenez.com, 775-348-6673, Reno.

Wacky Waddler Wiver Wace, 775-885-2613, Minden.

A friendly poodle greets visitors to the Genoa Country Store and Crafters' Attic.

JULY

Artown, www.RenoIsArtown.com, 775-322-1538, Reno.

Bicycle Tours of the Carson Valley, 1-800-565-2704, Carson Valley.

Concert on the Green, 775-782-8696, Genoa.

Great Basin Chautauqua Festival, www.nevadahumanities.org, 775-784-6587, Reno.

Great International Chicken Wing Society Cook-off, www.thegreatinternationalchicken wingsociety.com, 775-358-8376, Reno.

Mason Valley Onion Festival, 775-463-5114, Yerington.

Minden Village Summer Concert Series, www.uncommonconcerts.com, 775-220-0995, Minden.

Movies In The Park, 775-782-7134, Gardnerville.

Pops In The Park, 775-782-8696, Genoa.

Reno Basque Festival, www.renobasqueclub.org, 775-762-3577 Reno.

Silver Dollar Car Classic, www.silverdollarcar.com, 1-800-638-2321, Carson City.

Summerfest Carnival in Lampe Park, 775-782-3416, Minden.

Volleyball Festival, www.volleyball-festival.com, 281-207-1070, Reno.

AUGUST

Annual Valley Cruisers Car Club Event, 775-220-0995, Minden-Gardnerville

Best in the West Nugget Rib Cook-Off, www.nuggetribcookoff.com, 1-800-648-1177, Sparks.

Carson Valley Antique Tractor Show, 775-267-4816, Minden.

Hot August Nights, www.hotaugustnights.net, 775-356-1956, Reno.

Hot August Nights Poker Run, 1-800-727-7677, Minden.

Jazz & Beyond Music Festival, www.breweryarts.org, 775-883-1976, Carson City.

Nevada State Fair, www.nvstatefair.com, 775-688-5767, Reno.

PGA TOUR's Reno-Tahoe Open at Montrêux Golf and Country Club, www.RenoTahoe Open.com, 775-322-3900, Reno.

Pyramid Lake Sprint Triathlon, www.renoareatriathletes.com, 775-852-5954, Sutcliffe Marina at Pyramid Lake.

Relay For Life, 775-315-2770, Gardnerville.

Reno Cowboy Poetry and Music Gathering, www.renocowboypoetry.com, 775-830-7087, Reno.

Reno Gay Pride, www.renogaypride.com, Reno.

Silver Dollar Car Classic, www.silverdollarcar.com, 1-800-638-2321, Carson City.

Volunteer Fire Department Fundraiser Dinner Dance, 775-265-2841, Sheridan.

Wakeboard World Finals, www.kingofwake.com, 407-628-4802, Sparks.

SEPTEMBER

Douglas County Senior Games, 775-783-6455, Carson Valley.

Genoa Candy Dance and Craft Faire, 775-782-8696, Genoa.

Great Reno Balloon Race, www.renoballoon.com, 775-826-1181, Reno.

National Championship Air Races, www.airrace.org, 775-972-6663, Reno.

Professional Bull Riders Built Ford Tough Series, www.pbrnow.com, 1-800-732-1727 Option 1, Reno.

Street Vibrations, www.road-shows.com, 1-800-200-4557, Reno.

The Curse of the Hanging Tree, 775-782-2555, Genoa.

Virginia City International Camel Races, www.virginiacity-nv.com, 775-847-0211, Virginia City.

OCTOBER

Great Italian Festival, www.eldoradoreno.com/events, 1-800-879-8879, Reno.

Harvest Festival, www.corleyranch.com, 775-265-3045, Gardnerville.

Haunted Gardnerville Ghost Walk, 775-782-2555, Gardnerville.

Kit Carson Trail Ghost Walk, 1-800-638-2321, Carson City.

Minden Douglas Elks Annual Luau, 775-782-3416, Minden.

Nevada Day Celebration, www.nevadaday.com, Carson City.

Old Town Days, 775-782-7134, Gardnerville.

Rhymer's Rodeer at the Carson Valley Inn, 775-783-6679, Minden.

Reno Celtic Celebration, www.renoceltic.org, Reno.

Scarecrow Festival, 775-782-7629, Minden.

DECEMBER

Christmas in the Sierras' Concert, 775-782-8696, Genoa.

Douglas High Christmas Craft Faire, 775-782-5136, ext. 1532, Minden.

Nevada Chamber Music Festival, 775-348-9413, Reno.

Parade of Lights, 775-782-8144 Carson Valley.

Sparks Hometown Christmas, 775-353-2291 Sparks.

Victorian Home Christmas, 775-882-1805, Carson City.

LEFT: *Reno annually celebrates the American Car Culture during Hot August Nights.* Heather Anderson

RESTAURANTS

Let's eat! The Biggest Little City and sur-rounding area offer a wide array of dining establishments, featuring cuisines from all over the globe. Pick from all-you-can-eat buffets or restaurants featuring steaks and seafood, Italian, Mexican, sushi, Asian, and more. One could almost "starve" to death just trying to decide! Fresh is the order of the day here, because the area is only a few hours from the fish markets of San Francisco and the verdant fruit and veg-etable fields in the San Joaquin and Salinas valleys. Most major restaurant chains have establishments here, but many local eater-ies have an aroma and taste all their own. What are you waiting for? It's time to dine.

Dining Price Code

The price range below is for a single dinner that includes an entrée, appetizer, and dessert. Tax and gratuities are not included.

Inexpensive Up to $15
Moderate $15–$30
Expensive $30–$50
Very Expensive $50 or more

Carson City

THE BASIL—CREATIVE THAI CUISINE

775-841-6100
311 N. Carson St., Carson City, NV
Open: Daily
Price: Inexpensive to Moderate
Cuisine: Thai
Serving: L, D
Reservations: No
Credit cards: MC, V

Slightly off the beaten path, The Basil is a local favorite. This is an excellent stop for an inexpensive lunch or a tasty dinner. The sample platter is a great way to kick off din-ner, and features a generous selection of their most popular appetizers; angel wings, spring rolls, shrimp, vegetable tempura, and more. All salads are made with the freshest ingredients and their Soup of Siam can be a meal on its own. A large selection of entrées, including seven varieties of curry dishes, can make final decision mak-ing difficult. How about abalone and snow peas, or ginger duckling? Whatever your selection, you won't go away hungry. Portions are ample.

RED'S OLD 395 GRILL

775-887-0395
1055 S. Carson St., Carson City, NV
Open: Daily
Price: Moderate
Cuisine: American Southwest
Serving: L, D
Reservations: No
Credit cards: AE, D, MC, V

A feast on your plate, and a feast for your eyes—Red's definitely has a unique look. Red has a penchant for good barbecue and collecting quirky stuff. Check out the host stand as you enter the eatery—it was sal-vaged out of the St. Francis Hotel in San Francisco. Order one of the house special-ties, such as the steamroller ribs with "howlin' coyote bar-b-que" sauce, and check out the 1923 Monarch steamroller. Brought in from New York City—the steam-roller, not the ribs—it was used to pave what is now the famous Wall Street. In spite of all the stuff, the joint is open and airy, with high ceilings. Even Shaq wouldn't bump his head on that Sterling Harvester dangling from above. It was found on the side of the road in Portland, Maine. Red's bar—dubbed by Red himself, as "the great-est bar on earth"—boasts 101 different beers, 67 premium tequilas, and a vast assortment of liquors. After a couple of samples at the bar, it might be time to order a starter, like the "fire pumper wings" or the smoked salmon. Soup, salads, and Red's "kick ass chili" are local favorites as well. Take another look at the ceiling and check out the big-wheeled cart. It was a prop in the original *Planet of the Apes* movie. What the heck, this is the kind of place for the whole gang, so chow down on Red's Colossal Que, a titanic assortment of barbecue ribs, chicken, and handmade sausages. Maybe a pizza is on your mind; how about the Boss Hawg? It includes savory pork, jalapeño jack cheese, onion strings, and of course, barbecue sauce. And for dessert, you can't pass up deep-fried *xangos*—a rich cheesecake rolled in a flaky pastry tortilla, served with fresh strawberries and caramel sauce. Now, about the old water pumper above the bar. It was built in 1907 and sold to the city of Waco, Texas. Red says, "They want it back, but that ain't ever gonna happen."

Gardnerville

J.T. BASQUE BAR & DINING ROOM
775-782-2074
1426 Main St, Gardnerville, NV.
Open: Mon.–Sat.
Price: Moderate
Cuisine: Basque
Serving: L,D.
Reservations: No
Credit cards: AE, D, MC, V

This is traditional Basque dining at its finest. Set in an old two-story house on the main drag, entering the bar is like walking into an old oater movie set. The high walls are adorned with cowboy hats and the ceiling is covered with dollar bills. It's a great place to sip pecan punch, a traditional Basque wine drink. Inside the dining room, red house wine and water are served at every table. The waiter takes your main entrée order as you munch on salad and bread. Traditional Basque dishes are served every night, including scampi, rabbit, sirloin, lamb shoulder, lamb chops, chicken, and sweetbreads. Meals also come with rice, vegetable soup, and French fries. After wrapping up the meal with a scoop of ice cream you'll need a long stroll around town

The Basques in Nevada

Nevada is home to a unique dining style called Basque, which is a warm and hearty family style of food. The Basques come from an area between Spain and France in the Pyrenees mountains, but Nevada is their homeland in the American West. Immigrants of the late 19th century left behind family and friends and many took up as sheepherders in Nevada. The Basque tradition of excellent food, hospitality, and unique atmosphere can be found in any of Nevada's Basque restaurants. Every summer in Reno, the streets come alive with the aromas of barbecue cooking during the annual Basque Festival. So, when you see a restaurant cuisine listed as "Basque," get ready for something a little different—but very flavorful. One last thing: don't look for a menu. In most Basque restaurants, the waitress will just tell you what is being served that day.

to let the meal settle. Or, perhaps, another pecan punch?

Genoa

DW'S DINNER HOUSE
www.davidwalleys.com
775-782-8155, ext. 8953
David Walley's Resort
2001 Foothill Rd, Genoa, NV
Open: Tues.–Sat.
Price: Expensive
Cuisine: American
Serving: D
Reservations: Encouraged
Credit cards: AE, D, MC, V

No wonder DW's received the *Wine Spectator* Award for Excellence. Featuring more than 300 wines, this is a casually elegant dinner house, on the grounds of a historic resort and spa. Prime rib, slow-roasted for 10 hours, is a house specialty, but their exten-

Western hats line the walls and dollar bills adorn the ceiling inside the J.T. Basque Bar & Dining Room in Gardnerville.

sive menu will suit just about any taste. If prime rib isn't what you are looking for, check out the angel hair pasta with smoked salmon, the rack of lamb, or sautéed elk medallions forestiere. Each evening, DW's chef creates a daily entrée special. As for appetizers, take your pick of shrimp, lobster cakes, escargot, or fried calamari. Now, if there's still room for dessert, treat yourself to the chocoholic's cake, amaretto cheesecake, or lemon meringue pie.

LA FERME

www.la-ferme-genoa.com
775-783-1004
2291 Main St, Genoa, NV
Open: Tues.–Sun.
Price: Moderate to expensive
Cuisine: French country
Serving: D
Reservations: Recommended
Credit cards: MC, V

Owner Gilles LaGourgue and chef Yves Gigot serve up delectable meals nightly in the former guest house in Nevada's oldest community. Genoa's La Ferme is well known to locals for its casual atmosphere and tremendous country-style French cuisine. Gilles and Yves opened the restaurant several years ago after many successful years in the French restaurant business in Beverly Hills, CA and Incline Village, NV. All menu items are homemade using the freshest ingredients available. Before dining, it might be fun to visit the farm animal menagerie next to the restaurant and say hello to Boomer the llama. But dining is why La Ferme is so famous, making menu selections difficult. While there are always daily menu specials, some of the traditional favorites include snails in garlic butter, cassoulet—white beans with duck confit and sausage—braised rabbit, and roasted duck breast with apple-honey sauce. A little homemade after-dinner ice cream is a must.

Minden

BARONE & REED FOOD COMPANY

775-783-1988
1599 Esmeralda, Minden, NV
Open: Mon.–Sat.
Price: Moderate to Expensive
Cuisine: American unique
Serving: L, D
Reservations: Recommended
Credit cards: AE, D, MC, V

This is a comfortable dining spot in the heart of historic downtown Minden. The restaurant was designed by architect Niccolo Valerio of Beverly Hills, CA and is divided into three dining sections: two bars, a private lounge, and the ever popular chef's table. When it gets chilly in the winter, the facility is kept warm and cozy by two large fireplaces. It's worth the effort to take a stroll through their well-stocked wine room and out on the balcony; the Tuscan mural painted by Kathleen King adds to the casual ambiance of the restaurant. Lunch

La Ferme in Genoa features some of the best French cuisine in the area.

lads, grilled panini sand-
and daily specials. A com-
nu is offered, featuring
steak and seafood creations. Barone & Reed
prides itself on unique appetizers and
nightly special creations. Take-out is available if you call ahead.

FIONA'S BAR AND GRILL

Inside the Carson Valley Inn
www.cvinn.com/dining/fionas
775-783-6650
1627 US 395, Minden, NV
Open: Daily
Price: Moderate to expensive
Cuisine: American
Serving: B, L, D
Reservations: Recommended
Credit cards: AE, D, MC, V

Fiona's specializes in its express lunch,
dinner, and Sunday brunches. Attention
steaks, chops, and seafood fans: look no
further—this is your dinner stop in the
Carson Valley. Fiona's wood-burning grill
seals in the juices, creating a wonderful flavor that can't be beat. Well-marbled steaks
come in various sizes and several different
cuts, including the T-bone, rib-eye, and top
sirloin. If it's prime rib you're looking for,
Fiona's is slow-roasted for half a day under
a crust of rock salt and spices, to bring out
the best in flavor. Also on the menu is the
"monster" pork chop, and lamb chops as
well. Something from the sea more to your
liking? Try the garlic shrimp, lobster tail,
crab, or the halibut. All are brought in fresh
daily. All dinners come with a wide selection of tasty side dishes. If you happen to be
in on a Friday or Saturday, give the smoked
buffalo prime rib a go. Dinner is served
nightly, 4:30-9 PM and their express lunch
is served buffet-style daily, from 11 AM to 2
PM. The lunch bar includes a broad assortment of salads, a soup of the day, pizza, and
panini sandwiches. Sunday brunch is
served 9 AM to 2 PM, and includes a vast
array of your favorite breakfast foods. One
local newspaper calls Fiona's Sunday
Brunch the best in the valley. Last, but not
least, appetizers are served in the bar from
10 AM to 10 PM.

FLORAL VINEYARD AND KHRISTOPHER'S CAFÉ

775-882-3333
963 Topsy Ln., No. 312, Minden, NV
Open: Daily
Price: Inexpensive
Cuisine: Northern Italian
Serving: B, L,(Daily), D (Tues.–Sat.)
Reservations: No
Credit cards: MC, V

Clean and simple restaurant, accented by
wonderful fragrances emanating from the
adjacent flower shop. Dinner specialties
include traditional spaghetti and meatballs
and Italian sausage with pasta—however,
the tortellini buongustaio is definitely a
local favorite. Enjoy your favorite beer or a
glass of wine with your meal. Breakfast
items include Italian sausage and roasted
red pepper omelet, pork chop and eggs, and
the egg croissant sandwich with sausage
and bacon. The lunch menu includes several salads, grilled eggplant, and ahi tuna
sandwiches.

Reno

AMELIA'S

Inside the Reno Jet Center
775-858-731655 S. Rock Blvd, Reno, NV
Open: Daily
Price: Moderate
Cuisine: American
Serving: B, L, D
Reservations: No
Credit cards: AE, D, MC, V

Sip a cocktail from the full bar or have
breakfast, lunch, or dinner while watching
airplanes take off and land at Amelia's in
the Reno Jet Center. The atmosphere is

casual, and it is a favorite among the city's professionals for lunch and as an after-work hangout. The dinner menu is extensive, offering pasta dishes, fish and seafood, steaks, poultry, veal, and vegetarian cuisine. House specialties include the fettuccine alfredo, seafood platter with pasta, broiled Alaskan halibut, Veal Amelia, Flightline Chicken, and also hand-cut New York steak.

BEAUJOLAIS BISTRO

www.beaujolaisbistro.com
775-323-2227
130 West St, Reno, NV
Open: Tues.–Sun.
Price: Moderate to Expensive
Cuisine: French
Serving: L, D.
Reservations: Recommended
Credit cards: MC, V

Situated in a renovated building, Beaujolais Bistro is designed to be small, casual, warm, and friendly. The décor is French casual, with posters and some original works adorning the walls. French music plays in the background, as diners settle into the ambiance of the place. Welcome to the dream come true of chef-owner Bill Gilbert, who has spent many years mastering the art of French cuisine. The wine list is extensive, but more importantly, the staff is trained to assist wine lovers in pairing the right French or domestic wine with their meal. The dinner menu is conveniently divided between larger and smaller portions. House specialties include hazelnut-crusted venison chop with huckleberry sauce; frogs' legs with white wine and garlic herbs and portobello mushroom with spinach; and goat cheese baked in phyllo. For a real gourmet treat, try the roasted rack of lamb with nicoise olives and breadcrumbs. It's no wonder the bistro has garnered some outstanding reviews from such publications as *Bon Appetit* magazine and *Best Bets*.

BREW BROTHERS

Inside Eldorado Hotel Casino, Reno
www.eldoradoreno.com
775-786-5700
324 N. Virginia St., NV
Open: Daily
Price: Moderate
Cuisine: American
Serving: L, D
Reservations: No.
Credit cards: AE, D, MC, V

Offering eight microbrews, a creative menu, and cool ambiance, Brew Brothers was recently named Best Brewpub in America by *Nightclub & Bar* magazine. The menu is packed with brewpub favorites to suit every taste, including soups and salads, starters, sandwiches and burgers, gourmet pizza, and pasta dishes. Full entrées include fajita tacos, St. Louis-style spareribs, and grilled pork chops. Most evenings, live rock and blues bands get the joint jumpin' with contemporary hit tunes.

CAFÉ ALFRESCO

Inside Atlantis Casino Resort Spa
www.atlantiscasino.com/dining/cafe
alfresco.asp
775-825-4700
3800 S. Virginia St., Reno, NV
Open: Daily
Price: Inexpensive to moderate
Cuisine: Italian American
Serving: L, D
Reservations: No
Credit cards: AE, D, MC, V

Café Alfresco is near the top of the list when it comes to serving up pizzas, pasta dishes and great salads. They have 14 different pizza variations on the menu, all brewed in their wood-fired brick pizza oven. Not hungry for pizza? No problem. Their hearty café-style pasta dishes include ravioli alfresco, pasta rustica, and California chicken. For dessert, Café Alfresco offers ten flavors of homemade gelato, all served from their see-through gelato case. For a special treat, have it served in an almond-brittle basket—*yum*!

HARRAH'S STEAK HOUSE
Inside Harrah's Reno
www.harrahsreno.com
775-788-2929
219 N. Center St., Reno, NV
Open: Daily
Price: Expensive
Cuisine: American
Serving: D.
Reservations: Recommended
Credit cards: AE, D, MC, V

Steak lovers unite. This is your place. Harrah's Steak House is a genuine, award-winning, gourmet dining experience. The service is prompt but not intrusive, and the wine list is more than ample. For a special treat, kick the dining experience off with a cold appetizer such as the Cabo prawn cocktail, or the seafood platter on ice. If a hot appetizer is more to your liking, oysters Rockefeller or the escargot should fill the bill. Before your entrée arrives, a daily fresh sorbet is served to refresh and cleanse the palate. From the broiler, steak offerings include an Angus rib-eye, Angus T-bone, teriyaki flat iron steak, chateaubriand, or the classic favorite, steak and lobster. Each evening the chef creates a complete dessert selection to top off your meal.

JOHNNY ROCKETS
Inside Grand Sierra Resort and Casino
www.johnnyrockets.com
775-789-2555
2500 E. Second St., Reno, NV.
Open: Daily
Price: Inexpensive
Cuisine: '50s Americana
Serving: B, L, D
Reservations: No
Credit cards: AE, D, MC, V

Turn back the clock, pull on your socks, and get ready to do the bop, at Johnny Rockets 1950s retro burger shop. The bill of fare is what it should be: cheeseburgers, chili dogs, fries, rings, malts, melts, and Cokes. All this, right in the middle of the casino floor at Grand Sierra Resort where you have a clear view of the Race and Sports Book action. The food is prepared and served by an oldies-singing staff. Tabletop juke boxes belt out oldies favorites for only a nickel. This is guaranteed fun for the entire family. Kids menu on request.

LA STRADA
Inside Eldorado Hotel Casino, Reno
www.eldoradoreno.com
775-786-5700
345 N. Virginia St., Reno, NV
Open: Nightly
Price: Moderate to Expensive
Cuisine: Italian
Serving: D
Reservations: Recommended
Credit cards: AE, D, MC, V

Enjoy the taste and romance of old Italy at La Strada, Eldorado's signature restaurant since 1978. The restaurant was recently named one of the top 10 Italian restaurants in the country and its wine list is a six-time Award of Excellence winner from *Wine Spectator* magazine. This is authentic northern Italian cuisine prepared by chef from Milan. The décor is classic Mediterranean with many beautiful archways and subtle lighting creating an intimate atmosphere to enjoy a gourmet meal. All pasta is made fresh daily in the pasta store. Among the entrée classics are the roasted petit rack of veal, with potato and porcini gratin and veal au jus; pan-roasted quail, served over braised radicchio; guanciale in a Madeira wine reduction over polenta; and the Genova specialty ravioli, filled with greens, fresh herbs, and ricotta cheese in a toasted-walnut cream sauce.

LEGENDS GRILL, SPORTS & SPIRITS

www.legendsgrillsportsandspirits.com
775-853-5550
6010 S. Virginia St., #J, Reno, NV
Open: Daily
Price: Inexpensive to Moderate
Cuisine: American
Serving: B, L, D
Reservations: No
Credit cards: AE, D, MC, V

Legends is a classic sports bar serving
plenty of beer and spirits, ubiquitous TV
sports, inexpensive food, fantasy football
and live music on selected nights. This isn't
an ordinary sports pub, Legends recently
won five "Best of Reno" awards. The atmosphere is open and the ambiance friendly.
Located near the University of Nevada, so
get ready to meet some ardent Wolf Pack
fans. Open for breakfast, lunch, and dinner, the menu is loaded with something to
please just about everybody. Some menu
favorites include the Buffalo chicken salad,
sampler platters, and homemade taquitos.
For an appetizer, Legends recommends
their huge dry-rub chicken wings served
with Texas barbecue sauce and ranch dress-
ing. The menu also includes a big selection
of salads, burgers, hot and cold sandwiches, and sandwich wraps. Dinner
entrées include the New York steak platter,
St. Louis pork-rib platter, and assorted
pasta dishes.

LEXIE'S ON THE RIVER

Inside Siena Hotel Spa and Casino
www.sienareno.com/dining/lexies.html
775-321-5831
1 S. Lake St., Reno, NV
Open: Daily
Price: Moderate to Expensive
Cuisine: International
Serving: D
Reservations: Recommended
Credit cards: AE, D, MC, V

Inside Lexie's you can enjoy a serene view
of the Truckee River, or just watch the chefs
in the open kitchen create delightful cuisine from around the world. All this while
sipping a glass of wine selected from the
Wine Spectator Award for Excellence wine
list. As for the food, Lexie's strives for
artistically pleasing presentations created
from the freshest ingredients. The appetizer menu includes some creative dishes.
Antipasti Siena includes a selection of
Tuscan-style cured meats and marinated
grilled vegetables, with mascarpone herb
dip and black olive crostini; while the fritto
misto mare is a seafood adventure, including calamari, shrimp, and halibut with
caper parsley dip and savory yellow pepper
ketchup. For a dinner entrée, Lexie's offers
pasta dishes, such as ocean ravioli with
crab, lobster tail, scallops, sweet clams,
mussels, and shrimp; and their famous
tortelli d'anitra—roasted duck in tomato,
caper, and olive sauce. Seafood selections
include braised swordfish; shrimp ala
Siena with mostrada di Cremona; and
prawns with fontina cheese wrapped in
bacon on asparagus risotto. From the hills
and valleys, meat entrées include Black
Angus steak and beef dishes, as well as
lamb, pork, and quail selections, all cooked
to your taste. From the dessert menu, treat
yourself to the vanilla or chocolate soufflé,
or the vanilla panna cotta.

LOUIS' BASQUE CORNER

775-323-7203
301 E. 4th St., Reno, NV
Open: Tues.–Sat.
Price: Moderate
Cuisine: Basque
Serving: L, D
Reservations: No
Credit cards: MC, V

Louis' isn't going to win any awards for
outside decor, but *The Frugal Gourmet*
knew what he was talking about in

Kayak paddlers take on Truckee River rapids in downtown Reno.

recommending this eatery. Everything changes once you're inside. The bar area is warm and friendly, and the dining room has dark red walls decorated with examples of Basque art. This is not a place for a quiet, intimate meal. Diners sit at long rows of tables and benches, often next to complete strangers. The servers wear outfits in keeping with the atmosphere. Service is prompt, kicking off with salad and bread, quickly followed by pasta soup. Diners select their main entrée from among lamb stew, roast lamb, paella, steak, lamb chops, pork chops, brochette, tripe, and sweetbreads. Fries and Basque beans are always served with the meal. Service may be prompt, but diners are never rushed. Why not enjoy some friendly conversation with total strangers? It's more fun that way.

P.F. CHANG'S CHINA BISTRO
www.pfchangs.com
1-866-732-4264
5180 S. Kietzke Ln., Reno, NV
Open: Daily
Price: Moderate to Expensive

Cuisine: Chinese
Serving: L, D
Reservations: Recommended
Credit cards: AE, D, MC, V

P.F Chang's strives for a total culinary experience in its Chinese cuisine. The goal is to balance the ancient Chinese principles of *fan* and *t'sai* to achieve a harmony of taste, texture, color, and aroma. *Fan* foods include rice, noodles, grains, and dumplings; while *t'sai* foods include vegetables, meat, poultry, and seafood. Menu items feature traditional Chinese dishes, as well as innovative dishes that reflect the emerging influence of Southeast Asia on modern cuisine. Understanding that in addition to taste, the health value of their preparations is important as well, P.F. Chang's lists the nutritional values of their entrées right on the menu. While most entrées contain meat, poultry, or seafood, vegetarian dishes are a favorite with many diners. They also offer a gluten-free menu. The wine selection is extensive, and includes a "flavor first" list. By this they mean that wines are categorized from the lightest to the most intense to make it easier for diners to make their selections. Enjoy.

SILVER PEAK RESTAURANT AND ✓ BREWERY
www.silverpeakbrewery.com
775-324-1864
124 Wonder St., Reno, NV
Open: Daily
Price: Moderate
Cuisine: American
Serving: L, D
Reservations: No
Credit cards: MC, V

This brewpub is the dream come true for chef David Silverman and brewmaster Trent Schmidt. First the beer: Silver Peak brews both ales and lagers The ales tend to be more robust in flavor, while the lagers are smoother. One is not necessarily better than the other, they're just different in taste and texture. Of the 20 different styles of beer brewed at Silver Peak, some of the most popular include Red Roadster, XXX Blonde, and Silver Peak IPA. While great beers and cozy atmosphere are one thing, it all comes together with their food. Chef David sticks to one important principle, "Start with premium ingredients and don't screw them up." He doesn't. Silver Peak's dinner menu is constantly evolving to take advantage fresh seasonal products, but some of the standard favorites include the mixed seafood grill, smoked pork chops, and the seared filet mignon. Be sure not to pig out on the main course, because the desserts are to kill for. Check out the caramel apple upside-down cake served with Tahoe Creamery vanilla bean ice cream.

SUNDANCE CANTINA
Inside Boomtown Casino & Hotel
www.boomtownreno,com
775-345-8699
Interstate 80, Exit 4, Reno, NV
Open: Daily
Price: Inexpensive to Moderate
Cuisine: Mexican American
Serving: B, L, D
Reservations: No
Credit cards: AE, D, MC, V

¡Viva la comida buena! When you've got a major appetite for Mexican food—even at 3 o'clock in the morning—head on down to the Sundance Cantina. A great first stop is at their Margarita Bar where you can wrap a lip around one of the restaurant's signature margaritas brewed with your favorite tequila, including Don Julio, Cabo Wabo, or Herradura Silver. On the menu, you will find a tremendous assortment of favorite dishes from south of the border. Entrées include all your favorites: fajitas, pork carnitas, chimichangas, carne asada, and,

of course, a host of burrito combinations. Not in the mood for Mexican food? Not a problem. Sundance Cantina also serves a wide variety of hot and cold sandwiches, pizza, and much more.

WILD RIVER GRILLE

www.wildrivergrille.com
775-284-7455
17 S. Virginia St., 180, Reno, NV
Open: Daily
Price: Inexpensive to Moderate
Reservations: No
Serving: L, D
Credit cards: AE, D, MC, V

Dine inside or out on the expansive patio overlooking the Truckee River, Wild River Grille is a casual, contemporary dining establishment, nestled in the Riverside Artist Lofts Building. Enjoy a handcrafted cocktail, while reviewing the creative offerings on the menu. Soups are made from scratch daily, and the salad and veggie offerings are made from the freshest ingredients available. The signature entrée offerings include rainbow crab cakes, hand-breaded coconut shrimp, and cold-smoked chipotle salmon. Steak and pasta dishes are available as well. Smoking is allowed on the patio. The wine list is extensive, and the daily specials are well worth consideration.

Sparks

GREAT BASIN BREWING COMPANY

www.greatbasinbrewingco.com
775-355-7711
846 Victorian Ave., Sparks, NV
Open: Daily
Price: Inexpensive to Moderate
Cuisine: American
Serving: L, D
Reservations: No
Credit cards: AE, D, MC, V

This is a great stop for suds and grub any time of year. When the weather is warm, Great Basin's patio is the place to enjoy a cold one and listen to live jazz. Their beers have won too many awards to list but favorite selections include Nevada Gold, Ichthyosaur IPA, Jackpot Porter, and Wild Horse Ale. Among their seasonal offerings are the Cerveza ChileBeso, Oktoberfest, Rail City Raspberry, and Wheeler Peak Wheat. And for the kids, try their Great Basin honey birch-style root beer. Great Basin serves both lunch and dinner. Their dinner menu includes a wide variety of soups, chili, salads, sandwiches, wraps, burgers, and pizza. Some of the favorite dinner entrées include salmon tacos with fresh mango salsa, shepherd's pie, broccoli garlic fettuccine, and Jamaican jerk-style chicken.

VISTA GRILLE RESTAURANT

vistagrille.com
775-626-9922
1250 Disc Dr., Sparks, NV
Open: Daily
Price: Moderate to Expensive
Cuisine: American
Serving: L, D
Reservations: Suggested
Credit cards: AE, D, MC, V

This is a locally owned, casually elegant spot, to enjoy a long lunch or tasty dinner. When the weather is right, their patio bar is an excellent stop before sitting down for a meal. In addition to a full-service bar, Vista Grille also offers affordable wines by the glass or bottle. Enjoy an appetizer such as calamari strips or bruschetta—sweet French bread baked with blue cheese, tomato, and basil—while deciding on an entrée. Some of the favorites at Vista Grille include baked halibut, stuffed salmon, barbecue pork ribs, and any one of their pasta dishes. Vista is designed to accommodate entire families, or the couple looking for a romantic evening.

FOOD PURVEYORS

Bakeries

Josefs Vienna Bakery & Café, 775-825-0451, 933 W. Moana Ln., Reno, NV. Voted best bakery in Reno. Specialties include European breads, cakes, fruit tarts, Danish pastries, croissants, scones, and bagels. Every item cooked from scratch.

Krispy Kreme Doughnuts, 775-853-9111, 5050 Kietzke Ln., Reno, NV. Famous for great doughnuts, pastries, and coffee.

Cake & Flower Shoppe, 775-323-8951, 519 Ralston St., Reno, NV. Great assortment of cakes for all occasions as well as other fine pastries. Flowers add to the wonderful aromas emanating from the shop.

House of Bread, 775-322-0773, 1185 California Ave., Reno, NV. Great assortment of fresh breads and rolls, including French and sourdough.

Madeleine's Cookies, 775-884-9036, 3680 Research Way, Suite 5, Carson City NV. Great selection of cookies, brownies, cakes, and seasonal goodies brewed up under the watchful eye of Madeleines de la Torre.

Sugarplum Bakery and Treats, 775-783-8828, 2292 Main St., Genoa, NV. Known throughout the Carson Valley for their fresh-baked French bread, hard rolls baguettes, French pastry, cakes, pies, candied pretzels, and much more.

Sweetie Pies by Wendy, 775-265-0731, 1281 Kimmerling Rd., Suite 11, Gardnerville, NV. Pies are the specialty here, but you'll find great breads, rolls, cakes, and pastries as well.

Sweet Sensations by Sue, www.sweetsensationsbysue.com, 775-883-4900, 1800 US 50 E. Suite 7, Carson City, NV. Sue Streck specializes in creative wedding cakes. Elegant or whimsical, she creates cakes for all occasions.

Coffee Houses

88 CUPS Coffee & Tea (Internet Café), 775-783-0688, 1663 Lucerne St., Minden, NV. Home of the Sip-N-Surf that includes large latte or cappuccino and one hour of surf time on the net. Also offers tea service with a traditional flair. Don't miss the BOBA Chilly, a refreshing ice drink.

Aroma Club, www.aromaclubreno.com 775-825-7725, 4001 S. Virginia St., Reno, NV. Kick back and enjoy a latte, cappuccino, or blended drink and maybe have a bite to eat in the comfortable confines of this establishment. Always free Wi-Fi. Be sure to check out the large selection of fragrances.

Barista Brothers Coffee, 775-841-1818, 1825 N. Carson St., Carson City, NV. Quaint spot to stop for a latte, espresso, or non-coffee drink. Fine assortment of pastries to choose from.

Dreamer's Coffee House, Deli & Art Gallery, www.dreamerscoffeeandart.com, 775-322-8040, 17 S. Virginia St., Reno, NV. comfortable sofas and free wireless Internet greet visitors to this coffeehouse located in the Riverside Artist Lofts. In addition to a full coffee bar and deli menu, Dreamer's also serves juices, soda, beer, wine, salads, soups, cheesecakes,

A quaint little store in Genoa serves coffee and other goodies.

and other pastries. Check their Web site for live entertainment, artist receptions, and other activities.

Electronic Espresso, www.electronicespresso.com 775-322-7587, 134 W. 2nd St., Reno, NV. This is the spot to feed your bites and bytes, right in the heart of downtown Reno. Plenty of hot and cold drinks to choose from, a tasty menu, and also Internet access. Did somebody say Martini Lounge? Yep—they've got one.

Esoteric Coffee House & Gallery, 775-322-8999, 135 N. Sierra St., Reno, NV. Here the walls are adorned with wonderful art. Kick back and enjoy a fresh brewed coffee or any one of their many offerings. Check out the light-food menu, and don't be surprised if the evening is filled with live entertainment.

Holey Grounds Coffee House, 775-782-1961, 1267 US 395, Suite H, Gardnerville, NV. Check out the Alpen Sierra coffee or any of the smoothies, Italian sodas, and pastries. Wireless Internet available.

Java Jungle, www.javajunglevino.com, 775.329.4484, 246 West 1st St., Reno, NV. Locals refer to Java Jungle as the ultimate coffeehouse and a haven from the surrounding urban jungle. Features great coffee, espresso, and gourmet sandwiches. Check out the weekly poetry, art, and music offerings. Of course, free Wi-Fi.

Moxie Java, www.moxiejavareno.com 775-852-0375, 465 Southmeadows Blvd., Reno, NV. This is the home of the "moxie moment," where you enjoy a gourmet beverage in a comfortable atmosphere. Top beverage selections include the flavored latte, flavored mocha, and the white mocha. Free Internet.

Shady Grove Coffee Company, 775-782-8000, 1411 US 395 N, Gardnerville, NV. Organic coffees and teas along with fresh pastries and homemade crêpes. Relax in the reading room/book exchange.

Starbucks Coffee, 775-841-6557, 3228 N. Carson St. Suite 15, Carson City, NV. Large selection of coffee drinks in a casual atmosphere. The blueberry muffins and scones are always great selections.

The Bank Parlor and Pub, 775-783-4770 1596 Esmeralda Ave., Minden, NV. This is a fun stop for everybody. Offerings include specialty coffees, pastries, sandwiches, wraps, and more. Full bar open in the evening, featuring wine by the glass and a large selection of imported beers.

Walden's Coffeehouse, www.waldenscoffeehouse.com 775-787-3307, 3940 Mayberry Dr., Reno, NV. Great atmosphere to enjoy a fresh cup of coffee, tea, or a cold drink. Plenty of munchies on the menu as well. Free wireless access with your purchase.

Farmers' Markets

Carson Farmers Market, 775-746-5024, Pony Express Pavilion, Highway 50, Carson City, NV. Seasonal. Wed. 3:30–7:30 PM.

Custom Gardens On-Farm Green Market, 775-577-2069, 3701 Elm Street, Silver Springs, NV. Ray and Virginia Johnson maintain a large farm where you can pick your own fresh produce. Be sure to visit their demo garden stocked with many heirloom vegetables. Seasonal. Sun. 9 AM–1 PM.

Lampe Park Farmers' Market, 775-782-9828, 1328 Waterloo Lane, Gardnerville, NV., Rapidly becoming a shoppers favorite stop for 'seriously' fresh produce and other goodies. May-Sept. Wed. 8 AM–1 PM.

Sparks Hometowne Farmers Market, 775-353-2291, Downtown Sparks, NV. This is the granddaddy of farmers' markets in northern Nevada. Wander through the town square, listen to live music and sample fruits, veggies, and other goodies. The kid's area features arts, crafts and a bouncing platform. Seasonal. Thur. 4–9 PM.

Reno Farmers Market, 775-746-5024, Village Center, California and Booth Streets, Reno, NV. June-October. Sat. 8 AM–1 PM.

Frozen Desserts

Ben & Jerry's, 775-853-1266, 720 W. Meadows Pkwy., Reno, NV. It's best to have adventurous taste buds here. Long known for ever-changing, often eclectic flavor creations. How about some raspberry chocolate chunk? Organic ingredients only.

Carvel Ice Cream & Bakery, 775-852-7595, 1131 Steamboat Pkwy. Reno, NV. This is a sure cure for the sweet tooth. Carvel features ice cream products, as well as baked goods. Don't miss the Carvelanches, freshly made ice cream with your choice of candy mix-ins.

Cold Stone Creamery, 775-267-6690, 693 Topsy Ln., Suite 318, Carson City, NV. Well known for its ice cream, shakes, cakes and refreshing smoothies. Traditional and off-the-wall flavors and combinations.

Marble Slab Creamery, 775-851-7566, 6637 S. Virginia St., and 191 Damonte Ranch Pkwy. Reno, NV. Whether you're looking for the decadence of a banana split or a guilt-free nonfat frozen yogurt, this is an excellent stop. Also features homemade cookies, brownies, and pies. Even the waffle cones are homemade.

TCBY, 775-829-7447, 900 W. Moana Ln., Reno, NV. Dessert is the order of the day here including cakes, pies, and all kinds of ice cream products. You can't go wrong with a Beriyo smoothie, made with fresh fruits and premium frozen yogurt.

RECREATION

Ballooning, Flying, and Gliding

Balloon Nevada, www.balloonnevada.com, 775-790-7572. P.O. Box 2718, Gardnerville, NV. Take in a bird's-eye view of the beautiful Carson Valley and the majestic eastern Sierra Nevada in a hot-air balloon. All flights are for two persons and a pilot. Rise into the clouds early in the morning when the air is cool and stable. Flights offered seven days a week all year long. Reservations required. Rates: $475 ($237 per person).

Soar Minden, www.soarminden.com 775-782-7627, 1138 Airport Road, Minden, NV. Glider rentals, instruction and scenic flights are available all year long. No experience necessary. The facility boasts some of the best soaring conditions anywhere, and welcomes pilots from around the world specializing in record high-altitude and cross-country flights. Glider rentals start around $40 per hour.

Sierra Biplane Adventures, www.sierrabiplane.com, 1-800-922-3598, P.O. Box 50495, Reno, NV. Take a nostalgic ride in a 1941 Waco open-cockpit biplane. A great way to enjoy the beauty of the Carson Valley, Lake Tahoe, and the Sierra Nevada. Experience flying as it was in the golden days of aviation. Flights start at $49. Kids welcome.

Batting Cages

Line Drive U Indoor Batting Cages, 775-267-3331, 2577 Nowlin Rd., Minden, NV. Features three public batting cages equipped for both softball and baseball. Hitting, pitching, and fielding clinics, and also private instruction by appointment.

Tommy's Grand Stand Batting Cages & Grill and Deli, www.tommysgrandstand.com 775-355-7323, 830 Meredith Way, Sparks, NV. Eat, drink, and take a few cuts at the ole baseball. Tommy's is for the casual hitter looking to work off a hard day at work, or the serious ball player intent on honing his batting eye. Private lessons and group rates available. Hungry? Drop in the deli for a hot dog, hamburger, or one of their specialty sandwiches.

Bicycling

Big Daddy's Bicycles and Fitness, www.bigdaddybicycles.com, 775-782-7077, 1546 US 395 S, Gardnerville, NV.

College Cyclery, www.collegecyclery.net, 775-323-1809, 22 S. Virginia St., Reno, NV. Large selection of bicycles, accessories, and expert service.

Genoa Peak Trail, Ride along the ridgeline and check out the Lake Tahoe Basin to the west and the Carson Valley to the east. Spur roads off the main road connect to several peaks, Genoa Peak being the highest at 150 feet. From the Carson Valley, take NV 207 (Kingsbury Grade) west and turn right on North Benjamin Rd. The road becomes Andria Drive. Park when the pavement ends.

Prison Hill Recreation Area, The main parking and staging area is located just off Koontz Lane, Carson City, NV. The area offers 2,450 acres of trails open to hiking, bicycling, and horseback riding. Separate trails open to off-road vahicles.

Bird Watching
Lahontan Audubon Society, www.nevadaaudubon.org. Northern Nevada's Great Basin, Sierra Nevada, and numerous lakes and marsh areas offer birdwatchers a plethora of opportunity, and far too much information to list here. The Lahontan Audubon Society offers plenty of information on where to go and what to see. You won't be disappointed.

Boating
Topaz Lake Park, www.topazlake.com, 775-782-9828, 3700 Topaz Park Road, Gardner-ville, NV. This 90-acre park on the California/Nevada border attracts fishermen and water sports enthusiasts alike. The lake is stocked with rainbow trout, but don't be surprised if you come up with a nice brownie or bass.

Washoe Lake State Park, www.parks.nv.gov 775-687-4319, 4855 E. Lake Blvd., Carson City, NV. Launching ramps and docks are located at the main day-use area and at the North Ramp.

Boat Rental
Topaz Landing Boat Rentals, 775-266-3550, 3505 Topaz Lane, Gardnerville, NV. Motorized aluminum fishing boats hold up to four people. Fishing licenses may be purchased at the Topaz Lodge. Open seven days a week, 7 AM–5 PM. Reservations suggested.

Bowling
National Bowling Stadium, www.go-nevada.com/, National-Bowling-Stadium, 300 North Center Street, Reno, NV. This is the place the Los Angeles Times billed as the Taj Mahal of Tenpins. Opened in 1995, this four-story facility is devoted to all things bowling. The fourth floor houses the 78-lane tournament center, and the Lane 81 Pro Shop where the latest and greatest in bowling equipment is on display.

Grand Sierra Bowl, www.grandsierraresort.com. Inside the Grand Sierra Resort and Casino 775-789-2296, 2500 E. Second St., Reno, NV, Fifty professional-caliber lanes, computerized scoring, pro shop, and professional instruction by appointment.

Silver Strike Entertainment Center, www.silverstrikelanes.com, 775-265-5454, 1281 Kimmerling Rd., #8, Gardnerville, NV. State-of-the-art facility featuring 26 Brunswick synthetic lanes. Private party room has four lanes, blacklights, and a great sound system. Great arcade room for the kids. Hungry? Check out Piggy's Sports Bar & Grill.

Campgrounds

Hope Valley Campground, 1-877-444-6777, from Minden take US 88 about 21 miles west to Blue Lakes Road, turn left about two miles to the campground. Has 20 sites and one group site. Drinking water, no flush toilets. Bear-proof food storage locker at each site.

Washoe Lake State Park, www.parks.nv.gov, 775-687-4319, 4855 E. Lake Blvd., Carson City, NV. Open year around and available on first-come, first-serve basis. Each of the 49 sites has a table, grill, and fire ring. Some sites have shade structures. Two comfort stations with showers. Seven day limit.

Court Sports

JOGO, 775-849-9488, 11565 Old Virginia Road, Reno, NV. Jogo (Portuguese for "play") is a public facility in the business of fun. Try your hand at a variety of court sports, including racquetball, handball, squash, walleyball, basketball, court soccer, badminton, dodgeball, paddleball, pickleball, and table tennis.

Fishing

Angler's Edge, www.theanglersedge.com, 775-782-4734, 1506 US 395 S., Gardnerville, NV. Great stop for all your fly-fishing supplies. Fishing excursions available for individuals and groups. Nevada, California, and Pyramid Lake licenses available. Equipment repair for rods and reels.

Crater Lake, CA 88, Hope Valley, CA. Great spot for brook trout. Located about six miles off CA 88, take Alpine Mine Road. Half-mile hike to the lake.

Washoe Lake State Park, www.parks.nv.gov, 775-687-4319, 4855 E. Lake Blvd., Carson City, NV. The lake is stocked with channel catfish, bass, and Sacramento perch. Nearby Little Washoe Lake provides good fishing opportunities as well.

Four-wheeling

Elite Desert Tours, www.EliteDesertTours.com, 775-265-9307, 1329 Highway 395 North, Suite 10-274, Gardnerville, NV. Enjoy the beauty of the desert backcountry in a guided four-wheel-drive tour. Prepare to get dirty, as tours visit ghost towns and abandoned mines. Elite features Tomcars, all terrain vehicles designed maneuverability, endurance, and comfort. Bring the whole family; all ages welcome.

Golf

CARSON CITY

Eagle Valley Golf Course–East Course, www.eaglevalleygolf.com, 775-877-2380, 3999 Centennial Park Dr., Carson City, NV. Public 18-hole course. Par 72, 6658 yards, rating 69.6, slope 120. Pro shop, cart rentals, driving range, putting green, restaurant. Open Jan.–Dec. Rates, $15–$30.

Eagle Valley Golf Course–West Course, www.eaglevalleygolf.com, 775-877-2380, 3999 Centennial Park Dr., Carson City, NV. Public 18-hole course. Par 72, 6885 yards, rating 72.3, slope 140. Pro shop, cart rentals, driving range, putting green, restaurant, spa, lodging. Open Jan.–Dec. Rates, $25–$35.

Empire Ranch Golf Course, www.empireranchgolf.com, 1-888-227-1335, 1875 Fair Way, Carson City, NV. Public 27-hole course. Par 72, 6840 yards, rating 71.8, slope 129. Pro shop, cart rentals, driving range, putting green, restaurant. Open Jan.–Dec. Rates $40–$45.

Silver Oak Golf Club, www.silveroakgolf.com, 775-841-7000, 1251, Country Club Dr., Carson City, NV. Public 18-hole course. Par 71, 3504 yards, rating 70.1, slope 131. Pro shop, cart rentals, driving range, putting green, restaurant. Open Jan.–Dec. Rates $25–$50.

Sunridge Golf Club, www.sunridgegolf.com, 775-267-4448, 1000 Long Dr., Carson City, NV. Semi-private 18-hole course. Par 72, 6914 yards, rating 72.7, slope 138. Pro shop, cart rentals, driving range, putting green. Open Jan.–Dec. Rates $50–$60.

CARSON VALLEY

Carson Valley Golf Course, www.carsonvalleygolf.com, 775-265-3181, 1027 Riverview Drive, Gardnerville, NV. Public 18-hole course. Par 71, 6020 yards, rating 66.8, slope 111. Pro shop, cart rental, practice facilities, snack bar. Open Jan.–Dec. Rates $27–$33.

Genoa Lakes Golf Club Lakes Course, www.genoalakes.com, 775-782 4653, 1 Genoa Lakes Dr., Genoa, NV. Semi-private 18-hole course. Par 72, 7357 yards, rating 74.6, slope 133. Pro shop, cart rentals, driving range, putting green, restaurant, lessons. Open Jan.–Dec. Rates $60–$120.

Genoa Lakes Golf Club Resort Course, www.genoalakes.com, 775-782 4653, 1 Genoa Lakes Dr., Genoa, NV. Semi-private 18-hole course. Par 72, 7358 yards, rating 75.1, slope 136. Pro shop, cart rentals, driving range, putting green, restaurant, lessons. Open Jan-Dec. Rates $50-$105.

RENO/SPARKS

Arrowcreek Country Club Legend Course, www.arrowcreek.com, 775-850-4653, 2905 Arrowcreek Pkwy, Reno, NV. Semi-private 18-hole course. Par 72, 6937 yards, slope 73.4, rating 136. Pro shop, cart rentals, driving range, putting green, restaurant, lessons. Open Jan.–Dec. Rates $90–$145.

Brookside Golf Course, www.cityofreno.com, 775-856-6009, 700 S. Rock Blvd., Reno, NV. Public 9-hole course. Par 35, 3018 yards. Rating 67.3, slope 111. Practice green. Open Jan.–Dec. Rates $8–$19.

D'Andrea Golf Club, www.dandreagolf.com, 775-331-6363, 2900 S. D'Andrea Pkwy., Sparks, NV. Public 18-hole course. Par 71, 6849 yards, rating 71, slope 133. Pro shop, cart rentals, driving range, putting green, restaurant. Open Jan.–Dec. Rates $35–$105.

Lakeridge Golf Course, www.lakeridgegolf.com, 775-825-2200, 1218 Golf Club Dr., Reno, NV. Public 18-hole course. Par 71, 6715 yards, rating 71.6, slope 136. Pro shop, cart rentals, driving range, practice green, lessons available, restaurant. Open Jan.–Dec. Rates $40–$100.

Northgate Golf Club, www.renolaketahoe.com, 775-747-7577, 1111 Clubhouse Dr., Reno, NV. Public 18-hole course. Par 72, 6956 yards, rating 73.1, slope 133. Pro shop, cart rentals, driving range, putting green, restaurant. Open Mar.–Nov. Rates $27–$48.

Rosewood Lakes Golf Course, www.rosewoodlakes.com, 775-857-2892, 6800 Pembroke Dr., Reno, NV. Public 18-hole course. Par 72, 6693 yards, rating 70.7, slope 125. Pro shop, cart rentals, driving range, putting green, restaurant. Open Jan.–Dec. Rates $20–$40.

Sierra Sage Golf Course, www.sierrasagegolf.org, 775-972-1564, 6355 Silver Lake Blvd., Reno, NV. Public-18 hole course. Par 71, 6604 yards, rating 70.4, slope 122. Pro shop, cart rentals, driving range, putting green, restaurant. Open Jan.–Dec. Rates $13–$35.

The Resort at Red Hawk, Lake Course www.resortatredhawk.com, 775-626-6000, 6600 Wingfield Pkwy., Sparks, NV. Public 18-hole course. Par 72, 7140 yards, rating 70.7, slope 131. Pro shop, cart rentals, driving range, putting green, restaurant. Open Jan.–Dec. Rates $50–$100.

Washoe County Golf Course, www.washoegolf.org, 775-828-6640, 2601 S. Arlington St., Reno, NV. Public-18 hole course. Par 72, 6695 yards, rating 70.9, slope 124. Pro shop, cart rentals, driving range, putting green, restaurant. Open Jan.–Dec. Rates $18–$31.

Wildcreek Golf Course, www.renolaketahoe.com, 775-673-3100, 3500 Sullivan Ln., Sparks, NV. Public 27-hole course. Par 72, 6993 yards, rating 72.5, slope 133. Pro shop, cart rentals, driving range, putting green, restaurant. Open Jan.–Dec. Rates $30–$78.

Wolf Run Golf Club, www.wolfrungolfclub.com 775-851-3301, 1400 Wolf Run Rd., Reno, NV. Public 18-hole course. Par 72, 7100 yards, rating 73.1, slope 133. Pro shop, cart rentals, driving range, putting green, restaurant. Open Jan.–Dec. Rates $40–$80.

Hiking

Fay-Luther Canyon Trail, NV 207 (Kingsbury Grade) at Foothill Road. This is a popular gateway to the rugged Carson Range. The hike is considered strenuous after the first mile. The trail is open to hikers, horseback riders, mountain bikers, and, in winter, snowshoeing and backcountry skiing. Dogs are welcome.

Job's Peak Ranch Trail, US 395 south to NV 88, turn right to Foothill Road and left 2.5 miles to trailhead. The trail is family friendly (light to moderate) and runs through sage-covered open space. After crossing a small creek the 1.5 mile climb to the peak begins. The trail is for hikers only and dogs are welcome. At the trail's highest point, hikers take in a grand view of the Carson Valley.

Horseback Riding

Galena Farms, 775-267-4007, 2666 Billy's Road Minden, NV. Learn to ride or polish your pleasure or show skills. Galena features top reining and western performance trainer Mike Baker, along with award-winning Arabian trainer Chris Malysheff. Beginning children and adult horsemanship programs.

Kirkwood Corrals, L.L.C., 775-265-2664, Foothill Road, Gardnerville, NV. Ride the range and get-along with the little doggies, at this fifth-generation working cattle ranch. Two-hour minimum ride; take part in the daily ranch activities, including branding and cattle drives. Great for the whole family. Advanced reservations required.

Pony Express Stables, 775-783-0015, 1974 Foothill Road at Muller Lane, Genoa, NV. Plan a special event with a Wild West flair, or just take a relaxing horseback ride along a

100-year-old country ranch trail. Pony Express Stables offers guided trail rides, old-fashioned hay-wagon rides, and fun for the whole family. Lunch, dinner, and entertainment available upon request.

Verdi Trails West, www.verditrailsranch.com, 1-888-345-7603, 175 Trelease Lane, Verdi, NV. This full service equestrian center is located 10 minutes west of Reno just north of US 80. Verdi West offers trail rides, day camps, riding instruction, hay-wagon rides, barbecues, and parties. Tall trees shade a huge picnic and barbecue area. Open to individual families and large groups.

Rafting

Great Basin Sports, www.greatbasinsports.com, 775-782-5657, Markleeville, NV. Take a rafting trip down a 30-mile stretch of the east fork of the Carson River. This beautiful high-desert trip is suitable for the whole family. The rapids are gentle and the rock formations fantastic. Take a dip in the hot springs along the way.

Tennis

John D. Winters Centennial Park and Archery Complex, 775-887-2363, The Tennis Complex is located at the intersection of Centennial Park Drive and Heritage Way, Carson City, NV. Includes eight courts, covered pavilion, and restrooms.

Lampe Park, dcparks-recreation.co.douglas.nv.us, 775-782-9828, 1325 Waterloo, Gardnerville, NV. Located just west of US 395 on Waterloo Lane. This sprawling 32-acre facility includes several tennis courts.

Water Sports

Carson Valley Swim Center, www.carsonvalleyswimcenter.com, 775-782-8840, 1600 NV 88, Minden, NV. This facility has four indoor pools and two outdoor pools plus an activity pool for children. Two water slides and an exercise area assure fun for all ages. Facilities include a warm pool, fully accessible with a ramp, pool lift, and stairs for seniors and the disabled. Indoor pools are open year-round, two outdoor pools open April–Oct.

Ski Oasis Water Ski Lake, 775-882-0482, 2900 US 395, Minden, NV.

Truckee River Whitewater Park, 775-787-5000, Downtown Reno, NV. Hop on a kayak, canoe, raft, or inner tube and take a refreshing ride down the Truckee River in the heart of downtown Reno. Opened by the city in 2007, the park offers a variety of whitewater activities for all skill levels. Although the entire course can be run in two to three minutes, most people take their time and enjoy hours of whitewater fun in the 11 different pools. Equipment rentals and lessons are available at the park.

SHOPPING

In many ways, this region is shoppers heaven especially for those seeking antique glassware and china, Victorian pieces, or Western art and memorabilia. At the same time, there are a number of art studios and outlets for local artists. May we suggest not wearing those new Western boots into a fine china shop until you've broke 'em in a bit.

Antiques

Antique Elk, 775-324-1980, 1313 S. Virginia St, Reno, NV. In association with the Reno Tahoe Gaming Academy, this shop features casino memorabilia.

Antique Market Place, 775-348-6444, 1301 S. Virginia St. Reno, NV. Excellent store to shop for old world antiques, china, vintage clothes, antique lighting, art glass, and pottery.

All "R" Yesterdays, 775.827.2355, 1215 S. Virginia St, Reno, NV. Located in the heart of the Reno antique district this shop offers a wide variety of antiques, collectibles, and memorabilia.

Brick House Antiques, 775-783-3438, 1461 US 395 South, Gardnerville, NV. Large collection of quality furniture, opera glasses, books, western memorabilia, hand-painted porcelain, and much more.

Carson Valley Auctions, www.auctionzip.com, 775-450-1911, 3180 US 395 North, Minden, NV. Features auctions and appraisals of antiques and art. A fun place to wander through old "treasures" from all over the country. Call for auction schedule.

Cheshire Antiques, www.cheshireantiques.com, 775-782-9117, 1423 US 395 Gardnerville, NV. Specializing in European antiques, as well as offering a great selection of local items. Voted best antique store in the Carson Valley two years in a row.

Comstock Antique Mall, 775-322-5223, First and Sierra Streets, Reno, NV. On any given day, you can find stuff you always wanted and plenty of goodies you never knew you wanted until now. Located in the vibrant Downtown Art District.

Heirloom Jewelry, 775-329-4441, 1211 S. Virginia St., Reno, NV. Specializing in custom jewelry design, repair, and vintage collectibles. Check out the antique and handmade collection.

Joyce's Antiques, Gifts and Jewelry, 775-782-5631, 1503 US 395 North, Suite A, Gardnerville, NV. Something for just about everybody can be found at Joyce's, specializing in fine jewelry, home furnishings, unique collectibles, and spectacular Christmas collections during the holiday season.

Julie's Collectibles, 775-329-2661, 1274 S. Virginia St., Reno, NV. Return to the 50s in a poodle skirt, and other great trinkets from those bygone days. Nice collection of glassware, Hummel figurines, and china.

Laura Springs & Doctor's House Antiques, 775-782-2893, 1456 Foothill Road, Gardnerville, NV. This is a must visit for folks with a taste for Old West antiques. Located on a historic Carson Valley ranch, this huge barn is overflowing with a great collection of antiques, collectibles, and country primitives. The old ranch house is also filled with antique furnishings, vintage clothing, and accessories. Be sure to check out the furniture and English glassware.

Memory Lane, 775-337-6400, 1286 S. Virginia St., Reno, NV. Light up your day with an antique lamp, light fixture. Also features antique furniture, glassware, and kitchen gizmos.

Orchard Antiques, 775-782-6191, 1459 U.S. Highway 395, Gardnerville, NV. You'll want to spend some time browsing through Orchard's great array of antique furniture, books, and holiday décor. Don't stop there, they also feature firefighter antique memorabilia, Western collectibles, Victorian boxes, vintage linens, and kitchen kitsch.

Those Were the Days, 775-825-7755, 2700 S. Virginia St., Reno, NV. Featuring antiques and collectibles ranging from Mapes Hotel antiques to oak and walnut furniture. Here you will find gaming memorabilia, vintage tools, and sporting goods. Area's largest collection of vintage costume jewelry.

Tumblewind Antiques and Collectibles, 775-782-2444, 1600 Esmeralda Ave., Minden, NV. For more than 35 years, Tumblewind has done business in historic downtown Minden. This quaint shop offers more than 4,000 square feet of eclectic collectibles, including Heritage Lace linens, western memorabilia, glassware, books, Native American items, gaming collectibles, toys, and more.

Arts & Crafts

Michael's Arts and Crafts, www.muchaels.com, 775-267-1938, 955 Topsy Lane, Jacks Valley, NV. From beads to floral to framing, large selection for all your crafting needs.

Pioneer Yarn Company, 775-782-1221, 1687 US 395 North, Suite 3, Minden, NV. Full stock of knitting, crocheting, and sewing supplies.

Art Galleries

Art!Rageous, 775-783-4700, 1685 US 395 #5 Minden, NV. Showcasing a large selection including more than 150 framed pieces. Collection includes limited editions and originals, from watercolors to oil paintings.

Artisans International, www.artisansinternationalinc.com, 1653 Lucerne St. Suite B in Minden Village, Minden, NV. This is a gallery of world art, jewelry, and home décor. Specializing in 3-D art and jewelry, including fiber, glass, ceramics, metal, and wood. Collection includes the work of artists from more than 35 countries.

Artistic Viewpoints Gallery and Studio, 775-783-0633, 1368 US 395, Building B, Gardnerville, NV. Gallery offers an eclectic mix of fine art. Also offers art classes and workshops.

Davis Gallery of Fine Art, www.thedavisgallerygenoa.com, 775-782-0568, 2285 Main St., Genoa, NV. Davis Gallery features original works by nationally known plein-air and figurative artists. Works include landscapes, still life, florals, and sculptures.

East Fork Gallery, 775-782-7629, 1503 US 395, Suite K, Gardnerville, NV. This gallery is a non-profit cooperative showcasing the works of Nevada artists. The collection includes oils, watercolors, pastels, photography, pottery, and stained glass.

Great Basin Gallery & Frame, www.nevadaweb.com/gbart, 775-882-8505, 110 S. Curry St., Carson City, NV. Specializing in the fine art of Nevada featuring historic and contemporary works, and limited editions. Also offers framing and art restoration.

Lone Tree Frame Company and Gallery, www.lonetreegallery.net, 775-782-2522, 1598 Esmeralda, Old Town Minden, Minden, NV. Lone Tree specializes in Native American and Old West art and furniture. Much of their collection is produced by local artists.

Books

ASUN Bookstore (University of Nevada Reno), www.asunbookstore.com, 775-784-6597, N. Virginia St., & Artemesia Way, Reno, NV. Of course, tons of textbooks, UNR apparel, and gear. Also, boasts a large collection of books for the general public.

Barnes & Noble Booksellers, 775-826-8882, 5555 Virginia St., Reno, NV. Well-stocked bookseller with all the latest titles. Also carries music for all tastes.

Borders, 775-448-9999, 4995 S. Virginia St., Reno, NV. Carries a large inventory of books, movies, and music. Kick back in the coffeehouse, and check out a favorite book or magazine.

Borders Express, 775-826-5690, 5320 Meadowood Mall Circle, Reno, NV. A smaller version of its big brother.

Dharma Books, www.dharmabooks.biz/, downtown: 775-786-8667, 11 N. Sierra St., Suite 107; and 775-324-1990, 310 S. Arlington Ave., Reno, NV. Owners Tony Hall and Cheron Taylor are proud of their used and rare bookshop. They specialize in classic and modern literature, art and photography, history, Beat Generation literature, and Nevada/regional titles.

Eddy Street Book Exchange, 775-782-5484, 1225 Eddy St., Gardnerville, NV. Featuring new and used books, along with a wide variety of knickknacks.

Mark Twain Bookstore, www.marktwainbooks.com, 775-847-0454, 111 South C St., Virginia City, NV. Featuring an excellent collection of books on the Old West including ghost towns, Comstock history, Mark Twain, and children's books.

Sundance Bookstore, www.sundancebookstore.com, 775-786-1188, 1155 W. Fourth St., #106, Reno, NV. Dedicated to the service of books and book lovers, Sundance stocks a huge selection of mainstream books. Also stocks magazines, newspapers, unique greeting cards, and music. Lots of special events throughout the year.

The Book Den, 775-783-1100, 1328 US 395, #305, Gardnerville, NV. Large selection of the latest titles.

Fashion

Corral West Ranchwear, 775-852-0666, 3345 Kietke Ln., Reno, NV. Hey, buckaroo—in need of new jeans, a Western belt, or some genuine cowboy boots? This is Reno's top stop for all your Western-style apparel.

Countryside Bridal and Formal Boutique, 775-783-1948, 1491 US 395 South, Gardnerville, NV. Wedding coordination, bridal wear, and tuxedos; by appointment only.

Jos A. Bank Clothiers, 775-852-6835, 13945 S. Virginia St., Suite 632, Reno, NV. This is a great spot to peruse the latest in men's fashion. Good selection of both formal and casual wear.

Shoes-n-Feet, 775-853-5077, 770 S. Meadows Pkwy., C2, Reno NV. Feet hurt from too much sightseeing? Specializing in fashionable, foot-healthy shoes. Customer assistants have at least 160 hours of training on shoes, shoe construction, and also foot biomechanics.

Studio Couture Boutique, 775-336-4420, 18146 Wedge Pkwy., Reno, NV. A quaint boutique specializing in active wear, yoga apparel, and designer sweatshirts.

Teaz n Pleaz, 775-323-8329, 440 N. Virginia St., Suite B, Reno, NV. An upscale, ultra-chic retail clothing and gift boutique, catering predominately to women and couples, Teaz offers a full collection of quality women's garments (including plus sizes), corsetry, separates, lingerie, accessories, jewelry, and a tastefully fun collection of novelty gifts.

The Summit Sierra Store, 775-853-6893, 13925 S. Virginia St., Reno, NV. Featuring men's and women's casual clothing by J. Crew and CrewCuts for children. Also features a full line of shoes and accessories.

Jewelry

Michael & Sons Trading, 775-786-5110, 2001 E. Second St., Reno, NV. One of northern Nevada's leading purveyors of fine jewelry and Native American Art. Full-time jewelers on staff for all repair needs. Appraisals are performed by certified gemologists.

Rogers Jewelry Co., www.rogersjewelryonline.com, 775-851-8555, 6520 S. Virginia St., Reno, NV. Elegant collection of fine jewelry for men and women. Custom designs and repair on site.

Van Rensselaer Jewelers, 775-782-3476, 1452 US 395, Gardnerville, NV. Custom jewelry design and repair. Also watch repair.

Specialty and Eclectic

The Watermelon Patch, 775-782-8900, 1671 US 395, Minden, NV. A nursery and gift shop featuring clocks, soaps, baby creams and much more.

Sporting Goods

REI Recreational Equipment Inc., 775-828-9090, 2225 Harvard Way, Reno, NV. REI specializes in equipment for mountain climbing, camping, and backpacking. Also offers a wide variety of bikes, skis, snowboards, and paddling equipment. Clothing and footwear also in stock.

Reno Mountain Sports, www.renomountainsports.com 775-825-2855, 155 E. Moana Ln., Reno, NV. Ready to go hiking, biking, skiing, or kayaking? This is the stop for all your sports needs. Also store employees will help you find the best trails, water runs, and mountain climbs in the area.

5

Gold Country

Mining The Mother Lode

Yes, there is still gold in them thar hills and frogs are still a-jumpin' in Calaveras County. Although there's still plenty of gold underground, the real treasure in today's Mother Lode lies in all the possibilities for adventure. Cruising—by bicycle or motorcycle— along Highway 49, and its seemingly endless tributaries, is always a popular activity. Who knows where you'll end up; a new fishing spot, a historic park, or maybe trying your luck at a Native American casino?

Long gone are the thousands of miners, and their often treacherous competition for a fortune in gold. What exists today is the culture that has evolved from the diverse mining society. Shopping, dining, and great theater are alive and well in the Gold Country. Gold panning is, too.

Mother Lode and the Gold Country
Originally the term "Mother Lode" covered an area of about 120 miles from Bear Valley, north to Auburn. It probably came from the Mexican miners in the area who called it *La Veta Madre*. Today, however, the term denotes the entire SR 49 corridor. Gold Country, California Gold Country, and Mother Lode are all used interchangeably.

Each little town along the highway has a story to tell. As a matter of fact, step into the candy store in Jackson, the bookstore in Sonora, or the Miners Emporium in Sierra City, and not only will the attendant tell you about the items they offer for sale, they'll proudly tell you the history of the building you are in—because, just as every town has its own story, so does each building. What you experience traveling about the Gold Country isn't somebody's Hollywood-style, made-up version of the real thing—this *is* the real thing.

However, that is not to say that Hollywood doesn't visit and utilize the authenticity of the Gold Country. You've seen it many times. *High Noon*, The *Wild Wild West*, and *Back to the Future Part III* all had segments filmed at Railtown 1861 State Historic Park, near Jamestown. As a matter of fact, their trains have appeared in more than 300 feature films and television shows.

And, just like Hollywood, the Gold Country even has its own Walk of Fame. Take a stroll down Main Street in downtown Angels Camp, and check out the stars whose names mark the way along the sidewalk. Which stars? One might think they would be honoring the colorful characters who made the region famous, including Black Bart, Joaquin Murieta, and,

Not far now.

of course, Mark Twain, author of "The Celebrated Jumping Frog of Calaveras County." But no, the Walk of Fame doesn't honor those stars. It honors the likes of "John Hancock Special #3," a frog whose prodigious leap of 18 feet, 10½ inches captured top honors in the 1988 Calaveras County Fair & Jumping Frog Jubilee. The Jubilee is held every year during the third week of May.

Hollywood ain't got nothin' on the Gold Country.

LODGING

On the western slopes of the Sierra Nevada in the Gold Country, you won't find any of the glitzy resort-casinos so popular in Reno and Lake Tahoe. What you will find is a veritable treasure trove of quaint B&Bs, small recreational resorts, and some great restored grand hotels. Many of the B&Bs are restored and renovated homes first built in the late 1800s. Most have kept their period charm, while upgrading with modern conveniences. In the summer, daytime temperatures can top the century mark, so air conditioning comes as a welcome break with the past.

Credit cards are abbreviated as follows:
AE: American Express
D: Discover Card
MC: MasterCard
V: Visa

Colfax

ROSE MOUNTAIN MANOR

www.rosemountainmanor.com
Innkeeper: Barbara Bowers
1-866-444-7673

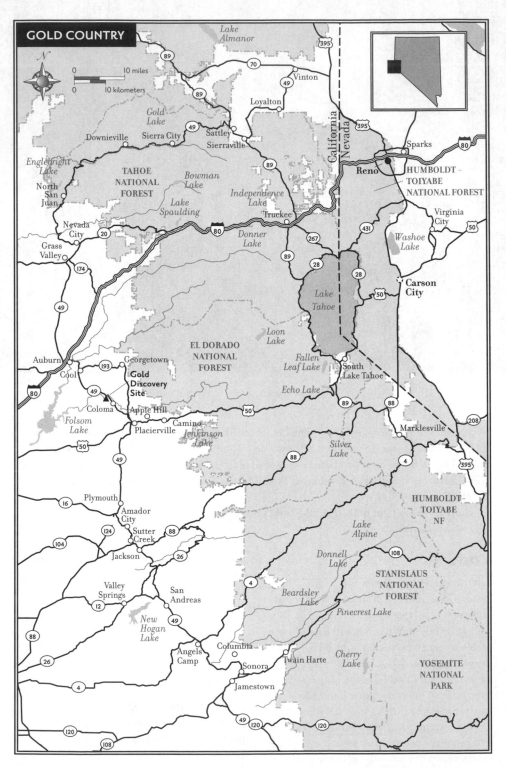

233 Plutes Way, Colfax, CA
Price: $99 and up
Credit cards: AE, D, MC, V
Children: Yes
Pets: No
Handicap access: Limited

Nestled in the secluded Sierra foothills, Rose Mountain Manor is an excellent location for a romantic getaway, or a retreat from the hustle and bustle of everyday life. The three guest rooms overlook the garden below and down into the woods. Each room has a private bath, a combination of antique and modern furnishings, down comforters, and plush terry robes. The Bear Hugs room contains a treasured collection of handsome bears, the Seashore Serenity room sports a soothing ocean theme, and the Guardian Angels Room has a private whirlpool bath. In the parlor, you'll find a wood-burning stove and TV. Take a stroll outside, down the quarter-mile Contemplation Walking Path, and enjoy the English garden. Rose Mountain offers a special feature in addition to the traditional B&B breakfast—they host afternoon tea, complete with handmade scones and tea breads, each day at 4 PM.

Coloma

COLOMA COUNTRY INN BED & BREAKFAST

www.colomacountryinn.com
530-622-6919
345 High Street, Coloma, CA
Price: $110 and up
Credit cards: MC, V
Children: Yes
Pets: Yes
Handicap access: Limited

Spend a romantic getaway in the place where the Gold Rush actually began. The

A replica of the original Sutter's Mill is on display at the Marshall Gold Discovery State Historic Park near Coloma.

The curtain still goes up most weekends at the Olde Coloma Theatre.

Coloma Country Inn is located in the Marshall Gold Discovery State Historic Park, commemorating the place where James Marshall first discovered gold in 1848. The inn itself is not a fancy Victorian, but a warm and historic farmhouse, having been built in 1852. Today, the inn offers four guest rooms in the main house, and two suites a short walk away in the Carriage House. Guest rooms in the main house offer a nice mix of American and English antiques. The Rose Room features a claw-foot tub and a private brick courtyard over-looking the garden gazebo. The adjacent Carriage House was built in 1898 and is connected to the main house by a winding brick path. The Garden Suite can accom-modate up to five people and features a kitchenette, pine floors, and a private patio. It also has a laundry facility, satellite TV, and wireless Internet access. In the morning, enjoy a sumptuous country breakfast, including an entrée and home-made baked goods, seasonal fruits, and plenty of other goodies.

THE SIERRA NEVADA HOUSE
www.sierranevadahouse.com
530-626-8096
835 Lotus Rd., Coloma, CA
Price: $89 and up
Credit cards: AE, D, MC, V
Children: Yes
Pets: No
Handicap access: No

The Sierra Nevada House offers the beauty of the Sierra foothills and a wide variety of outdoor activities at a reasonable price. Their stated goal is recreation by day, and restoration by night. This historic facility is a lodge, restaurant, and bar where one might spend a day rock climbing, horseback riding, or kayaking in the morning, and taking a photography, yoga, or nature class in the afternoon. Guests are welcome to partake in organized activities such as walking tours or nature hikes, or hop on a mountain bike and explore the area on their own. The six guest rooms are located above the bar and restaurant, and have recently been renovated. They are roomy, comfortable, and each has a private bath. Each room has its own theme and a story to go with it. The stories behind each room—whether fact, or Western lore—are based on people who once made The Sierra Nevada House their home.

Columbia

COLUMBIA CITY HOTEL & FALLON HOTEL
www. foreverlodging.com
1-800-532-1479
22768 Main St., Columbia, CA
Price: $90 and up

Credit cards: AE, D, MC, V
Children: Yes
Pets: No
Handicap access: Limited

The Columbia City Hotel and its sister, the Fallon Hotel, are authentically restored country B&Bs located in Columbia State Historic Park. Some concessions have been made with the authenticity, and modern conveniences like indoor plumbing, heating, and air conditioning have been added. Each room has a half bath, and a shower basket is provided for the trip down the hall to the shared shower. Both are small hotels—the City Hotel offers three rooms, and the Fallon, four rooms. Some of the upstairs rooms have balconies where one might enjoy an afternoon lemonade and watch the goings-on of an authentic Gold Rush-era town. Both hotels have lovely parlors for reading or playing one of the many board games the hotels have in stock. Guests of both hotels are welcome to a hearty buffet breakfast served up each morning in the City Hotel restaurant.

Downtown Coulterville boasts the Magnolia—California's oldest operating saloon.

Originally built in the late 1840s as a cantina and fandango hall, The Hotel Jeffery in Coulterville remained in the Jeffery family for decades after its construction.

Coulterville

HOTEL JEFFERY
www.hoteljefferygold.com
Innkeepers: Peter and Cherylann
Schimmelfennig
209-878-3471
1 Main Street, Coulterville, CA
Price: $70 and up
Credit cards: AE, D, MC, V
Children: Yes
Pets: By arrangement
Handicap access: Limited

The Hotel Jeffery is about as historically authentic as you can get. The original hotel was built in 1851 as a "saloon and fandango hall." Renovated and reopened in 2004, the hotel features rooms with queen beds and two-room suites. Each room is individually decorated, but all feature hand-stitched quilts for warmth and comfort. In the morning, wake up to the aroma of fresh-baked cookies and bread. No problem getting a little work done, the hotel offers free Wi-Fi. Be sure to check out the Magnolia Saloon and Grill, located next door and decorated with a flare for the rustic charm of the Old West. The menu features American cuisine including big burgers, Philly cheese steak, pizza, and a variety of salads.

Fair Play

FITZPATRICK WINERY AND LODGE
www.fitzpatrickwinery.com
Innkeepers: Diana and Brian Fitzpatrick
1-800-245-9166
7740 Fair Play Rd., Fair Play, CA
Price: $89 and up
Credit cards: AE, D, MC, V
Children: Yes
Pets: No
Handicap access: Yes

Spectacular views, great wine, and Irish hospitality are the order of the day at Fitzpatrick's. This is a working winery with a five-room B&B lodge, nestled in the heart of the El Dorado wine country. The hand-crafted log lodge is situated atop the underground wine cellar, and includes the wine-tasting room. Five themed rooms offer incredible views of the wine country and the Sierra Nevada. A made-to-order full breakfast is included in the price of your stay. The most elegant of the guest rooms is the Winemaker's Suite, where you will find great views from the private balcony and a room decorated in a wine fantasy theme. Another favorite is the French Basque Room decorated in bright, happy colors, with a window seat, a warm fireplace, and a balcony to enjoy the setting sun. When the weather is warm, sip a glass of wine and spend an evening out on the deck gazing into a star-filled sky. Later, it might be time to enjoy a water massage in the spa. The Great Room offers a warm fire, and a massive Irish pine table to enjoy a game of cards or chat with friends.

7UP RANCH BED & BREAKFAST
www.7upranch.com
1-800-717-5450 or 530-620-5450
8060 Fair Play Rd., Fair Play, CA
Price: $140 and up
Credit cards: MC, V
Children: Yes
Pets: Yes
Handicap access: Limited

Situated on 145 idyllic acres in the heart of the Sierra foothills, the 7Up Ranch is a great place for a romantic getaway, family gathering, or special event. There are more than 30 wineries within a three mile radius of the ranch, and whitewater rafting, gold panning, hiking, and mountain climbing can be found within minutes of the facility. The ranch is dotted with picnic areas, and the main cabin provides a great setting for the complimentary gourmet breakfast served every morning. The six guest rooms are located in three separate cabins, each with a private entrance and bath. The rooms are decorated in Old West/Gold Rush themes, and include old-fashioned wooden porches, queen and king beds, and in-room coffee and tea.

Grass Valley
ANNIE HORAN'S BED AND BREAKFAST
www.anniehoran.com
530-272-1516
415 W. Main St., Grass Valley, CA
Price: $99 and up
Credit cards: AE, D, MC, V
Children: Yes
Pets: No
Handicap access: Yes

Beautiful and historic, Annie Horan's was originally built in 1852. Recently refurbished, the Victorian B&B retains the charm and style of the Old West, but with modern amenities including central heat and air conditioning and wireless Internet access. The four guest rooms are theme decorated and each has a private bath. The Cloud Room offers enormous bay windows, while Annie's Room boasts a claw-footed bathtub for a long soak. A complimentary breakfast is served each morning. Annie's is centrally located with easy access to downtown dining and shopping.

THE HOLBROOKE
www.holbrooke.com
1-800-933-7077 or 530-273-1353
212 Main St., Grass Valley, CA
Price: $90 and up
Credit cards: AE, D, MC, V
Children: Yes
Pets: No
Handicap access: Limited

Established in 1851, The Holbrooke has seen it all. One of the earliest guest books

The National Hotel in downtown Grass Valley is a classic example of a grand hotel of the 1800s.

lists two presidents, Benjamin Harrison and Grover Cleveland, who spent at least one night here. Scores of miners and numerous major celebrities of the day made the hotel, restaurant, and saloon their headquarters. Today, The Holbrooke retains its Gold Rush-era charm, while adding many modern amenities. Each of the 28 rooms is decorated in the Victorian tradition of that era. All rooms have private baths, most with claw-foot tubs for a long soak after a day or night on the town. Some rooms have private balconies overlooking the historic downtown, while other are equipped with fireplaces. All rooms have cable TV and wireless Internet access. Numerous old photographs and other artifacts from the late 1800s are on display throughout the facility.

SIERRA MOUNTAIN INN

www.sierramountaininn.com
530-273-8133
816 W. Main St., Grass Valley, CA
Price: $148 and up
Credit cards: AE, D, MC, V
Children: Yes
Pets: No
Handicap access: Yes

Sierra Mountain Inn boasts five-star quality rooms in a restful atmosphere nestled among towering redwood trees. Recently refurbished, but keeping with its theme as a 1930s-style motor court, the inn offers 12 rooms and one cottage, all with private baths, kitchenettes, cable TV, individually controlled heating and air conditioning, and free wireless Internet access. Many of the rooms feature marble bath fixtures and king-size beds. Some rooms adjoin, creating lovely suites. A complimentary continental breakfast is served daily.

VICTORIAN LADY BED & BREAKFAST
www.victorianladyinn.com
530-477-8181
304 S. Church St., Grass Valley, CA
Price: $125 and up
Credit cards: MC, V
Children: Yes
Pets: No
Handicap access: Limited

Formerly known as Comeback Jacks, this quaint and cozy B&B now features three guest rooms and a suite, with themes based on bygone Hollywood divas. The Marilyn Monroe room is done in pink with a portrait of the starlet above the four-poster queen bed. Other guest quarters include the Lotta Crabtree Room, Sally Stanford Suite, and the Lola Montez Room. Great for get-togethers, the common areas include the parlor, country kitchen, and breakfast and dining rooms. Outside, the pool, spa, and gardens are great for kicking back on a hot summer afternoon. The inn is within easy walking distance to the downtown historical district.

Kit Carson

KIT CARSON LODGE
www.kitcarsonlodge.com
530-676-1370 or 209-258-8500
Hwy. 88 at Silver Lake, Kit Carson, CA
Price: $105 and up
Credit cards: AE, D, MC, V
Children: Yes
Pets: No
Handicap access: Limited

Clear blue skies, rugged granite peaks, and a beautiful alpine lake provide the

An interesting collection of cocktail shakers on display in the National Hotel in Grass Valley.

unbelievable setting for the Kit Carson Lodge. This is the place to really get away from everyday life, and enjoy nature's beauty at its finest. The lodge is both rustic and elegant at the same time. Lake Tahoe may possess similar beauty, but the emphasis here is on the peacefulness of nature. You'll find no slot machines or gaming tables in the lodge, but you will find an art gallery, and numerous art programs are offered throughout the summer. The gallery features artists who specialize in the local area. Enjoy the paintings, sculpture, ceramics, and photography. No loud speed boats or Jet Skis roar across Silver Lake, but canoes are available to rent for a fishing expedition or an evening paddle on the lake. Nestled among the pines at 8,000 foot elevation, the moon and stars provide the only light show in town. This is the place you might bring your child or a loved one to have that special talk or pull the whole family together for a reunion. The lodge features both a hotel and individual cottages which can accommodate from two to six people. The hotel rooms are furnished in knotty pine with exposed beam ceilings. Large windows look out across your deck, the lake, and the soaring peaks in the distance. The cottages have the same decor and also include full kitchens, fireplaces, and spacious decks. A restaurant, store and gift shop are open throughout the season. So, load up the fishin' gear, put on your hikin' boots, and leave all those electronic gizmos at home—especially the cell phone—it

won't work here anyway. No TVs here either. The Kit Carson Lodge is a place to connect with yourself and those around you. The lodge season runs from mid-June through mid-November.

Kyburz
STRAWBERRY LODGE
www.strawberry-lodge.com
530-659-7200
17510 Highway 50, Kyburz, CA
Price: $69 and up
Credit cards: MC, V
Children: Yes
Pets: Yes
Handicap access: Limited

Once a stop for Pony Express riders, the historic Strawberry Lodge is nestled high in the Sierra pines, along the banks of the cascading American River. The lodge has a restaurant, bar, 44 guest rooms, and one riverside cabin. This is a scenic, yet affordable, spot for family reunions, weddings, corporate retreats, or just a weekend getaway. This is a rustic facility so the rooms do not have TV or telephones, and Internet access is out of the question. The lobby is warmed by a fireplace and stocked with plenty of reading material. The large patio is a great place for gathering and offers tremendous views of the Sierra Nevada. During summer months, fly fishing, hiking, and mountain climbing are favorite activities, and when the snow arrives, the trails make for great snowshoeing and cross-country skiing.

Creature comforts.

Mokelumne Hill

THE LEGER HISTORIC HOTEL

www.hotelleger.com
209-286-1401
8304 Main St., Mokelumne Hill, CA
Price: $55 and Up
Credit cards: AE, D, MC, V
Children: Yes
Pets: No
Handicap access: No

It's off the beaten path, the walls are thin, the rooms a little small, there's no TV or telephone service in most of the rooms, and, it is said, ghosts roam the rooms and hallways when the moon is just right. It's no wonder The Leger (pronounced "luh-zhay") was voted a whole bunch of "Best of" awards for Calaveras County. A visit to the bar alone is worth the trip. Built in 1851, and last remodeled in the 1870s, it is the real deal—right down to the beautiful stained glass above the bar. Today, it's a cheery, sunny spot to enjoy a drink or a bite to eat, but in its day, this was a rowdy, hell-raising, Western gold-diggers' bar. The present hotel facility is actually three separate buildings, one of which housed the county courthouse, complete with downstairs dungeon and a hangin' tree out back. The 13 rooms come in various sizes and configurations. Some private baths. All the rooms are furnished with beautiful Victorian-era antiques.

Murphys

MURPHYS HISTORIC HOTEL

www.murphyshotel.com
1-800-532-7684 or 209-728-3444
457 Main St., Murphys, CA
Price: $69 and up
Credit cards: AE, D, MC, V
Children: Yes
Pets: No
Handicap access: Limited

Mark Twain slept here. Really. So did Black Bart and Ulysses S. Grant. For a true taste of the Gold Rush days, Murphys Historic Hotel is as good as it gets. Murphys boasts 29 guest rooms, nine of which are located in the original stone building. The other rooms are in the "modern" wings that have been added over the years. Fine dining is found in the renovated dining room, and the old-fashioned saloon is a nice stop for a cocktail and some live music on the weekends. The historic rooms and suites are furnished with authentic antiques from the 1800s. In the grand suite, you will find an antique grand piano, decorative potbelly stove, and an authentic barber chair. In keeping with the ambiance of the period theme, these rooms do not have TVs, telephones, alarm clocks, or coffeemakers. And no, they do not have private baths. Business is taken care of just down the hall—be thankful you don't have to go outside! If you can't live without a private bath and all that other newfangled stuff, the "modern" lodge will suit you just fine.

Nevada City

BELLA ROSA INN

An Intimate and Luxurious B&B
www.bellarosainn.net
Innkeepers: Gina and Ben
1-866-696-9055
517 West Broad St., Nevada City, CA
Price: $189
Credit cards: AE, D, MC, V
Children: Yes
Pets: No
Handicap access: Yes

Upon completion of their recent remodel, the innkeepers have created a very upscale B&B at the Bella Rosa Inn. Each of the six guest rooms has its own unique theme and color palette. Imagine snuggling into a comfy bed with fine linens and extra pillows in the Black and White Room, the Chocolate Room, or the Pink and Sage Room. All rooms come with wall-mounted, flat-screen TVs, private bath and shower, and wireless Internet access. A small fridge contains complimentary beverages. The tea and coffee bar is open 24-hours and you must try the fresh-baked cookies. Other amenities include an on-call massage therapist, a sauna room, and a large, private, beautifully landscaped outdoor sitting area that's ideal for parties or family gatherings. In the evening, relax in the beautifully appointed dining room or outside on the patio and sample complimentary wine and hors d'oeuvres. The inn is located in the downtown district, within walking distance to shopping and dining. Each morning, a complimentary gourmet breakfast is served.

THE DEER CREEK INN

www.deercreekinn.com
Innkeepers: Eileen and Ken Strangfeld
1-800-655-0363 or 530-265-0363
116 Nevada St., Nevada City, CA
Price: $160 and up
Credit cards: AE, D, MC, V
Children: No
Pets: No
Handicap access: Yes

No wonder Deer Creek was voted Best Bed and Breakfast in Nevada County. A stay here is a special treat. This Queen Anne Victorian offers romance and peace amid beautiful gardens and tastefully appointed rooms. The innkeepers have made it their personal goal that all guests relax and enjoy their stay. Each of the five guest rooms is uniquely decorated, with the idea that this is your home away from home. The guest rooms are named for former owners, and they include the Sheryl, Lela, Winifred, Ida, Elaine, and Eileen Rooms. The upstairs rooms all have private balconies that overlook the creek. Elaine's Room, with its Roman bathtub, private entrance, and canopy bed, is the most requested room; but Winifred's Room, which

Gold Country humor. Or maybe they aren't kidding.

includes the house's original claw-foot tub, and French doors leading to a private balcony, holds the record for the most marriage proposals *and* acceptances. Each evening, Ken and Eileen invite their guests to sit with them in the parlor or out in the garden, to enjoy a glass of Nevada County wine. They are very helpful when it comes to finalizing arrangements for dining and a night on the town. Over a gourmet breakfast in the morning, they enjoy discussing local points of interest so guests can prepare for an enchanting day of exploration. Deer Creek is a place where you stop and smell the roses.

EMMA NEVADA HOUSE

www.emmanevadahouse.com
Innkeeper: Susan and Andrew Howard
1-800-916-3662
528 East Broad St., Nevada City, CA
Price: $169 and Up
Credit cards: AE, D, MC, V
Children: Yes
Pets: No
Handicap access: Yes

This enchanting Victorian B&B retains its 1860s charm, with rich carpeting and Douglas fir flooring, while still treating guests to many modern amenities. The house includes three rooms on the main floor, and three upstairs rooms. The Empress Chamber on the main floor is one of the most popular rooms. Big windows let in the morning sun to this regal ivory and burgundy chamber. Recline on the antique bed and enjoy a soak in the Jacuzzi tub-shower. For something a little more eclectic, relax in Emma's Hideaway, a cozy upstairs room reminiscent of *Alice in Wonderland.* Central air conditioning keeps the house comfortable in the summer, and wireless Internet access is free. Each day begins with a delectable breakfast made with all fresh ingredients. Recline in the dining room or enjoy a cup of custom-blended coffee on the cozy sun porch. Be sure to take a stroll through the inn's beautiful gardens.

OUTSIDE INN

www.outsideinn.com
530-265-2233
575 E. Broad St., Nevada City, CA
Price: $75 and up
Credit cards: AE, D, MC, V
Children: Yes
Pets: Yes
Handicap access: Yes

Maybe you've had enough Gold Rush history and really don't care for the idea of keeping your little finger cocked while sipping tea at some fancy-schmancy B&B. Like, enough of Victorian-era, highbrow stuff already—it's time for some real fun, like kayaking, mountain biking, and fishing. A great place to start this adventure is by checking into the Outside Inn, a fully renovated 1940s-era motor court. Each of the 15 rooms has a theme of its own, many leaning toward the slightly eclectic. Aging hippies will love the Celestial Room, with glowing stars overhead, beaded curtains, and colorful upholstery celebrating the 1960s. (Far out, man.) For the outdoor nut, how about the Rock Climbing Suite. Here you'll find a king bed, kitchenette, private patio and (no kidding) your own private climbing wall. And then there's the Anglers' Room, celebrating all things fishy. The inn also has a couple of detached cabin/suites for families or romantic getaways. Sorry to say, the Creekside Hideaway was recently renovated into a Victorian boudoir. The inn also boasts a knowledgeable staff ready to set up bike rentals or kayak lessons. A short stroll gets you to all the downtown action and attractions.

THE PARSONAGE BED & BREAKFAST

theparsonage.net
Innkeeper: Susan Shea
530-265-9478
427 Broad St., Nevada City, CA
Price: $90 and up
Credit cards: D, MC, V
Children: Yes
Pets: No
Handicap access: Yes

Originally built in 1865, this little blue house at the top of Broad Street served as home to the town's Methodist minister for more than 80 years. Today, after two renovations, the home retains the original Victorian look and feel—right down to the embossed wallpaper and the furnishings in each room. The six guest rooms are uniquely furnished, and all have private

Union Lake high in the Sierra is a favorite for kayak enthusiasts. Dan Stephens

baths. The Master's Room overlooks Broad Street, the Balcony Room features a balcony and a gas log stove, while the Miner's Cabin is a casual and private retreat. Complimentary breakfast is served each morning, featuring fresh eggs from the Shea's Wandering Star Ranch in nearby Penn Valley. During summer months, fresh blueberries and strawberries are also on the menu.

RED CASTLE HISTORIC LODGINGS

www.redcastleinn.com
1-800-761-4766 or 530-365-5135
109 Prospect St., Nevada City, CA
Price: $120 and up
Credit cards: MC, V
Children: 12 and older
Pets: No
Handicap access: No

Red Castle was the first B&B in Nevada City and one of the first in the state of California. It is a beautiful four-story, 1860 Gothic Revival mansion, surrounded by incense cedars and rustic terraced gardens. The inn has received awards and rave reviews from such publications as *Gourmet* magazine, The *Sacramento Bee,* and the *Los Angeles Times*. Rooms and/or suites are located on all four floors. Each room has a private bath and access to private or shared verandas. Each room is artfully arranged reflecting the refinement of the 19th century. A favorite for couples traveling together is the Garret Suite on the top floor, featuring a two bedrooms, where large windows and a tree-top veranda provide magnificent views. One of the most romantic settings is found in the Forest View Room, where a canopy bed surrounded by lace and a crystal chandelier enhance the mood. Experience your romantic Victorian dream in the Rose Room, where tall French doors open to a private veranda, and a four-poster featherbed awaits your slumber. Breakfast at the castle is not a meal, it's a six-course event featuring a wide variety of treats prepared by a culinary academy-trained chef. Enjoy your meal in the terraced gardens, common social areas, or in the seclusion of your own room.

US HOTEL B&B INN

www.ushotelbb.com
Innkeeper: Katie Bennett
530-265-7999
233 B Broad St., Nevada City, CA
Price: $99 and up
Credit cards: MC, V
Children: Yes
Pets: Yes (on a limited basis)
Handicap access: Yes

Originally built in 1953, the inn is a California State Historic Landmark. Each of the seven rooms has a private bath, TV, and Internet access. French doors in the Empire Room lead to two balconies overlooking the historic downtown area. Take an afternoon nap on the full-size couch, or sleep the night away in the comfy king-size featherbed. A quiet retreat is found in The Garden Room. Bathed in soothing sunlight, the room features windows overlooking the rooftops and a fan-back wicker chair for reading, or just relaxing. Always available for comfort and reading, the common living room features an extensive collection of books, games, and memorabilia. Ready for a snack, but it's midnight? No problem. The community kitchen is always open, and stocked with snacks and refreshments. A hearty gourmet country breakfast is prepared daily and served family style around the hotel's dining table. No one leaves the table hungry.

Quaint shops occupy the bottom floor and rooms to rent on the second floor at Nevada City's US Hotel.

Placerville

BLAIR SUGAR PINE BED & BREAKFAST

www.blairsugarpine.com
Innkeepers: William and Kay Steffen
530-626-9006
2985 Clay St., Placerville, CA
Price: $120 and up
Credit cards: AE, D, MC, V
Children: No
Pets: No
Handicap access: No

This quaint Queen Anne Victorian house is steeped in history and romance. Built in 1901 by James Blair for his soon-to-be-wife Erla, the house is constructed of quality sugar pine. The Blairs went on to raise their family and lived in the house for many years. The "Honeymoon Tree" Erla planted adorns the property now, as a tall, stately redwood. Today, the home offers visitors a homespun-style of warmth and comfort. The original, handcrafted woodwork is still found in the entry, living room, and parlor. The three guest rooms all have private baths, queen feather beds, and down comforters. The entire house, including the guest rooms, features a tremendous collection of artwork and collectibles. Wireless Internet access is available throughout the house. Visitors are greeted with a tin of chocolates upon arrival, and evening refreshments include award-winning wines from local wineries. Early morning coffee and a gourmet breakfast are included in your stay. When it's time for a little exploration, the historic downtown district is a short stroll away.

HISTORIC CARY HOUSE HOTEL

www.caryhouse.com
530-622-4271
300 Main St., Placerville, CA
Price: $96 and up
Credit cards: AE, D, MC, V
Children: Yes
Pets: No
Handicap access: Yes

Today's visitors to the Cary House will appreciate all the modern conveniences, because when this hotel was built back in 1857, it had 77 guest rooms—but only one bath on each floor. Today, this beautifully restored hotel has 38 guest rooms and suites, each of them with private baths. Additionally, all rooms come with newfangled items never even dreamed of by the 49ers, including TVs, telephones, wireless Internet access, and individually controlled heating and air conditioning. No two rooms are the same at the Cary House, and each has been individually decorated with antiques selected to create a desired mood; something the managers like to call "affordable elegance." A person gets the idea of what the Cary House is all about the moment they enter the lobby. Large stained-glass windows, elegant furniture, and a baby grand piano set the tone. Located in the heart of the historic downtown district, it's an easy stroll to nearby dining, shopping, and entertainment.

ROBIN'S NEST RANCH B&B

www.robinsnestranch.com
Innkeepers: Mark and Susan Miller
530-344-0943
3170 Newtown Rd., Placerville, CA
Price: $130 and up
Credit cards: AE, D, MC, V
Children: Yes
Pets: Yes
Handicap access: Limited

For the outdoor or horse enthusiast, the award-winning Robin's Nest is a cool B&B located on an 11-acre horse ranch. The ranch house is a renovated 1883 homestead outfitted with period antiques and comfortable furnishings. Guest rooms are located in the main house and in the adjacent bunkhouse. Beautiful French-Swiss antiques adorn the Oak & Rose room, including a lovely hand-carved bed frame.

A stately Victorian B&B in Placerville is one of many found throughout the Gold Country.

Upstairs, the Lover's Fancy and Flower Garden rooms share a common balcony, where one can enjoy morning coffee or a cool drink in the afternoon. Out in the bunkhouse, only a few steps from the main house, guests may choose from one of two rooms, both furnished tastefully in the Western theme of this former working cattle ranch. The guest rooms have private baths and share a deck overlooking the horse pasture. Greeting treats and a full breakfast, including seasonal fresh fruit, are part of the package. If you need to get a little work done, fire up your laptop; the Wi-Fi is free. At Robin's Nest there's plenty of room to park your horse trailer and the dog is welcome, in the bunkhouse only.

THE SEASONS

www.theseasons.net
530-626-4420

2934 Bedford Ave., Placerville, CA
Price: $120 and up
Credit cards: AE, D, MC, V
Children: Yes
Pets: No
Handicap access: Limited

Beautiful gardens and a wraparound veranda welcome guests to The Seasons bed & breakfast. The inn is named for a series of paintings by artist and former owner Ann Gladwell, depicting life in El Dorado County at different times of year. Built in 1859, the house, although remodeled several times, is one of the oldest in Placerville. In addition to Gladwell's paintings, The Seasons is well-appointed with original art and unusual antiques. In the dining room where guests are served a complimentary breakfast, is a one-of-a-kind wrought iron chandelier made from an antique weather vane. One guest suite is located inside the main house, and the others are two buildings adjacent to the house. The Plumado Suite, named for the long-time owners of the property, has two rooms and its own private entrance overlooking the garden's flagstone patio. It has original wood floors, a wrought-iron queen bed, and a private bath. The Cottage is a separate wood-frame building surrounded by a white picket fence, and has a private deck with a pergola overhead. The Gardener's Cottage has two guest rooms, The Pomegranate and The Dreamer. A stroll through the inn's lavish garden is a must on any warm afternoon.

Sierra City
BASSETTS STATION
www.bassetts-station.com
530-862-1297
100 Gold Lake Rd., Sierra City, CA
Price: $80 and Up
Credit cards: MC, V
Children: Yes
Pets: Yes
Handicap access: Limited

The site that today is Bassetts Station (five miles east of Sierra City) has served up food, shelter, fuel, and necessities since the 1870s. Located at the confluence of Howard Creek and the Yuba River, it provides easy access to the Lake Basin Recreation Area, where hiking, four-wheeling, biking, swimming, and fishing are always popular activities, until the snow arrives when it becomes one of the best cross-country skiing and snowmobiling facilities around. The motel rooms are comfortable, and are equipped with satellite TV. Some units have full kitchens. In addition to the motel, Bassett's also has a café—the milkshakes are to die for—and a well-stocked country store and gift shop, complete with fishing licenses, fishing gear, sno-park permits,

and just about any camping supplies you might have forgotten. Fuel services and propane station to get you going.

BUTTES RESORT
www.buttesresort.citymax.com
1-800-991-1170 or 530-862-1170
230 Main Street (SR 49),
Sierra City, CA
Price: $65 and Up
Credit cards: MC, V
Children: Yes
Pets: No
Handicap access: Limited

There are rustic mountain cabins that may be adequate for when the boys go hunting—and then there are the 12 warm, clean, and cozy cabins that make up Buttes Resort. Nestled beneath the Sierra Buttes, the resort is a mountain retreat overlooking the Yuba River. The recently refurbished cabins have all had a thorough scrubbing and are equipped with new beds, fireplaces, and other amenities. Some of the cabins have full kitchens and small barbecues. A few of the cabins are separated by a single door, making them ideal for a small group or the entire family. Some of the cabins have expansive views of the Yuba River below. Inside the recreation room, try your hand on the pool table or at the dart board. The library is well stocked, with plenty of good reading. A large deck adjacent to the rec room offers a beautiful river view and makes a great meeting place. Sierra City is situated above 4,000 feet, so evenings are cool even in the summer. The store and gift shop are kept well supplied with wine, beer, and all the necessary fixins for a great barbecue. The pace is slower here. You will find no malls, superstores, or crowds. It is possible, however, to walk or drive to one of the 45 surrounding lakes, catch a nice brook trout, and not ever see another person—even on the Fourth of July.

Sonora

BARRETTA GARDENS INN

www.barrettagardens.com
Innkeepers: Astrid and Daniel Stone
899-206-3333 or 209-532-6039
700 South Barretta St., Sonora, CA
Price: $135 and up
Credit cards: MC, V
Children: Yes
Pets: No
Handicap access: Yes

Situated on a hillside overlooking the town of Sonora, Barretta Gardens is very popular among American and European visitors. The beautifully landscaped garden—complete with two patios, a barbecue area, fish pond, and fountain—add a park-like setting to the inn. Recline on the balcony and enjoy a beautiful High Sierra sunset. Comfort is the goal here and each of the five guest rooms is unique in its décor and ambiance. The down stairs Tempranillo Room is a romantic hideaway with a private entrance. The mahogany bedroom set and queen-size bed are complemented by the burgundy, green, and white color scheme. Forget taking a shower—have a long soak in the two-person whirlpool spa. The old master bedroom is now the Cabernet Sauvignon Suite, and is a symbol of Victorian elegance, complete with crystal chandelier and 10-foot-high ceilings. This suite also features a two-person whirlpool spa, so you can relax and watch the sun set from your bath. All rooms include fresh flowers, bottled water, candy, satellite TV, wireless Internet access, and comfy bathrobes. A complimentary, delicious, and healthful breakfast is served each morning.

THE GUNN HOUSE

www.gunnhousehotel.com
Innkeepers: Mike and Shirley Sarno
209-532-3421
286 S. Washington St., Sonora, CA
Price: $69 and up
Credit cards: MC, V
Children: Yes
Pets: No
Handicap access: Yes

This is one of the most historic buildings in the area. Built in the early 1850s by Dr. Lewis C. Gunn, publisher of the first newspaper in the Mother Lode area, the *Sonora Herald*. After an extensive renovation, the house has become a wonderful B&B offering several tastefully decorated rooms along with reasonable rates. The innkeepers have retained the historic charm of the place and although the inn is quite large, guests will find it warm and comfortable. Each guest room is different, but all are appointed with antiques and theme colors. All rooms have modern private baths, cable TV, and heating and air conditioning. Relax in the heated swimming pool and enjoy the stonework and river rock surrounding it. Several balconies overlook the gardens' flowers and greenery. Complimentary breakfast is served each morning in the Victorian parlor. Located downtown, the inn is short walking distance to some great shopping, local theater, and restaurants.

Sutter Creek

SUTTER CREEK BED AND BREAKFAST AT THE GREY GABLES INN

www.greygables.com
1-800-473-9422 or 209-267-1039
161 Hanford St., Sutter Creek CA
Price: $120 and up
Credit cards: AE, D, MC, V
Children: No
Pets: No
Handicap access: Yes

This award-winning B&B brings grace, elegance, and a touch of merry ole England to the gold country. In keeping with true English fashion, afternoon tea with cakes or scones is served in the parlor each day. Early in the evening, wine and hors d'oeuvres are available. Red-brick pathways lead to a terraced garden, making for a wonderful stroll and quiet conversation. Every morning a full breakfast is served on fine bone china in the dining room or, if you prefer, in the privacy of your own room. The guest rooms—each named for prominent 19th-century English writers, poets, and artists—has its own fireplace accented with wood trim and marble tile, a private bath (some with tubs), and tasteful furnishings including roomy beds and antique accessories. The Browning room, on the main floor, has lavender and teal green décor and a marvelous garden view. The Rossetti Room is a Victorian suite with green carpet, soft pink walls, a four-poster king bed, and a table for tea and breakfast tucked away in the alcove.

HANFORD HOUSE INN
BED & BREAKFAST

www.hanfordhouse.com
Innkeepers: Bob and Karen Tierno
1-800-871-5893 or 209-267-0747
61 Hanford St., Sutter Creek, CA
Price: $109 and up
Credit cards: AE, D, MC, V
Children: Yes
Pets: No
Handicap access: Yes

Nestled into the foothills of the gold country, the Hanford House is a beautiful brick inn, offering 10 themed rooms and suites. This is a great place for a romantic getaway, a relaxing weekend, or to use as your headquarters while exploring the many sights and activities in the area. It also has facilities to accommodate weddings, reunions, seminars and conferences. All guest rooms have private baths, telephone, cable TV, and wireless Internet access. A few of the rooms have fireplaces and spa tubs. Guests also have access to the sunny parlor, a roof-top sun deck with grand views, and a shaded patio. Afternoon refreshments are served upon arrival, and in the morning enjoy a great cup of coffee or tea before sitting down to a gourmet breakfast prepared by a local chef. If you need to take care of some business, the inn has a business center equipped with a copier, PC, printer, and fax service.

Volcano
ST. GEORGE HOTEL

www.stgeorgehotel.com
209-296-4458
16104 Main St., Volcano, CA
Price: $60 and up
Credit cards: AE, D, MC, V
Children: Yes
Pets: Yes
Handicap access: Limited

Built in 1862, the St. George Hotel, located in the heart of the Amador Wine Country, is an award-winning landmark. Recent honors include Best Historic Hotel, Best Place to Take a Date, and one of the Top 10 Bars in the world worth flying to (by *GQ* magazine). Here you can stay in the main three-story hotel, which, as a landmark, is rich in authenticity, and share a bath, or retire to one of the six rooms in the garden annex, each with its own bath. The 12 rooms in the main structure occupy to the top two stories, with the parlor, dining room, and saloon on the ground floor. For a nice, romantic touch, check into a second-or third-story balcony room. Enjoy the sights and sounds of this quiet hamlet and let Sutter Creek flowing in the distance lull you to sleep. No worry about the noise from a neighbor's TV spoiling the ambiance—there are no TVs or phones in the main hotel rooms. Outside, the grounds surrounding the hotel are beautifully maintained. Hundreds of daffodils and tulips bloom in the spring, and majestic trees provide shade in the summer. There are a also number of cozy sitting areas throughout the garden.

CULTURE

Architecture

Fortunately, you won't find many strip malls and no skyscrapers in the Gold Country. The main streets of the towns retain their Gold Rush theme. Although the theme is pretty much the same, each community has its own personality, inviting visitor investigation.

Cinema

Del Oro Theatre, 530-273-6932, 165 Mill St., Grass Valley, CA. This Art Moderne theater was built in 1941, and although remodeled several times on the inside, it is still an area landmark. Shows first-run movies on its three screens.

Music & More Theatre Dewitt, 11596 D Ave., Auburn, CA. Home to concerts, local symphony, plays, and film screenings.

Regal Auburn Stadium 10, 530-745-0156, 500 Nevada St., Auburn, CA. One of the most modern movie houses in the Sierra foothills. Features stadium seating, digital 3D, IMAX, and giant screens.

Regal Placerville Stadium 8, 530-621-9853, 337 Placerville, CA. Shows first-run movies, has a game room on premises, and has listening devices available. Also hosts the El Dorado County Independent Film Series.

Gold Mine Tours

Hangtown's Gold Bug Park and Mine, www.goldbugpark.org, 530-642-5207, 2635 Goldbug Lane, Placerville, CA. Step back in time and experience what hardrock gold miners felt as they picked, shoveled, and blasted their way deep into the earth. This is a great place to take the kids. The tour isn't too long or difficult, but is extremely informative. Adjacent to the mine, the old stamp mill is beautifully restored, and in operation. (Please pass the ear plugs.) Where's Hangtown? You're already there—that was Placerville's original name, and some say they should have left well enough alone. The mine and stamp mill are located on 60 acres, and outside there's a covered picnic area and a stream for a little gold panning. The grounds and facilities are owned and operated by the city of Hangtown . . . ahh . . . err . . . make that Placerville. Open daily April–Oct., 8:30 AM–5:30 PM. Admission: Adults $4, kids 7–16, $2. Audio tape for self-guided tour is $1, and well worth it. There is no charge for entrance into the park, parking, or use of the picnic areas and trails.

Kennedy Gold Mine, www.kennedygoldmine.com, 209-223-9542, P.O. Box 694, Jackson, CA. Kennedy Gold Mine is famous because it is one of the deepest mines, at nearly 6,000 feet. The mine itself has been closed since 1942, but a great deal of its rich history remains. It is said that in excess of $34 million in gold was extracted from the mine. Visitors will tour the stamp and gold recovery mills, the buildings where gold flakes were melted into large bricks for shipment, and the huge steel head frame, whose pulleys once guided miners into the bowels of the earth. The facility is open on weekends, March–Oct. Admission is $9 for adults, and $5 for kids 6–13.

Sutter Gold Mine, www.caverntours.com, 13660 Historic Highway 49, Sutter Creek, CA. Cinch up your hardhat (provided) and climb aboard the Boss Buggy Shuttle. This is no

A docent leads visitors on a guided tour of the Hangtown's Gold Bug Park & Mine near Placerville.

replica—this is a honest-to-goodness modern goldmine. The one-hour guided tour takes visitors more than 1,200 feet into the actual mine. Here visitors receive a comprehensive look at a modern goldmining operation. See the 15-yard haul truck and learn how to distinguish between real gold deposits and pyrite (fool's gold). Open daily, year round. Adults $15.95, kids (4–12) $10.50.

Historic State Parks
CALAVERAS BIG TREES
www.parks.ca.gov
209-795-2334
SR 4, Arnold, CA
Open: Daily, sunrise to sunset
Admission: $6 per vehicle

Talk about awesome—you can't help but feel humble among these leviathans. Guided and self-guided tours help navigate you through the splendor of the Big Trees. These massive relics soar 300 feet into the sky, and have bases as much as 33 feet in diameter. Some of the trees are believed to 2000 years old. There are many miles of trails with varying degrees of difficulty. The North Grove features a 1.5 mile, self-guided trail. The Three Senses Trail

LEFT: *A docent demonstrates the use of an audio stick which tells about the Gold Bug mine in four languages.*

allows you to experience the feel, smells, and sounds of this incredible forest. The largest trees—"Agassiz" and "Palace Hotel"—are located in the South Grove. The North Grove Campground has 74 campsites, and can accommodate tents and RVs up to 30 feet. All campsites have fire rings, picnic tables, piped water, flush toilets, and coin-operated showers.

COLUMBIA STATE HISTORIC PARK
www.parks.ca.gov
209-588-9128
11255 Jackson St., Columbia, CA
Open: Daily 10 AM–4 PM
Admission: Free

Take a step back in time to the 1850s. Columbia's business district has been preserved with shops, restaurants, and two hotels. Here you can watch store keeps in period clothing conduct business in the style of yesteryear. Take a ride on a 100 year-old stagecoach, or hire a "fine steed" for a horseback ride through the "diggins." Stop for a bit, have a picnic, and pan for a little gold. Free town tours are offered year-round on Saturday and Sunday at 11 AM; and every day at 11 AM, from July 5 through Labor Day. Many period-themed special programs are offered throughout the summer. You might enjoy joining the Bucket Brigade, where you'll get wet and learn about firefighting in the 1850s. Another favorite program that runs throughout the summer is History Mysteries. The whole family joins in to investigate, solve, and bring to trial an 1850s Columbia criminal.

A miner's cabin at Columbia State Historic Park.

A family picnic at Columbia State Historic Park.

EMPIRE MINE STATE HISTORIC PARK

www.parks.ca.gov
530-273-8522
10791 E. Empire St.
Grass Valley, CA
Hours: Daily 10 AM–5 PM
Admission: Adults $3, children $1

About 5.6 million ounces of gold was taken from Empire Mine, making it one of the state's richest mines. It's also among the oldest, largest, and deepest mines in the state. The mine was in continuous operation for more than 100 years until it closed in 1956. Today, visitors will see many of the building, the owner's house, restored gardens, and the entrance to the 367 miles of tunnels. All of the lower shafts are now flooded. At the visitor center, don't miss what was once housed in the "secret room"—this is a scale model of the mine and all its shafts, and was once used to keep track of all the underground activity taking place when the mine was still in operation. Guided tours and audiovisual presentations are offered at various times throughout the day. The park facility also contains eight miles of forested trails for hiking, horseback riding, and mountain biking.

INDIAN GRINDING ROCK STATE HISTORIC PARK

www.parks.ca.gov
209-296-7488
14881 Pine Grove-Volcano Rd., Pine Grove, CA.
Hours: Daily 11 AM–3 PM, Weekends, 10 AM–4 PM
Admission: $6 per vehicle

To find this park, take SR 88 east, from Jackson to Pine Grove, and turn left at Pine-Grove-Volcano Road. This site was once a major, if primitive, sort of food processing plant for Native Americans. The open meadows and large valley oaks provided an ample supply of acorns. The outcropping of marbleized limestone contain more than 1,100 mortar holes, the largest of bedrock mortars in North America. The Chaw'se Regional Indian Museum, designed to reflect the architecture of the traditional roundhouse, contains a beautiful collection of Sierra Nevada Indian artifacts, reflecting their technology and crafting ability. Several times a year, ceremonies are held by local Native Americans, including dancing, hand games, singing, and storytelling. The park also contains two self-guided nature trails.

MALAKOFF DIGGINS STATE HISTORIC PARK

530 265-2740
23579 North Bloomfield Road
Nevada City CA 95959
Open: Daily (hours vary depending on the season)
Admission: $6 per vehicle

From Nevada City take SR 49 east and turn right on Tyler Foote Road; follow signs to park. This 3,000-acre forested park is the scene of California's largest hydraulic goldmine. Here you can see huge cliffs carved by mighty streams of water that once washed away entire mountains. Ensuing legal battles between mine owners and downstream farmers led to the end of this practice. Also located in the park is a 7,800-foot bedrock tunnel that served as a drain. The visitor center houses exhibits on life in the nearby town of Humbug, later renamed North Bloomfield. The large park also offers miles of hiking, mountain biking, and horseback riding trails.

MARSHALL GOLD DISCOVERY STATE HISTORIC PARK

www.parks.ca.gov
530-622-3470
310 Back St., Coloma, CA
Open: 8 AM–sunset March–Labor Day; 10 AM–4:30 PM Sept.–Feb.
Admission: Parking $5; Museum, park entrance $2

No trip to the California Gold Country would be complete without a stop at the place where it all began. This is it—Ground Zero. James Marshall, the foreman of the lumber mill he was building for John Sutter, was inspecting a newly built tailrace on the morning of Jan. 24, 1848, when a glittering object in the water caught his eye. The rest is history. Today, visitors will find a full-scale replica of the sawmill, a museum filled with historical memorabilia, and a number of historic buildings including Marshall's cabin. A nice walk or short drive up CA 153—California's shortest state highway—brings you to an enormous statue of Marshall

An old handcar and other movie memorabilia are on display at Railtown 1897 State Historic Park near Jamestown.

pointing to the exact spot where he first found gold. His body is buried beneath the monument. The park itself includes most of the historic town of Coloma, plenty of hiking trails, picnic tables, a store and gift shop, and some good spots to try your hand a gold panning. The park is handicap friendly and—no kidding—Wi-Fi access is available near the museum.

RAILTOWN 1897 STATE HISTORIC PARK
www.csrmf.org/railtown
209-984-3953
Jamestown, CA
(three miles south of Sonora)
Hours: Daily 9:30 AM–4:30 PM April–Oct., 10 AM–3 PM Nov.–March
Admission: $2

This is a one-of-a-kind attraction, known as "The Movie Railroad" because Railtown owes its continued survival in part to the film industry. The historic locomotives and railroad cars are all beautifully restored, and have appeared in more than 200 films and TV shows. Still a popular Hollywood location site, Railtown 1897 has been called "the most photographed railroad in the world." *Petticoat Junction*, *The Wild Wild West*, *High Noon*, *The Virginian*, and *The Unforgiven* were all filmed here. More recently, movie crews produced the railroad sequences in *Back to the Future Part III* at Railtown. Home to the historic Sierra Railroad, visitors are welcome to check out the authentic roundhouse, climb aboard historic railroad cars, and learn about the railroad's history in the interpretive center. On weekends, for a nominal fee, climb aboard an authentic steam locomotive and ride through the Sierra foothills.

A docent discusses one of the many displays at Railtown.

Museums

AMADOR COUNTY MUSEUM
www.co.amador.ca.us
209-223-6386
225 Church St., Jackson, CA
Hours: Tues.–Sun., 10 AM–4 PM
Admission: Free

Overlooking downtown Jackson, the classic Greek Revival-style building was originally built in 1859 as a home for Armstead C. Brown, one of the community's settlers. The towering cedar trees that line the walkway leading to the entrance are believed to have been planted by Brown himself, after the house was completed. Visitors are welcome to wander about through the 15 rooms, where fascinating artifacts from the county's early days are on display. The museum collections include a gold history exhibit, fashions from the past, a sewing and quilt exhibit, a Chinese American collection, a re-created school room, a Victorian bedroom, and much more.

LEFT: *Authentic Gay Nineties attire worn by a docent at Railtown, CA.*

BERNHARD MUSEUM COMPLEX

www.placer.ca.gov
530-889-6500
101 Maple St., Auburn, CA
Hours: Tues.–Sun., 11 AM–4 PM
Admission: Free

A rich history surrounds the Bernhard Museum Complex. The house was originally built in 1851 as the Traveler's Rest Hotel, and is today one of Auburn's oldest surviving buildings. In the 1870s the house was sold to the Bernhard family, and Mr. Bernhard became a pioneer vintner. The two-story winery was built in 1874. The family and their descendants occupied the house for nearly 100 years. Today, the Victorian house, winery and other buildings contain tons of artifacts. Wine lovers will enjoy touring the wine processing building, where many artifacts pertaining to wine and barrel making are housed. The complex is also home to the Placer County Museum's Living History Program.

CALAVERAS COUNTY MUSEUM

www.calaverascohistorical.com/museum.html
209-754-3910
30 N. Main St., San Andreas, CA

Live fiddle music sets the authentic tone at Railtown.

Jackson has its own National Hotel. Will they leave the light on?

Hours: Daily 10 AM–4 PM
Admission: $3

Operated by the county historical society, the Calaveras County Museum complex includes displays of pioneer 19th-century life in the Mother Lode. Among the exhibits you will find the geology of the Gold Country, artifacts of the Miwok Indians, early mining artifacts, photographs, and the jail cell where Black Bart was held to await trial for stagecoach robbery.

EL DORADO COUNTY HISTORICAL MUSEUM

www.co.el-dorado.ca.us/museum
530-621-5865
104 Placerville Dr., Placerville, CA
Open: Wed.–Sun. 10 AM–4 PM
Admission: Free

Life in El Dorado County didn't start with the discovery of gold a few miles up the road in Coloma in 1848, though that event definitely changed everything. The museum features a great collection of baskets and tools made by the skilled artisans of the Maidu, Miwok, and Washoe Native American tribes, who lived in the region prior to its "discovery" by the rest of the world. And the growth and development of the region didn't end, once the Mother Lode was played out. Museum exhibits chronicle the Gold Rush era as well as those who eventually settled in the region and established ranches, vineyards, orchards, schools, churches, and commercial business. Old stagecoaches, farm wagons, and carriages depict transportation in the area before the automobile. This museum seeks to capture the big picture of the evolution of the region.

FOREST HILL DIVIDE MUSEUM
www.placer.ca.gov
530-367-3988
24601 Harrison St., Foresthill, CA
Hours: May–Oct., Weekends noon–4 PM
Admission: Free

The museum is located amid rugged river canyons that are especially rich in goldmining sites dating back to the time when gold was first discovered in the Sierra foothills. Some of the early mining communities included Yankee Jim's (1849), Todd's Valley (1849), Deadwood (1852), and Bird's Store (1849). The museum complex consists of the museum facility, a reconstructed Livery Stable/Blacksmith Shop, and the original Foresthill Jail, which was moved to the site. Over time, the town of Forest Hill became Foresthill, but the museum retains the area's original name.

GOLD COUNTRY MUSEUM
www.placer.ca.gov
530-889-6500
1273 High St., Auburn, CA
Hours: Tues.–Sun. 11 AM–4 PM
Admission: Free
Gold Panning: $2

This is an interpretive museum of Placer County's Gold Rush history. It is housed in the old Works Progress Administration (WPA) building. The tour begins inside a dark, repli-cated hardrock mining tunnel. Once out of the tunnel, you visit the stamp mill and assayer's office, where the raw ore was processed. Other exhibits include a miner's cabin and a mining camp saloon where a game of faro, a card game popular at the time, is in progress. Now, it's time to grab a pan and see it you can't locate a little color, panning for gold in the indoor stream. Don't want to pan for gold? Kick back and watch the video on Gold Rush history.

IMAGINARIUM OF NEVADA COUNTY
www.nevco.k12.ca.us/imaginar.htm
530-478-6415
112 Nevada City Hwy., Nevada City, CA

RIGHT: *A guide escorts tourists through a working stamp mill near Placerville.*

Hours: By appointment
Admission: Free

This is an interactive, hands-on science museum and includes 20 or more science exhibits. Guests will literally have a hair-raising experience in the Van De Graf Generator, shrink themselves in the Distortion Room, and play mind games at the Color Wall. The exhibits are designed for kids of all ages.

MINERS FOUNDRY CULTURAL CENTER
www.minersfoundry.org
530-265-5040
325 Spring St., Nevada City, CA
Open: Mon.–Fri. 10 AM–4 PM

The Foundry's museum displays a rich collection of photographs and artifacts, featuring the building's history from the time it was built in 1855 to serve the needs of the miners and other businesses through the Sierra foothills. Located in the heart of downtown, the Nevada City Miners Foundry retains the character of the Gold Rush days, with its rough-hewn beams, heavy metal doors, and antique fixtures and furnishings. The cultural center sponsors numerous private and public special events throughout the year.

NORTH STAR MINING MUSEUM
530-273-4255
End of Mill St. at Allison Ranch Rd., Grass Valley, CA
Open: Daily 10 AM–4 PM, May–Sept.
Admission: Donations

Designated as a Historical Landmark, the museum contains a large display of mining equipment and artifacts from the 1880s. Among the displays is the largest Pelton Wheel ever constructed, and used to generate power for the mine. Also on display is a Cornish pump and stamp mill. A really cool picnic area is located just over the bridge crossing Wolf Creek.

PLACER COUNTY COURTHOUSE MUSEUM
www.placer.ca.gov
530-889-6500
101 Maple St., Auburn, CA
Hours: Daily 10 AM–4 PM
Admission: Free

Located on the first floor of Auburn's Historic Courthouse, the building was completed in 1898. After nearly 100 years of use, the building's future came into question in the 1980s, but thanks to some civic-minded citizens, repairs were made and today it is open to the public. The Museum Gallery is located in the space that once housed the jail, and provides an overview of the county's history. Some of the highlights include a diorama depicting a Nisenan Indian family, the stagecoach that ran from Auburn to Michigan Bluff and a video on the history of the transcontinental highway system that runs through the county. Don't miss the tremendous collection of Native American art and the Auburn Centennial painting by renowned artist Thomas Kinkade.

Another don't-miss exhibit is the Placer County Gold Collection on permanent display inside the gift shop. Placer County purchased the largest pieces in 1921 for $3,500 to preserve samples of the raw material that drew people from around the world. Today, the collection contains nearly 200 troy ounces of gold, all from Placer County Soil. The collection was appraised in 1996 at $343,500 based on weight and historical relevance.

SIERRA COUNTY HISTORICAL PARK & MUSEUM
530-862-1310
SR 49, one mile east of Sierra City
Hours: Daily 8 AM to Sunset, May–Oct.
Admission: Free

Now a park, the facility is located on the site of the Kentucky Mine which is listed in the National Register of Historic Places. The park includes a great museum featuring documents, photographs and artifacts depicting the life and times of the early days of the county and the discovery of gold. Also on the grounds are a working stamp mill, mine tunnel, blacksmith shop, and trestle from the mine to the stamp mill.

A museum occupies the first floor of the Placer County Courthouse, built in 1894.

SIERRA NEVADA LOGGING MUSEUM
sierraloggingmuseum.org
209-795-6782
2148 Dunbar Road, White Pines, CA.
Hours: Daily 8 AM–sunset
Admission: Free

This is a locals' favorite for picnicking and family gatherings. The six-acre museum site includes logging and mining artifacts, kiosk, picnic tables and barbecues. Climb aboard the historic Shay locomotive. The museum and park are located on the shores of beautiful Pine Lake just a mile from Arnold on Dunbar Road.

UNDERGROUND GOLD MINERS MUSEUM
www.undergroundgold.com
530-287-3330
356 Main St., Alleghany, CA
Open: May–Oct. by appointment
Admission: $95 per person

Admission may seem rather pricey, but this is a full day emersion into underground mining. The tour begins in the museum where the history of the Sixteen to One mine is revealed. This mine has been in operation for more than 100 years and continues to produce quartz and gold. The actual excursion underground takes three to four hours. Special rates available for groups, nonprofits and children.

Music & Dance

Music in the Mountains, www.musicinthemountains.org 1-800-218-2188 or 530-265-6124, 530 Searls Ave., Nevada City, CA. Performs seasonal and holiday concerts at the Nevada County Fairgrounds. Specializing in a full spectrum of classical music including pops, jazz, big band and Broadway. Their shows have drawn rave reviews. They sell more than 12,000 tickets to more than 32 concerts and chamber concerts annually.

Saint Joseph's Cultural Center, www.saintjosephsculturalcenter.org, 530-272-4725, 410 S. Church St., Grass Valley, CA. Talk about diversity, one could easily spend a day just poking around all the venues that call the center home. Housed in a historic 1894 brick building, the center is devoted to cultural events, classes, and workshops. The center includes the Grass Valley Museum, John Olmstead's Earth Planet Museum, 13 artist's studios, an art gallery, and a dance studio. Outside, the historic Rose Garden contains statues, a fountain, more than 100 rosebushes, holly, crape myrtle, and cedar trees.

The Center for the Arts, www.thecenterforthearts.org, 530-271-7000, 314 W. Main St., Grass Valley, CA. Great performing arts venue. This is the jewel of the Sierra foothills for catching great concerts, dance performances and theatrical productions. The Main Stage Theater seats more than 300 people, while the Off Center Stage facility is perfect for performances for 50 to 100 people. The Main Gallery is an aesthetically pleasing facility featuring shows by local, regional, and international artists.

The Movement Alliance, www.themovementalliance.org, 530-277-2046. The Movement is a non-profit, modern dance company, dedicated to authentic American dance form.

Twin Cities Concert Association, www.tcca.net, 530-470-9454, P.O. Box 205 Nevada City, CA. The TCCA has brought excellent chamber music and concerts to the area for more than 60 years. They specialize on performing in intimate settings and conducting "meet the artist" forums.

Nightlife

Chief Crazy Horse Inn Saloon & Grill, www.chiefcrazyhorseinn.com, 530-470-8443, 230 Commercial St., Nevada City, CA. Live music almost every night makes this saloon one of the most popular watering holes in Nevada City. Musical styles vary broadly including classic rock, bluegrass, R&B, and surf music. Good food hot off the grill, and margaritas are among the top attractions. Now, about that name . . .

Coloma Club, www.colomaclub.com, 530-626-6390, intersection of CA 49 and Marshall Road, Coloma, CA. Restaurant and saloon are open seven days a week. Rustic atmosphere and friendly people make the club a cool stop after a day exploring Sutter's Mill. On Friday and Saturday nights belt out your favorite tune at the karaoke bar.

Historic Iron Door Saloon, www.iron-door-saloon.com, 209-962-8904, 18763 Main St., Groveland, CA. Among the oldest taverns in California, the Iron Door is family-friendly, serves food, and has live music every weekend of the year. Nice collection of historic photos and mining artifacts. And, yes, the front door *is* made of iron.

Main Event, 209-223-5775, 105 Main St., Jackson, CA. There are always different events going on at Main Event. Full bar and dining in a relaxed, casual atmosphere. Great place to catch your favorite sporting event via satellite TV.

Old Corner Saloon, www.oldcorner.com, 209-785-3311, 574 Main St., Copperopolis CA. Plenty of friendly company any night of the week and you never know what's on tap for entertainment. Karaoke anyone? The Old Corner Saloon is a favorite stop for area locals.

The Coloma Club is a popular eatery and meeting spot for locals and tourists alike.

Sutter Creek Palace, 209-267-1300, 76 Main St, Sutter Creek, CA. Despite many changes in its more than 100-year history, the Palace is a favorite for locals and tourists alike. The oak floors are complemented by historic stained-glass windows. The wall of historical photos is worth checking out. On weekends, the Palace turns into a piano bar and everybody has a good time.

The Old Stan, 536-9598, 177 South Washington St., Sonora, CA. Great fun in a casual environment, The Old Stan is family friendly. They specialize in locally made beer and wine. On Friday and Saturday nights, they also specialize in bringing local musicians to the stage.

The Rock of Twain Harte Pub & Restaurant, www.therockofth.com, 209-586-2080, 23068 Fuller Rd., Twain Harte, CA. Cozy, mountain lodge atmosphere makes The Rock a great place to kick back by the fireplace on a cold winter night. Shoot pool and toss darts upstairs, and when the weather warms up a bit, step outside and try your hand at horseshoes.

Theater

Black Bart Players, www.murphysblackbartplayers.com, 209-728-8842, 580 S Algiers St., Murphys CA. This is fun entertainment for the whole family. Quality productions that are exciting, thought-provoking, and innovative. The players excel at farce, comedy, and melodrama. Latest addition to the venue are the Black Bart Improvisers. The theater also hosts community events throughout the year.

Community Asian Theatre of the Sierra "CATS", www.catsweb.org 530-273-6362, 228 Commercial St., No. 88, Nevada City, CA. A staple for culture hounds in the Sierra. Throughout the year, CATS puts on plays, workshops, and special events focusing on cultural diversity.

Off Broadstreet, www.offbroadstreet.com, 530-265-8686, 305 Commercial St., Nevada City, CA. The neon lights may shine on Broadway, but an evening with Off Broadstreet is a fun adventure into the world of theater. The group produces only comedies—mostly musicals featuring hit songs from the 1950s and 60s. Intimate cabaret seating and a modestly priced selection of refreshments adds to the festivities.

Old Coloma Theatre, www.oldecolomatheatre.com, 530-626-5282, 380 Monument Rd., Coloma, CA. The theater is operated by the Coloma Crescent Players and their goal is to promote amateur performing arts in a traditional melodrama form, in a community, family theater atmosphere, and to encourage new talent in all aspects of the theater arts. Most performances are written, produced, directed, and performed by local talent. Doors open every Friday and Saturday night, and general admission is $10.

Millerosa's STAR for a Day, www.millerosa.com, 209-736-4758, 4625 Camp Nine, Vallecito. You'll never guess whose starring in this cowboy classic. That's right, you are! Rob a bank, save the distressed damsel, you are the star in your own "oater" classic. Millerosa provides great costumes, easy scripts, beautiful sets, and a heap of fun. Bring your friends, family, and the pets, too. Spend a day having fun as a cowboy actor, and take home a DVD of your excellent adventure. And if you're lookin' to get hitched, they'll even provide the minister.

Murphys Creek Theatre, www.murphyscreektheatre.org, P.O. Box 603, Murphys, CA. A must-do event is to catch the company's Theatre Under the Stars outdoor summer theater festival held at Cornelia B. Stevenot Performing Arts Center at Stevenot Winery. The beautiful amphitheater seats about 250 people and is renowned for its excellent acoustics. Their season runs from June through September.

Stage 3 Theatre Company, www.stage3.org, 209-536-1778, 208 S. Green St., Sonora, CA. Stage 3 bills itself as "the adventurous theatre company," striving to bring contemporary theater to the growing Sierra foothills audience. Productions include regional premiers of area playwrights as well works by established artists. The company annual Festival of New Plays attracts submissions from all over the world. The theater building has an intimate atmosphere and seats about 80 people.

Sutter Creek Theatre, www.suttercreektheater.com, 1-866-463-8659, 44 Main St., Sutter Creek, CA. This is the place to be in Sutter Creek for music, theater, films and special events. The theater is privately owned and operated by Laura and Byron Damiani Jr. who strive to offer quality and diverse productions. The venue comfortably seats 216 people, and is renowned for its excellent acoustics and intimate seating. The theater also supports local non-profit fund raising events for the Amador County Arts Council, Amador High School Drama Club, Sutter Creek Elementary School, Operation CARE, and many others. Originally four silent movie houses were built in the area during the 1920s. Information was lost on the exact location of the theater in Plymouth. The theater in Ione was torn down to make way for a parking lot in the 1970s, and fire destroyed the Ratto Theater building in Jackson on October 14, 1998. The SCT is the only remaining original former silent-movie house in the region—a real tribute to its 90-year history.

The Foothill Theatre Company, www.foothilltheatre.org, 530-265-9320, 401 Broad St., Nevada City, CA. For more than 30 years The Foothill Theatre Company has dazzled audiences with top-quality productions. Produces a full range of plays from classic to contemporary, originals and old favorites, comedies and dramas.

Volcano Theatre Company, www.volcanotheatre.org, 209-296-2525, P.O. Box 288, Volcano, CA. Enticing theater in a quaint, historic, cobblestone building is what's on tap when the curtain goes up at the Volcano Theatre Company. The company stages a wide variety of productions, from those scripted by local writers to favorite classics, and has won several awards. In addition to productions in the theater, summertime plays are held under the stars in the nearby amphitheater.

SEASONAL EVENTS

JANUARY

El Dorado Art & Wine Festival, www.morerehab.org, 530-622-4848, Placerville.

Gold Discovery Day, www.marshallgold.org. 530-295-2170, Coloma.

Sierra Writers Speaker Series, www.sierrawriters.org, 530-265-2982, Nevada City.

Wild & Scenic Environmental Film Festival, wildandscenicfilmfestival.org, 530-265-5961, Nevada City.

FEBRUARY

Arts & Wine Extravaganza, 209-532-6218, Sonora.

Behind the Cellar Door, www.amadorwine.com, 1-888-655-8614, Amador County.

Fireman's Ball, 209-532-7890, Sonora.

Code of the West Gun Show, 530-676-8762, Placerville.

Gala for Sierra Repertory Theatre, 209-532-3120, Sonora.

Mardi Gras, 530-265-2692, Nevada City.

Snowshoeing in the Sierra, 530-621-1224, Placerville.

Valentine Erotique, 530-265-8141, Nevada City.

MARCH

1850's Snow Ball, 530-644-3761, Pollock Pines.

Celtic Faire, www.calaverascelticfaire.com, 209-532-8375, Sonora.

Columbia Day Celebration, www.columbiacalifornia.com, 209-536-1672, Columbia.

"Humanity" Exhibition, www.neighborhoodcenterofthearts.com, 530-272-7287, Grass Valley.

Gather the Women, www.gatherthewomen.org, 530-477-7883, Nevada City.

Gem & Jewelry Show, 209-928-5579, Angels Camp.

Murphys Irish Day and Parade, murphysirishdays.org, Murphys.

Northern Sierra Winter Wine & Food Fest, www.northernsierrawinecountry.com, 1-866-355-9463, Grass Valley.

St. Piran's Day Festival, 530-272-8315, Grass Valley.

APRIL

Calaveras Follies, 209-736-6078 (Frogtown) Angels Camp.

Columbia State Historic Park Annual Wine Tasting, 209-588-5115, Columbia.

Earth Day Celebration, 530-620-4364, Placerville.

Georgetown Annual Easter Egg Hunt, 530-333-4000, Georgetown.

Grass Valley Car Show, 530-272-8315, Grass Valley.

Logging Modelers Convention, www.westsidereunion.com, 559-683-7764, Sonora.

Music in the Mountains Spring Fest, www.musicinthemountains.org, 530-265-6173, Nevada City.

New Morning Jamboree, 530-621-1130, Placerville.

Sonora Smokepolers Spring Rendezvous, 209-588-91190 or 209-878-0132, Chinese Camp.

Sonora Spring Festival Sonora, www.sonoraca.com, 209-532-7725, Sonora.

Spring Fishing Derby and Casting Contest, 530-642-5232, Placerville.

Teddy Bear Convention, www.teddybearcastle.com, 530-265-5804, Nevada City.

MAY

Calaveras County Fair and Jumping Frog Jubilee!, www.frogtown.org, 209-736-2561, Angels Camp.

California Cultural Days, 530-363-3257, Coloma.

Community Art Show, www.nevadacity chamber.com, 530-265-8141, Nevada City.

Garden Tour "Springtime in the Foothills", 530-344-1981, Placerville.

Hangtown Classic Car Show, 530-622-1731, Placerville.

Mother Lode Round-Up Parade & Rodeo, 209-928-9318, www.motherloderoundup.com, Sonora.

Museum Discovery Day, 1-800-655-4667, Grass Valley.

Old West Antique Show, 530-272-3243, Grass Valley.

Open Greenhouse & Plant Sale, www.omaricaranch.com, 530-274-9059, Grass Valley.

Penn Valley Rodeo, www.pennvalley rodeo.com, Penn Valley.

Pioneer Art Show, 530-274-8807, Grass Valley.

Banners celebrate the jumping frogs of Calaveras County.

JUNE

American River Festival, www.americanriverfestival.org, 530-626-6882, Placerville.

El Dorado County Fair, www.eldoradocountyfair.org, 530-621-5860, Placerville.

Fair Play Wine Festival, www.fairplaywine.com, Fair Play.

Father's Day Bluegrass Festival, 530-265-9073, Grass Valley.

Father's Day Fly In, www.columbiagazette.com/flyin.html, 209-533-5685, Columbia.

Nevada City Bicycle Classic, 530-265-2692, Nevada City.

Mother Lode Fair, www.motherlodefair.org, 209-532-7428, Sonora.

Music in the Mountains Summer Fest, www.musicinthemountains.org, 530-265-6173, Nevada City.

North Columbia Bluegrass Hootenanny, 530-265-8141, Nevada City.

Placerville Founder's Day & Annual Wagon Train, 530-672-3436, Placerville.

Rattlesnake & Roadkill Cook-off, 530-333-2167, Georgetown.

Secession Days Celebration, www.roughandreadychamber.com, 530-272-4320, Rough & Ready.

Wine Tasting-A Grape Affair, www.northernsierrawinecountry.com, 1-866-355-9463, Nevada County.

JULY

4th of July Parade and Celebration, 530-272-8315, Nevada City.

4th of July Celebration, 530-265-2692, Grass Valley.

4th of July Family Blast, www.eldoradocountyfair.org, 530-621-5860, Placerville.

4th of July Parade & Kids Fair, 530-644-6713, Pollock Pines.

4th of July Glorious Celebration, www.columbiacalifornia.com, 209-536-1672, Columbia.

Annual 49er Day, www.roaringcampgold.com, 209 296-4100, Pine Grove.

Arts & Wine Festival, www.fireonthemountain.com, 209-533-3473, Twain Harte.

Bear Valley Music Festival, 1-800-458-1618, Bear Valley.

Big Bad Bulls & Wild West Show, www.nevadacountyhorsemen.org 530-268-8785, Grass Valley.

Jazz Camp, www.sierrajazzsociety.com, 530-273-5489, Nevada City.

Jeepers Jamboree, www.jeepersjamboree.com, 530-333-4771, El Dorado County.

Red Hot Summer Dance Party, 530-889-1629, Pilot Hill.

Sierra Nevada Folk Art Festival, 925-372-8961, Angels Camp.

Sierra Storytelling Festival, www.sierrastorytellingfestival.org, 530-265-8141, Nevada City.

Summer Nights Celebration, 530-265-2692, Nevada City.

AUGUST

Blues Festival, www.fireonthemountain.com, 209-533-3473, Sonora.

Hangtown Destruction Derby, www.hangtowncops.org, 530-642-5210, Placerville.

Hot August Night Car Show & BBQ, 530-677-1868, Placerville.

Mine Yard Living History Days, www.empiremine.org, 530-273-8522, Empire Mine State Historic Park. Grass Valley.

The Walk of Fame in downtown Angels Camp honors past Jumping Frog Jubilee contest winners.

Motherlode National Art Expo, www.placervillearts.com, 530-626-3862, Placerville.

Nevada County Fair, www.nevadacountyfair.com, 530-273-6217, Grass Valley.

Sierra Art AfFaire, 530-344-0452, Placerville.

Sierra Blues and Brewfest, www.nevadacountyfair.com, 530-265-6124, Grass Valley.

Sierra Shakespeare Festival, www.foothilltheatre.org, 1-800-730-8587, Grass Valley.

SEPTEMBER
Americas Day for Kids, www.bgce.org, 530-295-8019, Placerville.

American River Music Festival,www.americanrivermusicfestival.org, Coloma-Lotus Valley.

Butterfly Concert Celebration, www.marblevalleycenter.org, 530-642-2431, Placerville.

Constitution Parade & Celebration, 530-265-2692, Nevada City.

Draft Horse Classic, 530-273-6217, Nevada County Fairgrounds, Grass Valley.

Foothill Farmlands Arts Festival, www.foothillfarmlandsartsfestival.org, 209-532-2787, various locations

Georgetown Divide Founders Day, 530-333-0402, Georgetown.

Gold Country Duck Race, 530-272-DUCK, Nevada City.

Gold Harvest Wine Trail, www.northernsierrawinecountry.com, 1-866-355-9463, Nevada County.

Horseback Ride-a-Thon, www.rideandshine.net, 530-676-1920, Placerville.

Me-Wuk Indian Acorn Festival, 209-928-3475, Tuolumne City.

Poison Oak Show, 209-533-4656, Columbia.

Railroad Days, 530-346-8888, Colfax.

Tomato Tasting & Workshops, 530-273-0919, Grass Valley.

OCTOBER
Apple Hill® season, www.applehill.com, 530-644-7692, Apple Hill.

Autumn Shindig, 530-265-8141, Nevada City.

Calaveras Grape Stomp and Gold Rush Street Faire, www.calaveraswines.org, 209-728-9467, Murphys.

Coloma Gold Rush Live, 530-295-2170, Coloma.

Downtown Placerville Spooktacular, 530-642-5232, Placerville.

Fiddle & Bango Contest, www.columbiacalifornia.com, 209-536-1672, Columbia.

Hangtown' Hold'em Poker Tournament, www.eldoradocounty.org, 530-621-5885, Placerville.

Hangtown Jazz Jubilee, www.hangtownjazz.com, 530-622-8186, Placerville.

OktoberFest Twain Harte, 209-586-4482, Twain Harte.

Rock & Gem Show, www.rockandgemshow.org, 530-676-2472, Placerville.

Run Through The Colors, 530-265-2666, Nevada City.

Salmon Tours, www.yubariver.org, 530-265-5961, Yuba River.

NOVEMBER
Apple Hill Harvest Run, www.applehillrun.org, 530-644-4552, Apple Hill.

Christmas Craft & Music Festival, www.fireonthemountain.com, 209-533-3473, Sonora.

Community Photography Exhibit, 530-265-8141, Nevada City.

Empty Bowls Supper, 530-642-1120, Placerville.

Music in the Mountains Fall Fest, www.musicinthemountains.org 530-265-6173, Nevada City.

DECEMBER
Bed & Breakfast Candlelight Tour, www.goldcountryinns.net, 530-477-6634, 1-800-250-5808, Nevada County.

Christmas in Coloma, www.marshallgold.org, 530-295-2162, Coloma.

Christmas Parade, 530-626-3849, Placerville.

Copper Run, 209-785-2236 or 209-785-2393, Copperopolis.

Cornish Christmas, www.downtowngrassvalley.com, 530-272-8315, Grass Valley.

Music in the Mountains Holiday Special, www.musicinthemountains.org, 530-265-6173, Nevada City.

Restaurants

Gold Country legend has it that one day a miner, who had just struck it rich, walked into a Hangtown (Placerville today) restaurant and asked the proprietor—also the cook—what the three most expensive items on the menu were. When informed they were eggs, bacon, and oysters, the miner bellowed, "Well, fry 'em up!", and the Hangtown Fry was born. A number of Gold Country eateries proudly serve this tantalizing concoction.

Now, if you're not in the mood for a Hangtown Fry, fear not. Dining in the Gold Country is as diverse as the culture itself. From new-wave vegetarian specialties to down-home barbecue steak and taters, you won't have to look too far to find exactly what your taste buds demand. Just make sure that if a waiter asks, "Want fries with that?" you know exactly what they mean.

Dining Price Code

The price range below is for a single dinner that includes an entrée, appetizer, or dessert. Tax and gratuities are not included.

Inexpensive Up to $15
Moderate $15–$30
Expensive $30–$50
Very Expensive $50 or more

Angels Camp

CAMPS RESTAURANT

www.greenhorncreek.com
209-729-8181
711 McCauley Ranch Rd., Angels Camp, CA
Open: Wed.–Sun. 11:30 AM–9 PM
Price: Moderate
Cuisine: American
Serving: L, D
Reservations: Recommended
Credit cards: AE, D, MC, V

Enjoy the view of Greenhorn Creek Golf Club (and the duffers hacking it up) from your table inside Camps Restaurant. Lots of windows create an open and airy ambiance, in a country club atmosphere. The adjacent Bistro Bar is an excellent choice for your favorite cocktail or glass of wine before your lunch or dinner. Should find yourself comfortable in the bar enjoying a game on TV, no problem—the bar has a dining menu of its own. The dinner menu at Champs runs the full gamut, from starters, soups, and salads, to complete entrées. A good way to get the meal going might be to start with their beef carpaccio, thin slices of raw filet drizzled with olive oil and lemon pepper sauce. In addition to their famous steaks, lamb, and seafood, Champs lets you build your own pasta creation. Start with bow-tie pasta and add the sauce of your choice plus other goodies, such as mushrooms, capers, bell peppers, and even shrimp, chicken, or fresh salmon. Live music on Friday and Saturday night really gets the joint jumpin'.

Arnold

SNOWSHOE BREWING COMPANY

www.snowshoebrewing.com
209-795-2272
2050 Highway 4, Arnold, CA
Open: Daily 11:30 AM–9 PM
Price: Moderate
Cuisine: American Fresh
Serving: L, D
Reservations: No
Credit cards: AE, D, MC, V

Lots of brick and an elegant wood bar give this brewpub a friendly atmosphere for catching a game with friends, or dining out with the entire family. The menu is a showcase of mass appeal and creativity. How about prime-rib nachos for an appetizer? Other appetizers include Buffalo wings, potato skins, and calamari strips. Burgers, Mexican grill specialties, and unique pizzas top the dinner menu. Let your culinary imagination run wild, building a pizza from their list of over 15 toppings. But, wait a minute. This is a brewpub—what about the beer? No disappointment here. The five main beers include Snoweizen Wheat Ale, Apricot Wheat Ale, Thompson Pale Ale, E.S.B. (Extra Special Blizzard), and Grizzly Brown Ale. They also feature a number of specialty and seasonal offerings.

TALLAHAN'S CAFÉ

www.tallahans.com
209-795-4005
1225 Oak Circle, Arnold, CA
Open: Fri.–Tues. 6 AM–9 PM
Price: Inexpensive to moderate
Cuisine: American Contemporary
Serving: B, L, D
Reservations: No
Credit cards: AE, D, MC, V

Tallahan's is about eating and drinking well, and having fun. Fun that is as long as you follow the rules: No kicking or spitting; no dancing without a partner; no throwing food at your children; *always* smile; have a good time; tip your server well; and call your Mom. The rules pretty much sum up the spirit and atmosphere at Tallahan's. Dine inside or, when the weather is right, relax on their spacious deck outside. For breakfast and lunch, the menu is pretty much standard café fare with a few tasty twists. But, when it's time for dinner, proprietors Karen Smith and Tony Fabbro have a few specials that deserve close attention. How about a shrimp cocktail fresca for an appetizer? This is created with bay shrimp, onion, garlic, fresh tomato, cilantro, and guacamole. Or try the grilled polenta, topped with shiitake, button and portobello mushrooms, with creamy gorgonzola sauce. Now for an entrée, locals rave about the risotto with prawns. This is made with Italian sausage, onions, mushrooms, and red bell pepper, in a roasted tomato pesto sauce with Parmesan cheese. Not feeling exotic? The menu is filled with burgers, sandwiches and vegetarian pastas. The wine list is very impressive and features an extensive number of offerings from Calaveras County.

Auburn

LATITUDES

www.latitudesrestaurant.com
530-885-9535
130 Maple St., Auburn, CA
Open: Wed.–Sun. 11:30 AM–10 PM

Early California-themed murals adorn many building walls in downtown Auburn.

Price: Moderate to Expensive
Cuisine: International
Serving: L, D
Reservations: Recommended
Credit cards: AE, D, MC, V

A remodeled, 1880s-era Victorian house situated in the heart of historic downtown Auburn provides a beautiful setting for Latitudes Restaurant, Gallery and Bar-Café. The establishment is the creation of Pat and Pete Enochs, who strive to bring a healthful, international flavor and culinary diversity to the Sierra foothills. In addition to their standard menu, they offer country-themed specials each month. Dinner entrées include such items as German-style cider chicken, East Indian curried tofu, teriyaki tempeh, and fettuccine alfredo just to name a few. Every Sunday, a sumptuous brunch is served most of the day, featuring Spanish and Greek omelets, scrambled tofu offerings, and crêpes. Enjoy a cocktail and an appetizer in the quaint bar located in the basement. Be sure spend a little time in the galleries, where the works of local artists are on display.

MONKEY CAT RESTAURANT

www.monkeycat.com
530-888-8492
805 Lincoln Way, Auburn, CA
Open: Daily 11:30 AM–9:30 PM
Price: Moderate
Cuisine: International
Serving: L, D
Reservations: No
Credit cards: AE, D, MC, V

Monkey Cat brings a unique dining experience to the Sierra foothills. A little taste of the islands awaits you in the Palapa Bar, where special house concoctions are served under the palm-frond roof supported by rustic tree pillars and *vigas*. Sip a Lemon Drop Martini, enjoy some Monkey Cat Crab Cakes, even get some work done plugging into the Wi-Fi Internet access. The bar area is even dog friendly. When it's time for a full meal, the tastefully decorated restaurant—with wood floors, white tablecloths, and friendly staff—is the place to be. Monkey Cat offers both a lunch and dinner menu. Entrées on the dinner menu range from several pasta dishes—including the Vegetable Wellington—to a chicken Cordon Bleu and veal scallopini. The wine list deserves special attention. A large selection of local wines from Sierra foothill vintners is always available, as are wines from many growing areas in California, but don't overlook the selections from France, Italy, South Africa, Australia, and New Zealand.

PASQUALE T'S

www.pasqualets.com
530-888-8440
905 Lincoln Way, Auburn, CA
Open: Daily 11:30 AM–9 PM
Price: Inexpensive
Cuisine: Italian
Serving: L, D
Reservations: No
Credit cards: AE, D, MC, V

Good Italian food, lots of it, and at affordable prices is the hallmark of Pasquale T's, in historic downtown Auburn. On a warm evening, dine out on the patio overlooking the intersection of Lincoln Way and High Street. Pasquale uses authentic Italian recipes and prepares his own sauces and pasta. The dinner menu is massive, offering everything from create-your-own pizzas and calzones, to veal piccata, several variations of fettuccini, lasagna, and linguine. Not in the mood for Italian? No problem; order a juicy filet mignon or the Fisherman's Wharf seafood platter. As if the menu wasn't already large enough, on the weekends Pasquale offers special dishes like tortellini gorgonzola with grilled chicken. Order your favorite beverage from the wine and beer bar. Enjoy.

Colfax

DROOLING DOG BAR B Q
www.droolingdogbarbq.com
1-888-33-1BONE or 530-346-8883
212 N. Canyon Way, Colfax, CA
Open: 11 AM–8 PM, Thur.–Sun.
Price: Inexpensive to Moderate
Cuisine: American Barbecue
Serving: L, D
Reservations: No
Credit cards: MC, V

Hungry for some good barbecue? This is the place: a nothing frilly, good old-fashioned rib joint. Drooling Dog is housed in a wood-framed, country-style building and located a bit off the beaten path, but it's worth the effort to find it. Dine inside, or sit out on the heated patio and chow down on some real Southwest barbecue served up by Linda and Doug Mason. The menu is pretty straightforward: barbecue ribs, chicken, tri-tip (beef), brisket, and pulled pork. Order size (and price) depends on how hungry you are. Also, a bowl of "Duwango Duwayne's" chili made with tri-tip, black beans, and chipotle makes a tasty addition to your meal. Sip on a cold brew from Eel River Brewing Company, or have a glass of Nevada City wine. The Dog also keeps a large supply of sodas, iced teas, and lemonade. For barbecue fans, this sure is some good eatin'.

Grass Valley

KAIDO JAPANESE RESTAURANT
www.kaidosushi.com
530-274-0144
207 W. Main St., Grass Valley, CA
Open: Tues.–Sat. 5–9 PM
Price: Moderate
Cuisine: Japanese
Serving: D
Reservations: No
Credit cards: MC, V

Dinner and a movie? How about an authentic Japanese dinner and a Japanese movie? That's what's on the menu nightly at Kaido, a quaint and clean restaurant in downtown Grass Valley. Locals may rave about the sushi, but a full line of entrées is offered. Another favorite are the sashimi dishes. These are raw, thinly sliced foods served with a dipping sauce and simple garnishes. Usually sashimi dishes are prepared with fish or shellfish, but they can be made from almost anything, including beef, or chicken. Kaido also offers and wide variety of cooked entrées including shrimp tempura, chicken teriyaki, salmon shioyaki, and spicy sesame chicken. Wine, Japanese plum wine, Japanese beer, and hot sake quench your thirst; and how about some green tea ice cream for dessert? A different movie is shown each week, and they are shown in the original Japanese with English translations. Many of the films are vintage classics from the 1930s and 40s.

SWISS HOUSE
www.swisschef.com
530-273-8272
535 Mill St., Grass Valley, CA
Open: Wed.–Sun. 5–9 PM
Price: Moderate to Expensive
Cuisine: Swiss German
Serving: D
Reservations: Yes
Credit cards: AE, D, MC, V

Well-traveled and classically trained in Europe, Chef Karl prepares some incredible meals from scratch, using the freshest and finest of ingredients. The ambiance is casual and the restaurant is decorated in Swiss-German tradition. For the past 18 years Karl has refined some of his finest dishes, including Swiss bratwurst, rahmschnitzel—a Swiss tradition—and beef bourguignonne. More traditional entrées are also served, including steaks, chops, and prawns. The wine list is extensive, so be sure to give yourself some extra time to look it over. Karl says the two Swiss wine offerings pair well with every entrée. Chef Karl also makes all the desserts—so be sure and save some room for the iced lemon soufflé, chocolate mousse, or the apple strudel with custard sauce. *Proscht*!

VILLA VENEZIA
www.villavenezia.info
530-273-3555
124 Bank St., Grass Valley, CA
Open: Daily 11:30 AM—8:30 PM
Price: Moderate
Cuisine: Italian
Serving: L, D
Reservations: Recommended
Credit cards: AE, D, MC, V

Located in the historic section of downtown Grass Valley, Villa Venezia brings the taste, ambiance, and flavor of old Roma to the Gold Country. This is a great spot to bring the entire family or for a romantic dining experience. The meals are all prepared from scratch using the freshest ingredients. The extensive wine cellar features quality selections from many of the local vineyards. For a real treat, set aside Tuesday night and enjoy the classic seafood cioppino. This is an old country favorite that includes lobster, mussels, clams, scallops, and white fish in a tomato, white wine, garlic, and olive oil broth. While all your favorite Italian dishes are available, some of their specialties include lamb shank braised in Chianti; gnocchi with prosciutto and cream sauce; chicken with Marsala sauce; homemade cannelloni; penne with fresh tomatoes and eggplant; and roasted pork loin with fresh herbs.

Murphys
MINERAL
www.mineralrestaurant.com
209-728-9743
419 Main St., Murphys, CA
Open: Wed.—Sun. 1—9 PM
Price: Very Expensive
Cuisine: Vegetarian
Serving: L, D
Reservations: Yes
Credit cards: AE, D, MC, V

Mineral is the type of restaurant one would expect to find in downtown San Francisco. It's small, nicely appointed, and exclusively vegetarian. Taste, texture, and style are the three elements Chef Steve Rinauro brings to his cuisine. Trained in San Francisco and Los Angeles, he creates flavors from many cultures including Indian, Mexican, and Asian, utilizing a primarily French technique in his preparation. All dishes are prepared using fresh and organic ingredients. The wine list is limited by design. Each offering is intended to blend with the meal. The menu changes often, and dinners are served in three-, five-, and seven-course offerings.

Nevada City
CITRONÉE BISTRO AND WINE BAR
www.citroneebistro.com
530-265-5697
320 Broad St., Nevada City, CA
Open: 5:30 PM to closing. Closed Tuesdays
Price: Moderate to Expensive
Cuisine: French
Serving: D
Reservations: No
Credit cards: AE, MC, V

French-country cuisine, world-class wines, and an elegant atmosphere are what Citronée brings to your table. Recommended by *The New York Times*, the *Los Angeles Times*, and *Sunset* magazine, Citronée has also won numerous honors including The Award of Excellence from *Wine Spectator* magazine. Classically trained Chef Robert Perez and his wife Marianna are dedicated to both presentation and preparation to assure guests a wonderful dining experience. Casual, café-style dining is offered in the front dining area, but for a more elegant experience, step into the brick-walled back room. The menu is seasonal, and designed around sustainable resources, utilizing the many organic farms in the area. The restaurant offers a tapas/grazing menu, and a full dinner menu. Featured smaller plates include the Catalan flatbread with roasted peppers, caramelized onions, anchovies and manchego cheese; and the bruschetta with herbed goat cheese, marmalade onions, and roasted garlic. From the dinner menu, one might enjoy free-range chicken breast stuffed with herbed ricotta on a bed of garlic mashed potatoes with natural pan juices; or maybe braised rabbit with cognac, orange, and dried prunes, with creamy papardelle. Of course, their wine list is extensive, featuring local varieties and selections of California and around the world. Be sure to stop by the wine shop.

SOPA THAI CUISINE
www.sopathai.com
530-470-0101
312-316 Commercial St., Nevada City, CA
Open: 11 AM–9:30 PM
Price: Moderate
Cuisine: Thai
Serving: L, D
Reservations: Suggested
Credit cards: AC, D, MC, V

Genuine Thai cuisine in the heart of the gold country is what Sopawon "Soupy" Savedra is serving daily in Nevada City. Sopa is an award winner having been written up in *Sunset* magazine and other travel publications. Her menu features more than 60 entrées, all made from traditional Thai ingredients, so there is something to please every palate. Variety and sharing are traditional values in Thai culture, and Soupy recommends dishes be shared, allowing everyone to experience the breadth of flavors that Thai cuisine offers. Among the appetizers and soups are steamed mussels,

crab rolls, spicy wings, and a Thai version of won ton soup. While the menu is extensive, which can make entrée selections difficult, a good bet is to opt for one of the house specialties, like the gai yang, barbecued chicken Thai style, or the pad talay—sautéed mixed seafood bathed in homemade spicy sauce. Other specialties include ho mok, a red curry paste mixed with coconut milk and served with a combination of seafood and vegetables; and the pai pae sa, a steamed whole fish flavored with plum sauce, topped with ginger, parsley, and steamed vegetables. For dessert, give the fried banana a try. This is a banana wrapped in rice paper, fried, and topped with honey, sesame seeds, or caramel.

SOUTH PINE CAFÉ
www.southpinecafe.com
530-274-0261
110 S. Pine Street, Nevada City, CA
102 N. Richardson St., Grass Valley, CA
Open: Mon.–Sun. 8 AM–3 PM
Price: Inexpensive
Cuisine: American
Serving: B, L
Reservations: No
Credit cards: MC, V

Breakfast and lunch to please all tastes is the goal at the South Pine Café. If you are a biscuit and gravy connoisseur or a devout vegan, there's something (probably many items) on the menu for you. At either location, you will find a comfortable, Southwestern design restaurant. Breakfast entrées range from lobster Benedict, spicy Jamaican tofu scramble, and the South Pine Sampler, featuring Louisiana hot sausage. Be sure to check out the omelets, tofu scrambles, and pancake offerings. Lunch offerings are equally creative. The lobster tacos, Thai chicken burrito, and vegan BLT with avocado are popular with the locals. For dessert, don't miss the "8,000 calorie rippin' South Pine cheesecake," featuring traditional cheesecake with a layer of chocolate cheesecake topped with a bitter-sweet chocolate shell. Order just one and several forks to share with friends? Naw, go for it. Eclectic menu of local beers and wines as well.

Placerville

COZMIC CAFÉ

www.thecozmiccafe.com
530-642-8481
594 Main St., Placerville, CA
Open: Daily 7 AM–8 PM
Price: Inexpensive
Cuisine: American vegetarian
Serving: B, L, D
Reservations: No
Credit cards: MC, V

Great food served in the ambiance of a historic Gold Rush-era building help make the Cozmic Café a popular stop with locals and visitors alike. Housed in the Pearson's Soda Works Building, constructed in 1859, the café is open daily for breakfast (served all day), lunch, and dinner. Recently voted best organic cuisine in Placerville, favorites include the tofu scramble and the Greek scramble for breakfast. Included in the house specialties are The Fit Fish, The Primo Portabella, and The Righteous Rice Bowl. Cozmic also serves up a wide variety of sandwiches, wraps salads, and combos. Upstairs, the pub opens on weekends, serving locally made beer and wine, often with special live music programs in the ballroom.

SEQUOIA

www.sequoiaplacerville.com
530-622-5222
643 Bee St., Placerville, CA
Open: Tues.–Sun. 11 AM–10 PM
Price: Expensive
Cuisine: American
Serving: L, D
Reservations: Yes
Credit cards: AE, D, MC, V

Located in the beautifully restored Bee-Bennett Victorian mansion, it's no wonder why Sequoia is voted "Most Romantic Restaurant in Placerville" year after year. Sequoia exudes taste and ambiance. The main dining room is set around the original 1853 fireplace where you can take in the wisteria blooms etched into stained-glass windows and peer out on the outdoor patio. Should you be seated out on the spacious veranda, enjoy warm summer breezes, the lulling sound of the nearby fountains and gaze out on Bee Street just beyond the herb garden. Take your time pursuing the extensive wine list and enjoy an appetizer. For a dinner appetizer, you can't go wrong with seared ahi, escargot and spring roll, or the fried sweet potatoes. Favorite dinner entrées include Mediterranean stuffed eggplant, steak Diane, or the Black & White—petit filet and prawns. Take your time and enjoy the ambiance; there's no reason to rush your dining experience at Sequoia.

TOMEI'S@384

www.tomeis384.com
530-626-9766
384 Main St., Placerville, CA
Open: Tues.–Sat., 11:30 AM–close
Price: Moderate to Expensive
Cuisine: International
Serving: L, D
Reservations: Recommended
Credit cards: AE, D, MC, V

Tomei's@384, located downtown in the historic Round Tent building, is fun and slightly different in terms of both décor and cuisine. This is where Gold Rush history collides with post-modern art. Art works (most by local artists) are displayed over the original brick interior of the building, and dining tables are set with black linen tablecloths and fresh flowers. The restaurant is comfortable and casual, with eclectic touches tossed in here and there. Owner

Mike Tomei is a huge supporter of local agriculture, so much of the wine list is comprised of varieties from the Sierra foothills (but definitely not exclusively), and the fresh ingredients used to prepare their menu items are as locally grown as possible. Tomei describes the menu as "Pangean Contemporary Cuisine" meaning their flavors and presentations are drawn from sources around the world. For example, the rib-eye steak grilled Argentinean style with house-made chimichurri sauce, crispy onions, grilled Yukon potatoes, and cumin-seasoned roasted fresh vegetables; and their ever popular grilled southwestern spice-rubbed all-natural pork tenderloin is served with guacamole and pepper sweet corn salsa, and a green onion potato cake. The lunch menu has the usual assortment of appetizers, salads, soups, sandwiches, and paninis. But a must-try is the chicken panini, with grilled chicken, apple horseradish spread, melted brie, and caramelized onions. It's a culinary list-topper. An excellent dessert selection is the flourless chocolate decadence cake, with chocolate sauce and fresh strawberries. Yum! As a value-added service, Tomei's@384 offers a foothill concierge service and will book wine country tours, limo service, local lodging, and set up golf and whitewater rafting packages.

ZACHARY JACQUES

www.zacharyjacques.com
530-626-8045
1821 Pleasant Valley Rd., Placerville, CA
Open: Wed.–Sun. 4:30–9:30 PM
Price: Moderate-Expensive
Cuisine: French
Serving: D
Reservations: Yes
Credit cards: AE, D, MC, V

John and Lynnette Evans bring the flavor of the French countryside to your table at Zachary Jacques. The casual ambiance and gourmet preparations are a refreshing discovery in the Sierra foothills. Beautiful stained-glass accents the wine bar, where you'll find some unique appetizers to go with your first glass of wine. Chef John suggests traditional "Burgundy style" snails baked with garlic butter and parsley, or the mushrooms stuffed with spinach, brie and sun dried tomatoes, baked in puff pastry. The extensive wine list features offerings from local wineries, as well as selections from California and France. A favorite main entrée is the filet of wild salmon baked in puff pastry with basil, sun-dried tomato, spinach, and mushrooms. However, the duck grilled with a brick weight, and served with preserved black walnuts, apples, red cabbage, and shallot vinaigrette is very popular as well. An à la carte menu is available as well. On the weekend, live music sets a mellow tone; and during the summer, try your hand a *petanque*, the French version of bocce ball. Never heard of *petanque*? No problem, Lynnette says, "It's a wine-friendly sport, and beginners are more than welcome."

Plymouth

TASTE RESTAURANT

restauranttaste.com
209-245-DINE
9402 Plymouth, CA
Open: Thur.–Mon. 4:30 PM–close
Price: Moderate to Expensive
Cuisine: American
Serving: D
Reservations: Suggested
Credit cards: AE, D, MC, V

This quaint and cozy restaurant serves up tasty, upscale food and has received rave reviews from both *The Sacramento Bee* and *Sacramento Magazine,* where it was named one of the best restaurants in the area. The 100-year-old building that houses Taste is tastefully decorated with wood-plank floors and ochre walls. The innovative menu is always changing depending on the season, but whatever time of year and whatever you order, it will be prepared from the freshest ingredients available. Chef Mark Berkner, who started the restaurant with his wife, Tracey, brings many years of experience to his kitchen. The Axis Venison, for example, is prepared with a sautéed loin, ancho chili Yukon Gold potato puree, caramelized Bartlett pears, and cocoa red-wine sauce. Another favorite is the cauliflower risotto prepared with parmesan, lemon, La Clarine goat cheese, chives, broccolini, and cauliflower florets. The wine list is extensive, but not overwhelming, featuring local, California, and European wines. Diners are also welcome to bring in their favorite wine for a corkage fee. For dessert, try the pear walnut ravioli, warm puff pastry pockets filled with ginger gelato and preserved walnuts.

Sonora

OUTLAWS BARBQ

www.outlawsbarbq.com
209-523-1227
275 S. Washington St., Sonora, CA
Open: Tues.–Sun. 11 AM–close
Price: Moderate
Cuisine: American Barbecue
Serving: L, D
Reservations: No
Credit cards: AE, D, MC, V

Whether you are just looking for a quick barbecue sandwich from the Pony Express lunch menu, or are ready to sit and chow down on a full dinner, Outlaws will fill the bill when it comes to homemade barbecue. Here you can take the whole family into the dining area, or relax with friends in the saloon. Be sure to check out the beautiful antique bar that proprietors Janet and Paul Kennedy say is, "old as the hills." Enjoy your favorite libation while reviewing the menu. Outlaws offers a large selection of local wines and beers. Maybe enjoy a bottle of Three Thieves wine. It's served in a retro glass jug to keep the snobs away. The main bill of fare is barbecue ribs, steak, brisket, pork, chicken, and seafood. They say the secret to excellent barbecue is in the smoke, and all Outlaws' meats are cooked up in their Texas-style smoke pits. There are plenty of appetizers and salads, as well as a whole slew of sides, such as their creamy coleslaw, chili, and, of course, Texas-style ranch beans. Yes, this may be a barbecue dinner house, but Outlaws also offers a number of vegetarian entrées for their "range-friendly" friends.

Sutter Creek

CAFFÈ VIA D'ORO

www.caffeviadoro.com
209-267-0535
36 Main St., Sutter Creek, CA
Open: Wed.–Sun. 11:30 AM–close
Price: Moderate to Expensive
Cuisine: American
Serving: L, D
Reservations: Recommended
Credit cards: AE, D, MC, V

Warm and comfortable, the Caffè is housed in the brick, Gold Rush-era Malatesta Building. A large mural greets visitors in the dining area, depicting the idyllic life style of the Sutter Creek area. The casual interior décor includes custom-made tables and chairs created by local artisans, and the high ceiling contains materials to improve the sound and ambiance. A full array of appetizers, soups, and salads are available. Popular selections include the Southern Style BBQ Shrimp, the Coastal Scallops, and the D'Oro Taster. Entrées feature many traditional favorites like steaks and chops, all with d'Oro's special touch. New Orleans-style cooking is very popular at d'Oro. Among the favorite entrées is the jambalaya, Baton Rouge pork chops, and trout Ponchetrain. The wine list is more than adequate, leaning of course to offerings from local wineries.

FOOD PURVEYORS

Bakeries

Andrae's Bakery, 209-267-1352, 14141 SR 49, Amador City, CA. Homemade breads, pastries, cakes, and other goodies are always fresh. Relax in this rustic, but comfortable establishment, and breath in the heavenly aromas.

Aria Bakery and Espresso Café, 209-728-9250, 458 Main St, Ste B, Murphys, CA. Daily offerings include desserts, pastries, breads, and Northwest espresso. Delicious little tarts, pies, cookies, as well as the cream puffs and éclairs. Croissants, Danish, bagels, and panini sandwiches are made from scratch daily. Ham and cheese croissants are a favorite with the locals.

Calamity Joan's Bakery, 209-795-9275, 925 Highway 4, Suite C2, Arnold, CA. "A jamboree of freshness from our mixing bowl to you!" Specializing in artisan breads, bagels, donuts, cinnamon rolls, and cookies all baked fresh daily. Breakfast and lunch sandwiches made to your specifications. Desserts by special order.

The Flour Garden Bakery and Cyber Café, www.flourgarden.com, 530-272-2043, 11999 Sutton Way (Inside Brunswick Longs Drugs), Grass Valley, CA. No corners cut here, all bakery items are made from scratch, blending European style with California health consciousness. Cruise the Web and munch some great bakery items.

The Grapevine Bistro and Bakery, 530-272-4470, 1041 Sutton Way, Grass Valley, CA. Features great line of homemade breads and pastries; also serves breakfast all day. Ask about their lunch alternative.

Wow! Bakery, 209-223-4619, 140 Main St., Jackson, CA. Oven fresh cakes, breads, and pastries will make you say, "wow." Great place for a mid-morning snack.

Coffeehouses

Back Roads Coffee House, 209-267-0440, 74A Main St. (Randolph at Main St.), Sutter Creek, CA. Friendly and comfortable, a great place to meet with friends. Large selection of coffees, teas, and much more.

Beanie's at Plymouth Hotel, 209-245-8805, 9356 Main St., Plymouth, CA. Quaint location inside a historic hotel featuring fresh, homemade breads, pastries, coffee, and espresso.

Gold Country Coffee Roasting Co., 209-728-8634, 90 Big Trees Rd., Murphys, CA. Established in 1994, daily offerings include fresh roasted coffee, espresso drinks, and tasty pastry. Live jazz groups get down most weekends.

Gold Rush Coffee Co. & Café, www.goldrushcoffeeco.com, 338 209-274-0799, Preston St., Ione, CA. This is a contemporary coffeehouse housed in a beautiful Gold Rush-era building featuring a full espresso menu, periodic live entertainment, and open-mike nights. Also serves breakfast and lunch.

Train Station Coffee House, 530-677-6287, 4274 Mother Load Drive, Shingle Springs, CA. Cozy atmosphere and great coffee greet visitors here. Be sure to treat yourself to one of their pastries.

On the Go Espresso, 209-295-2202, 24140 SR 88, Pioneer, CA. Featuring gourmet coffee and espresso. Order a deli sandwich for lunch.

The Koffee Nook, 209-736-0927, 1227 S. Main St., Angels Camp, CA. Specializing in fair trade coffee and teas. Also serves smoothies, soft serve ice cream, fresh baked treats, breakfast burritos, and bubble teas.

Farmers' Markets

Angels Camp CFM, 209-736-2580, 1192 S. Main St., Angels Camp, CA. June–Sept., Fri. 4:30–8:30 PM.

Arnold-Mountain Growers CFM, 209-728-9112, Cedar Center and SR 4, Arnold, CA. June–Oct. Sun. 10 AM–2 PM.

Auburn Farmers Market, www.foothillfarmersmarket.com, 530-823-6183, corner of Auburn Folsom Rd. and Lincoln Way, Auburn, CA. Sat., March–Nov. 8 AM–noon, Nov.–March, 9–1 PM.

Auburn Dewitt Center, www.foothillfarmersmarket.com, 530-823-6183, Bell Road off SR 49, June–Dec., Wed., 11 AM–2 PM.

Colfax Farmers Market, www.foothillfarmersmarket.com, 530-823-6183, Main Street, May–Oct., Wed., 4–7 PM.

Foresthill Farmers Market, www.foothillfarmersmarket.com, 530-823-6183, Main Street, Foresthill, CA, June–Aug., Wed., 4–7 PM.

Grass Valley Fairgrounds, www.thegrowersmarket.com, 530-265-5551, McCourtney Road, Gate 4, Grass Valley, CA. May–Oct., Sat. 8 AM–12 PM.

Ione CFM, www.cafarmersmarkets.com, 530-753-9999, W. Main and S. Sacramento St., Ione, CA. June–Oct., Mon. 3–6:30 PM.

Lake of the Pines, www.foothillfarmersmarket.com, 530-823-6183, Combie Center, June–Sept., Sat. 10 AM–2 PM.

Nevada City, www.thegrowersmarket.com, Sierra 530-265-5551, Presbyterian Church, 175 Ridge Rd., Nevada City, CA. July–Oct, Tues. 3–6 PM.

Placerville Certified Farmers Market, www.edc-cfma.org, 530-622-1900, Ivy House Parking Area, corner of Cedar Ravine and Main St., Placerville, CA., May–Oct., Sat. 8 AM–noon.

Pine Grove CFM, www.cafarmersmarkets.com, 530-753-1813. Pine Grove Community Park, Pine Grove, CA. June–Oct., Wed., 3–6 PM.

Sonora CFM, 209-532-7725, Theall and Steward St., Sonora, CA. May–Oct. Sat. 8 AM–noon.

Sutter Creek CFM, www.cafarmersmarkets.com, Eureka St. and SR 49, Sutter Creek, CA. June–Oct. Sat. 8–11 AM.

Tuolumne CFM, 209-928-4351, Tuolumne City Park, Fir and Main St., June–Oct., Wed. 4–8 PM.

Twain Harte CFM, 209-586-4482, Eproson Park, Twain Harte, CA. June–Sept. Fri.
3:30–6 PM.

Frozen Desserts

A & J's Yogurt/Deli, 530-295-1265, 7215 Hwy 49, Lotus, CA. Great for a refreshing yogurt
dessert. Full deli serves up sandwiches and much more.

Baskin Robbins 31 Flavors, 530-672-9295, 3378 Coach Ln., Shingle Springs, CA. A great
old-time ice cream shop, also featuring many health-oriented desserts.

Café at the Park, 209-245-6981, 18265 SR 49 (Far Horizon 49er Village RV Resort),
Plymouth, CA. Full-service deli and espresso bar and a cool old-fashioned ice cream parlor serving up refreshing sundaes, malts, and more.

Chatterbox Café, 209-267-5935, 39 Main St., Sutter Creek, CA. Original 1946 soda fountain, where ice cream, sundaes, and sodas are served the old-fashioned way. Also serving
breakfast and lunch.

Confectionately Yours, 530-274-3448, 146 Mill Street, Grass Valley, CA. Too many ice
cream flavors to list. Also builds great sundaes, yogurt desserts, and smoothies. Handmade
and sugar-free chocolate and fudge.

Dorado Chocolates, 530-272-6715, 104 E. Main St., Grass Valley, CA. This is the spot for
some unique chocolate confections. They feature two product lines and guarantee to satisfy
most everyone's sweet tooth.

Sutter Creek Ice Cream Emporium, 209-267-0543, 51 Main St., Sutter Creek, CA.
Sweet tooth acting up? Treat yourself to some fresh, homemade fudge, an ice cream
sundae, or a soda. Dessert is the specialty here, but the soups and sandwiches are also
very tasty.

RECREATION

Bicycling

BICYCLING ADVENTURES

Death Ride, www.deathride.com, 530-694-2475, 3 Webster St., Markleeville, CA.
Organized and staged every summer by the Alpine County Chamber of Commerce, the
Death Ride is a serious challenge for serious bicycling enthusiasts. The annual event takes
riders over five mountain passes including Monitor Pass (8,314'), Ebbett's Pass (8,730')
and Carson Pass (8,573'). The course begins and ends at Turtle Rock near Markleeville and
takes in 130 miles and more than 15,000 feet of lung-crushing climbing.

Yuba Expeditions, www.yubaexpeditions.com, 530-289-3131, 208 Main St., Downieville,
CA. Bike the high country with folks who know the trails and conditions. Yuba is the top
mountain bike shuttle service in the northern Sierra Nevada. Several great riding areas to
choose from. Also stocks rental and demo bikes, and provides sales and service. Peruse
their great selection of trail maps highlighting the Downieville trail system, and the latest
topo maps from the US Forest Service.

BICYCLE RENTALS AND REPAIRS

Auburn Bike Works, www.auburnbikeworks.com, 530-885-3861, 350 Grass Valley Hwy., Auburn, CA.

Mountain Pedaler, 209-736-0771, 352 S Main St., Angels Camp, CA.

Tour of Nevada City Bicycle Shop, www.tourofnevadacity.com, 530-265-2187, 457 Sacramento St., Nevada City, CA.

Campgrounds and RV Parks

Angels Camp RV and Camping Resort, www.angelscamprv.com, 1-888-398-0404 or 209-736-0404, 3069 Highway 49, Angels Camp, CA. Located adjacent to Calaveras County Fairgrounds off SR 49. RV sites with no restrictions on size or slideouts. Premium tent sites include electricity and water. Also comfy camping lodges and rustic log cabins. Swimming pool, showers, laundry, and kitchen pavilion. Rates: Tent sites $16–$30, RV sites $28–$46.

Auburn State Recreation Area, www.parks.ca.gov, 530-885-4527, 501 El Dorado St., Auburn CA. This massive park covers 40 miles at the confluence of the North and Middle Forks of the American River. Located in the heart of Gold Rush country, this area once teemed with miners seeking their fortune. Today, it is a preserved natural area, offering a wide variety of recreation opportunities to more than 500,000 visitors a year. Lake Clementine offers great opportunities for water activities, while dirt bikers head for Mammoth Bar OHV. Several great trails are open to mountain bikers. Hikers and horse-back riders cherish the area as well. Anglers find the lake and river waters golden with trout and other game fish, while gold panners seek a little color of their own. A number of private outfitters are licensed to offer whitewater trips. The area has numerous camping and day-use facilities. Fires are permitted where fire pits are provided, and all animals must be leashed. All campsites, except for those at Lake Clementine, are on a first-come, first-serve basis. Fee: $15 per night.

Auburn Gold Country RV Park, www.auburngoldcountryrvpark.com, 530-885-0990, 3550 KOA Way, Auburn, CA. For the RVer, the facility offers big pull-through sites with lengths of up to 60 feet, 50-amp full hookups, and plenty of shade trees. Also offers tent sites and camping cabins. Rates start at $27 for tents, and $33 for RVs (no hookups).

Coloma Resort, www.colomaresort.com, 530-621-2267, 6921 Mt. Murphy Rd., Coloma, CA. SR 49 to Coloma, go west on Murphy Road, cross a bridge and make an immediate right turn to the resort. The facility offers campsites, on site RV rentals, tent cabins, and bunkhouse. A great place to fish for trout, ride the wild whitewater, hike in the hills, take a bike ride, or pan for gold. Basic camping site $38, tent cabins $48.

Cisco Grove Camping and RV Park, www.ciscogrove.com, 530-426-1600, 48415 Hampshire Rock Rd., Soda Springs, CA. US 80 to Cisco Road exit, left to Hampshire Road. Basic RV sites include water and electric, while premium sites include sewer hookups. The campground is divided into nine sections, each site within easy walking distance to rest-room and shower facilities. Plenty of summer and winter outdoor activities close by.

Gold Strike Village Mobilehome and RV Park, www.goldstrikevillage.com, 209-754-3180, 1925 Gold Strike Rd., San Andreas, CA. Located just outside of San Andreas near the

There's gold in those hills. Washington Ridge near Grass Valley, viewed from SR 20 in the northern Sierra Nevada.

intersection of SR 49 and SR 12, this is a full-service camping and RV facility including Olympic pool, shady trees, heated restrooms, hot showers, laundry, and clubhouse. Also, Glory Hole goldmine and mining artifacts on the site.

Golden Pines RV Resort and Campground, www.goldenpinesrvresort.com, 209-795-2820, 2869 East Highway 4, Arnold, CA. On SR 4 just north of Arnold at 5,000-foot elevation, Golden Pines is open all year for RV and tend campers. Facilities include full hookups, tent sites, rental cabins, pool, rec hall, hot showers, and laundry. Rates: Tent sites $20, RV $35.

Marble Quarry RV Park & Cabins, www.marblequarry.com, 209-532-9539, 11551 Yankee Hill Rd., Columbia CA. The folks in charge like to call Marble Quarry a park, not just a place to park your RV and it's only a stone's toss from historic Columbia. This family-oriented facility is quiet, clean, and offers free gold-panning instruction (you keep the gold) and interpretive tours via covered wagon, of the historic marble quarry. Rates: Tent site $24, RV $34–$37.

Nevada County Fairgrounds, www.nevadacountyfair.com, 530-273-6217, McCourtney Rd., Grass Valley, CA. The facilities are nestled among tall pines. The RV park has 44 sites with full hookups, 100 sites with water and power, as well as numerous dry camping sites throughout the grounds. Rates: From $20 for dry camping to $28 for full hookups.

River Rest Resort, www.riverrestresort.com, 530-265-4306, P.O. Box 40, Washington, CA. From Nevada City/Grass Valley, take SR 49 east, merge with SR 20, about 20 miles to

Washington Road, turn left. Spread out along the south fork of the Yuba River, this is a beautiful place for fishing, hiking, swimming, ATV riding, and even a little gold panning. Some beautiful campsites right on the river. Rates: Campsites $25; RV sites, $30. Day-use, $10 per car.

Roaring Camp Mining Company, www.roaringcampgold.com, 209-296-4100, 12010 Tabeau Rd., Pine Grove, CA. This is a destination stop, featuring tent camping and cabins; no RVs. Located at Clinton Bar in the Mokelumne River Canyon via SR 88, east of Jackson. Accommodations are rented by the week. Experience the thrill of panning for your own gold, fishing, swimming, and exploring the rugged terrain. Lots of family and youth activities and adventure tours. Come Saturday night, join in the steak cookout. Open May–Sept. Rates: Tent, $450 per week; cabin, $550 per week.

Robbs Valley Resort, www.dorobbs.com, 1-866-978-5824, 14216 Ice House Rd., Pollock Pines, CA. Located 22 miles north of SR 50 on Ice House Road. Bring your own outdoor toys or use (rent) Robbs gear. Ideal spot for ATVs and all manner of water recreation activities. Be sure to try the prime rib, and get ready for karaoke or live music in The Waterin' Hole. Tent sites, $15, RV sites with hookups $25–$35.

Sierra Skies RV Park, www.sierraskiesrvpark.com, 530-862-1166, 100 Carrier Circle, Sierra City, CA. Go for a hike, or have a picnic along the shores of the beautiful Yuba River. This is a wonderful place to park the RV and kick back for a while. Facilities include 30 RV sites, some pull-through, electricity, water, and septic. Close to lakes, rivers, and fine dining. Open May through October.

Three Links Camp, www.caioof.org/Camp/3LinksCamp.html, 209-586-5500, 21950 Highway 108, Mi-Wuk Village, CA. The camp is located about 18 miles east of Sonora on SR 108, and was established in 1958 by the California Odd Fellows and Rebekahs Fraternal Order. It was designed and operates today as a peaceful retreat from the pressures of life. Here you don't even have to pitch a tent (they are provided) unless you want to. While the camp rents to individuals, it is especially good for family reunions, community and social groups, meetings, and weddings. It has a multipurpose building with full kitchen and dining facilities, chapel, swimming pool, amphitheater, and crafts building, Tent sites $12, RVs $20. The facility also offers dorm beds for $12 a night.

Cave Exploration

California Cavern, www.caverntours.com, 1-866-762-2837, 9565 Cave City Rd., Mountain Ranch, CA. This is huge cavern was the first to be opened to the public in 1850, and visiting dignitaries have included Mark Twain, Bret Harte, and John Muir. Today, guided tours and cave expeditions are offered for all levels of explorer, from casual visitor to guided spelunking treks. Some of the crystalline formations are very rare. Tours start at $12.95 for adults, $6.50 for children 3–12.

Mercer Caverns, www.mercercaverns.com, 209-728-2101, P.O. 509, Murphys, CA. Located just minutes from Murphys, these caverns offer an amazing look at this underground work of nature. Be sure to check out the Angel Wings—a nearly transparent crystalline formation, that is about 9 feet long. The Cathedral Room offers great examples of stalactites and stalagmites. The caverns are open daily, Memorial Day Weekend through September, 9 AM–6 PM. Admission is $12 for adults, and $7 for children 5–12.

Moaning Cavern, www.caverntours.com, 1-866-762-2837, 5350 Moaning Cave Rd., Vallecito, CA. Guided walking tours and expeditions are available every day of the year. The basic tour takes about 45 minutes and is professionally guided. The tour ends on the spot where scientific excavations revealed the bones of prehistoric people who apparently fell into the cavern thousands of years ago. If this sounds too tame, start your three-hour expedition with a 165-foot rope rappel into the cavern's gigantic main chamber. The chamber is large enough to house the Statue of Liberty. Regular tours are $12.95 for adults, and $6.50 for kids 3–12.

Gaming

Black Oak Casino, www.blackoakcasino.com, 1-877-747-8777 or 209-928-9301, 19400 Tuolumne Road North, Tuolumne, CA. Owned and operated by the Miwok band of Indians, this modern casino offers slots, card and table gaming, and live entertainment. Check out the great attractions for the kids, including the huge Underground Arcade and Black Oak Lanes bowling alley. Hungry? Take your pick from five restaurants. Relax and try your luck in the smoke-free lounge. Open 24/7; must be 21 to gamble.

Jackson Rancheria Casino & Hotel, www.jacksoncasino.com, 1-800-822-WINN, 12222 New York Ranch Rd., Jackson, CA. This is one of the best spots to try your luck in the entire Gold Country. The Rancheria has 48 gaming tables, 15 poker tables featuring Texas Hold 'Em, Live Bingo, and more than 1500 slot and video poker machines. Always plenty of headline entertainment and the kids can have a ball in the Minor's Camp Arcade. World-class dining is always close at hand, from high-end menus in Lone Wolf's Steakhouse, to tasty buffets and casual meals in Raging River. Stay a few days in the hotel or pull your rig into the RV park. Open 24/7; must be 21 to gamble.

Gold Mining

Gold Prospecting Adventures, www.goldprospecting.com, 209-984-4653, 18170 Main St., Jamestown, CA. Learn to pan for gold like the original 49ers, or get into the latest high-tech gear and see if you can turn up a little color (gold). For more than 25 years these folks have conducted school programs, family adventures, and taught prospecting courses on this authentic gold-mining site. Kids of all ages really enjoy the 1849 Gold Mining Camp, an exact replica of the original camp built in 1849. Guides are dressed in 49er garb, and you just might have a chat with Black Bart, James Marshall, or even Mark Twain.

Golf Courses

ANGELS CAMP

Greenhorn Creek Resort, www.greenhorncreek.com, 209-729-8111, 711 McCauley Ranch Road, Angels Camp, CA. Public 18-hole course. Par 72,. 6749 yards, rating 68.2, slope 123. GPS cart rentals, free range balls, three putting greens, and club rentals, pro shop. Stay in one of their beautiful villas overlooking this great course. Fine dining, pool, and tennis courts on the premises. Rates, $35–$90.

ARNOLD

Meadowmont Golf Course, www.meadowmontgolf.com, 209-795-1313, 1684 Highway 4, Arnold, CA. Public 9-hole course. 3200 yards, par , rating 66.8, slope 121. Pro shop, rental clubs, carts, lessons, and putting green. A scenic little course located in "the big trees" at an elevation of 4000 feet. Rates, $15–$19 per nine holes.

AUBURN

Black Oak Golf Course, 530-878-1900, 2455 Black Oak Rd., Auburn, CA. Public 9-hole course. Par 36, 3157 yards, rating, 36, slope 129. Clubhouse with bar, casual restaurant, cart rental, small driving range, and putting green. Very lush course with lots of big trees.

DarkHorse Golf Club, www.darkhorsegolf.com, 530-269-7900, 24150 DarkHorse Dr., Auburn, CA. Public 18-hole course. Par 72, 5180-7030 yards, rating 68.8, slope 126. Challenging layout with several streams and ponds. Pro shop, cart rentals, driving range, putting green, clubhouse, and restaurant. Rates, $29–$69.

The Ridge Golf Course, www.ridgegc.com, 530.888.7888, ext 3, 2020 Golf Course Rd., Auburn, CA. Public 18-hole course. 6,345 yards, rating 70.1, slope 132. Pro shop, cart rentals, driving range, putting green, lessons, and restaurant. This Robert Trent Jones II course will challenge golfers of all skill levels.

CAMINO

Apple Mountain Golf Resort, www.applemountaingolfresort.net, 530-647-7400, 3455 Carson Road, Camino, CA. This is an 18-hole public course. Par 70, 6176 yards, rating 67.2. Cart included with green fees. Driving range, putting green, restaurant for breakfast, lunch and banquets. Course runs through towering stands of pine, cedar, and madrone. Rates, $35–$59.

Camino Heights Golf Club, 530-644-0190, 3020 Vista Terra Drive, Camino, CA. Private club with limited public access. Course has 9 holes, 3715 yards, par 62, rating, 60.6, slope 101. Carts, putting green. Rates, $12.

COPPEROPOLIS

Saddle Creek Resort, www.saddlecreek.com, 1001 1-800-611-7722 or 209-785-7400, Saddle Creek Dr., Copperopolis, CA. Public 18-hole course. Par 72, 6035 yards, slope, 122. Pro shop, large practice facility, lessons, clubhouse, and restaurant. Located within a gated community, Saddle Creek Golf Club is a meticulously maintained facility, and has been written up in several popular golfing magazines. Rates, $40–$95 (cart and practice balls included).

GRASS VALLEY

Alta Sierra Country Club, www.altasierracc.com, 530-273-2041, 1897 Tammy Way, Grass Valley, CA. Private course with limited public access. An 18-hole course. Par 72, 6537 yards, rating 70.1, slope 127. Cart rentals, driving range, and putting green. Located above the valley fog, and below the Sierra snow, the course has a new pro shop, and clubhouse with a full-service bar.

IONE

Castle Oaks Golf Club, www.castleoaksgolf.com, 209-274-0167, 1000 Castle Oaks Drive, Ione, CA. 18-hole public course. Par 71, 6739 yards, rating 72.7, slope, 131. Pro shop, cart rentals, driving range, putting range, lessons, restaurant, and a full-service bar. Long course from the back tees, fairly flat terrain. Rates, $38–$58.

MURPHYS

Forest Meadows Golf Course, www.forestmeadowsgolf.com, 209-728-3439, 4 miles east of Murphys on Highway 4, Murphys, CA. Public 18-hole Robert Trent Jones II course. Par 60, 3221 yards, rating 62.5, slope 107. Cart rentals, putting green, and clubhouse. This is a fun and picturesque course, with some very challenging holes. Be sure to stop by Woody's Bar & Grill before, and after, year round. Rates, $20–$35.

PIONEER

Mace Meadows Golf & Country Club, www.macemeadow.com, 209-295-7020, 26570 Fairway Dr, Pioneer, CA. Public play is welcome at this 18-hole semi-private club. Par 71, 6310, rating 69.9, slope 128. Carts, pro shop, putting green, restaurant, and a full-service lounge. Course is located in a beautiful mountain setting, with lots of Douglas fir and cedar trees. Rates, $25–$35.

SONORA

Phoenix Lake Golf Course, www.PhoenixLakeGolf.com, 209-532-0111, 21448 Paseo De Los Portales, Sonora, CA. Public 9-hole golf course. Par 37, 2711 yards, rating 33.2, 115. Pro shop, cart rentals, driving range, putting range, lessons, and snack shop. This is a championship course with panoramic views, and some tough holes. Rates, $20–$33.

Mountain Springs Golf Course, www.mountainspringsgolf.com, 209-532-1000, 17566 Lime Kiln Rd., Sonora CA. Public 18-hole course. Par 72, 6665 yards, rating 71.9, slope 128. Pro shop, cart rentals, driving range, putting range, lessons, and a restaurant. Tough mountain course, with its share of blind shots. Rates, $36–$51.

VALLEY SPRINGS

La Contenta Golf Club, www.lacontentagolf.com, 209-772-1081, 653 Highway 26, Valley Springs, CA. Public 18-hole course. Par 71, 5895 yards, rating 68.5, slope 130. Cart rentals, well-stocked pro shop, driving range, and putting greens. Have a good round, and *la contenta* you will be. The La Contenta Bar & Grill overlooks both the first and ninth holes. Rates, $24–$34.

Lakes & Marinas

Lake Don Pedro, www.donpedrolake.com, 209-852-2396, 31 Bonds Flat Rd., La Grange, CA. Don Pedro is an expansive lake boasting 160 miles of shoreline and nearly 13,000 surface acres of water. Here you can enjoy your favorite water sports, including fishing, boating, swimming, water skiing, jet skiing, windsurfing, sailing, and houseboating. The lake has two full-service marinas, Moccasin Point Marina, just west of Jamestown, and Lake Don Pedro Marina on the lake's west side. Both marinas feature boat rentals, fuel, bait and tackle, mooring, store, and a café. The lake also has three campgrounds, and can accommodate tent campers, large groups, RVs, and motorhomes. Other features include a day-use/picnic area, swimming lagoon, amphitheater, and softball and volleyball facilities. The lake is open all year, and in-season fees apply April-Sept. Tent camping $20, day-use fee $6.

Lake McClure, www.lakemcclure.com, 209-378-2521, 9090 Lake McClure Rd., Snelling, CA. Located east of Coulterville, via SR 132. Lake McClure and the adjacent Lake McSwain offer all the water-related activities you can ask for. Nestled in the Sierra foothills, this is a great spot for boating, fishing, water skiing, windsurfing, sailing, and house boating. It's also a popular spot for hang-gliding, wildlife viewing, and hiking. Two marinas, Lake McClure Marina and Barrett Cove Marina are well stocked and offer ski boats and equipment as well as house and patio boats for rent. Over 600 spacious campsites are available in five campgrounds. Most come with tables, water, and barbecue grills. RV hookups also have electric and sewer hookups. Modern restrooms, hot showers, and laundry facilities add to a wonderful experience. Day-use and picnic facilities for families and large groups are available. Day-use, $6 per vehicle; $6 per boat. Overnight camping, $20; trailer hookup $26.

New Melones Lake, www.recreation.gov, 1-877-444-6777 or 209-536-9094, 6850 Stud Horse Flat Rd., Sonora, CA. Located off of SR 49, eight miles north of Sonora. At more than 12,000 acres, Melones offers all water sports, camping, and great fishing. Visitors center/museum offers interpretive programs all year. The lake has two campgrounds: Glory Hole, about six miles south of Angels Camp; and Tuttletown, about 8 miles north of Sonora. At a little over 1,000-foot elevation, temperatures can rise above 100 during the summer. Facilities include barbecue grills, comfort stations, drinking water, showers, and dump stations. The full-service marina at Glory Hole includes houseboat and boat rentals, fuel, boat storage, snack bar, and a store. Open year around 10 AM–4 PM. Standard family campsites, $16 per night.

Pinecrest Lake, www.recreation.gov, 1-877-444-6777, Located 30 miles east of Sonora on SR 108. Nestled in the tall pines at 5,600 feet, the facility offers a wide array of outdoor activities. Facilities include 300 campsites with tables, grills, and flush toilets, pay showers, day-use sites at the boat launch. The lake is stocked with rainbow trout and other fish. Rental boats available. Lots of hiking and biking trails and educational talks are hosted at the interpretive center. During the winter, this is a popular spot for Nordic skiing. Open all year. Fee: $19.

Rollins Lake, www.penresort.com, 530-477-9413, 21597 You Bet Rd., Chicago Park, CA. Located off Highway 174 between Grass Valley and Colfax, Rollins Lake (elev. 2100 ft.) has a 900-acre surface area and 26-mile shoreline. Rollins offers great camping, fishing, boating, and a variety of water sports. Crafts for kids and ice cream giveaways are among the summer events. The facility also has a volleyball court, horseshoe pit, and footballs and Frisbees to lend out. Campers may choose among more than 250 campsites at four separate campgrounds. Peninsula Campground features shaded lakeside and wooded campsites with spacious lake views, fishing, water sports, boat launch, and swimming beach. Launch your own boat at the marina or rent a fishing boat, patio boat, canoe, kayak, waterbike, or paddleboat for a day of fun and frolic on the lake. Facilities include tent camping, RV hook-ups, and small cabins. Rates: $32 and up for campsites, $6 per motorized watercraft.

Scotts Flat Lake, www.scottsflatlake.net, 530-265-5302, 23333 Scotts Flat Rd., Nevada City, CA. This is a beautiful spot to spend a relaxing day by the water, or a week or more as home base for a Gold Country vacation. Easy access via SR 20 east of Nevada City. The lake has a concrete boat ramp, and the marina store is well stocked for all your fishing and munching needs. Boat rentals are available, as are moorings and pre-mixed fuel. Dip a line, and see if you can't bring a rainbow trout or a nice base to cook over the barbecue. The camping facilities cater to RV and tent campers alike with clean water, flush toilets, hot showers, and a nearby playground. Fees: $6 day-use fee per vehicle; $6 boat launch; overnight camping starts at $19 per night.

Sly Park–Jenkinson Lake, www.eid.org, 530-644-2545, 4771 Sly Park Rd., Pollock Pines, CA. Sly Park, a few miles northeast of Placerville via SR 50, is a haven for outdoor activities, including camping, hiking, horseback riding, biking, and, of course, water recreation on the lake. The lake features 600 surface acres and nine miles of shoreline, a day-use area with picnic tables, and 10 individual campgrounds scattered around the lake. Be sure to check out the James Calvin Sly Museum and the adjacent Miwok Nature Trail. The lake has two boat launch ramps and boat rentals are available. Horse enthusiasts gather at the Black Oak Equestrian Center. Day use $8 per vehicle, $13 with boat. Premium campsite $25; regular campsite $20.

River Rafting

Sierra Mac River Rafting Trips, www.sierramac.com, 1-800-457-2580, P.O. Box 264, Groveland, CA. For more than 35 years, outfitter Marty McDonnell and his professional guides have led novice-to-expert rafting expeditions on the Tuolumne River and Cherry Creek. Trip rates include guided oar/paddle boats, Coast Guard-approved flotation vests, safety instruction, wilderness interpretation, killer meals, and van shuttle service. Climb aboard and experience some of the Sierra's greatest rapids including Nemesis, The Squeeze, Gray's Grindstone, and the notorious Clavey Falls (with optional footpath). One-day trips for novice rafters begin at $225 per person. Reservations are mandatory.

Tributary Whitewater Tours, www.whitewatertours.com, 1-800-672-3846, 20480 Woodbury Dr., Grass Valley, CA. Time to get wet and wild! Since 1978 Tributary has been guiding rafting trips throughout the Sierra Nevada and elsewhere. Rafting trips for all skill levels, even trips suitable for children. Favorite rafting rivers include the American, Truckee, Yuba, and East Carson rivers.

Zephyr Whitewater Expeditions, www.zrafting.com, 1-800-431-3636 or 209-532-6249, P.O. Box 510, Columbia, CA. Water enthusiasts ages 7 to 75 have enjoyed Zephyr's whitewater expeditions on the Tuolumne, Kings, Merced, and American rivers. They boast expert guides, state-of-the-art equipment, and their food is classified as "river gourmet." They offer everything from whitewater school to family outings, advanced trips, and special killer trips. One-half day express trips start at $95. Group discounts available.

Snow Skiing/Boarding

Bear Valley, www.bearvalley.com, 209-753-2301, Highway 4 at Highway 207, Bear Valley, CA. Boasting more than 1,200 skiable acres and a vertical drop of nearly 2,000 feet, Bear Valley offers plenty of powdery action for the ski enthusiast. The mountain is accessed via one high-speed quad, two triple chairs, six double chairs, and one carpet lift. Of the 67 trails, 25 percent are beginner, 40 percent intermediate, and 35 percent advanced. For the snowboarder, Bear's terrain parks include a 20-foot table top, the 20-foot Rainbow Rail, the 20-foot Battleship Box, and much more. Lessons are available—encouraged, for beginners—to get skiers tuned up for the slopes. Lift tickets are $59 adult, $49 teen, and $19 for children. Senior, super senior, and season passes are available. A full line of skiing and boarding equipment is available. Nearby Bear Valley Lodge and Village Resort are the place to kick back after a day on the slopes. In the Cathedral Lounge, enjoy the warmth of the four-story granite fireplace or slip into the Grizzly Bar for a toddy.

Dodge Ridge, www.dodgeridge.com, 209-536-5300, 1 Dodge Ridge Rd., Pinecrest, CA. One of the premier ski facilities on the west side of the Sierra Nevada, Dodge Ridge offers 60 trails on more than 800 acres accessed by 12 lifts. The mountain is family friendly with 40 percent expert runs, 40 percent intermediate, and 20 percent novice. The facility was designed more for the outdoor adventurer than the ski socialite. Aside from the lodge, there are few off-slope attractions. As for getting the youngsters into the sport, it boasts some of the best beginner terrain of any resort. SkiWee Land starter program is considered one of the finest ski and snowboard school programs around. For the serious skier, Boulder Creek Canyon offers some real thigh-burning exhilaration. Take the plunge into High Noon, the Granite Bowl, or plunge down Sonora Glades. Overall, the mountain boasts a vertical drop of 1,600 feet, 59 runs, and five freestyle terrain parks. Good food is found in the North Fork Bistro. Of course equipment rentals, lessons, and child care are available. All day lift tickets are $52 for adults, $39 for teens, $15 for youths. Half-day, season passes, and group discounts are also available.

Royal Gorge, www.royalgorge.com, 1-800-500-3871, 9411 Hillside Dr., Soda Springs, CA. More than 9000 acres of trails makes Royal Gorge the largest cross-country ski resort in North America. The facility offers hundreds of miles of groomed trails, where skiers enjoy striding, skating, diagonal stride, snowshoeing and telemarking. Here you will also find four surface lifts, two overnight lodges, eight warming huts, four trailside cafés, and several stimulating inn-to-inn trails. Rental equipment and lessons for kids and adults are available. Trail passes start at $25 for adults. Season passes, half-day passes, and group discounts are available.

SHOPPING

Arts & Crafts

Amador Fireside Center Inc., www.amadorfireside.com, 209-223-3806, 155 Main St., Jackson, CA. While the center's main focus is in fireplaces, spas, and outdoor patio furniture, they also offer a unique collection of gift items for the home. Definitely worth a look.

As Time Goes By, 530-823-7723, 321 Commercial St., Auburn, CA. Antique pine furniture, primitives, and American folk art pieces are the specialty here. It's a quaint gallery, and carries a beautiful selection of antiques and home accessories.

Auburn Old Town Gallery, www.auburnoldtowngallery.com, 530-887-9150, 218 Washington St., Auburn, CA. This artists' cooperative features the works of 60 local artists, and explores a wide range of media, including pastel, oil, and watercolor paintings, etchings, pen and ink drawings, pottery, unique jewelry, woodcarvings, photography, blown and fused glass, sculpture, painted silk, decorated gourds, and hand-woven baskets, shawls, and purses.

Bennett Gallery, www.bennettgallery.net, 1-888-848-1164, 440 Main St., Placerville, CA. Bennett Sculpture is created by world-renowned sculptors Bob and Tom Bennett, identical twins who share a singular artistic vision. A tasteful gallery houses their work as well as

work of other artists. Check out the modern sculpture, paintings, art glass, raku, ceramics, jewelry, and even art humor.

Copper Proper LLC, www.copperproper.com, 209-785-7690, 200 Town Square Rd., Copperopolis, CA. Get decorating ideas and fine gifts for your home in this shop. Offerings come from around the world, and they also feature eye-catching innovations from local artisans.

Exposure Gallery, www.exposuregallerync.com, 530-265-4342, 313 Commercial St, Nevada City, CA. This gallery of photography features the works of owner Shannon Perry and many other local photographers. Exhibitions change throughout the year.

Jerianne Van Dijk Illustrations, www.jerianne.net, 530-271-7128, 111 Mill St., Grass Valley, CA. Van Dijk is a self-taught artist whose favorite mediums include watercolor, gouache, ink, pastels, and some oil.

Julie Baker Fine Art, www.juliebakerfineart.com, 530-265-9ART, 246 Commercial St., Nevada City, CA. This lovely gallery focuses on exhibiting the works of emerging artists from California and across the country. Their primary goal is to identify and exhibit artists who present contemporary vision in their painting, drawing, and sculpture.

Mountain Harvest Co-op, www.mountainharvestcrafts.com, 530-289-3334, 154 School St., Downieville, CA. A cool little shop, where you can find handmade quilts, jewelry, wood art, knitted clothing, and much, much more. The store is owned and operated by a group of local craftspersons.

Mowen Solinsky Gallery, www.mowensolinskygallery.com, 530-265-4682, 225 Broad St., Nevada City, CA. John Mowen and Steve Solinsky are longtime residents and artists, with years of experience in their craft. The gallery features their work as well as the work of more than 100 regional and national artists.

Nicholson Blown Glass, www.nicholsonblownglass.com, 530-823-1631, 5555 Bell Rd., Auburn, CA. The dedication of Rick and Janet Nicholson to the art of glassblowing is evident in their small studio. Each piece is a freehand expression of the excitement and risk-taking, only found in an experimental glassblowing studio.

Sierra Experience & Old Town Cigar, 530-888-9681, 111 Sacramento St., Suite E Auburn, CA. This combination gift store and cigar shop carries a variety of one-of-a-kind gifts, as well as an incredible selection of cigars, including Arture Fuente, Dannenan, CAO, and Macanudo. All are kept fresh in a walk-in humidor.

Soiled Doves Parlour & Gifts, www.soileddovesparlour.com, Highway 49, Downieville, CA. A rather eclectic offering of Victorian gifts and clothing. Also features locally hand-crafted, 100 percent organic, body and bath-care products.

Wild Plum, www.wildplumonline.com, 530-273-5007, 111 Mill St., Grass Valley, CA. This fun little store specializes in unique home accessories, high-end silk florals and unusual furniture. Large selection of wreaths and silk arrangements.

LEFT: *A wooden Indian maiden greets visitors to Trader Stan's.*

Villa Mia Antiques, www.villamiaantiques.com, 209-728-1600, 237A Main St., Murphys, CA. The heritage of England and America is on display here including furniture, collectibles, art, jewelry, and gifts. Don't miss the European pottery collection, including hand-painted Quimper ceramics.

Books

Books & More, www.booksnmore.com, 209-736-9020, 328 North Main St., Angels Camp, CA. When they say "more" they mean lots more. Not only does this shop specialize in new and used books, they also stock gold-panning equipment, baseball cards, and DVD rentals.

Hein & Co. Used and Rare Books, www.abebooks.com/home/HEINCO/, 209-223-9076, 204-A North Main St., Jackson, CA. This bookseller specializes in used and rare books. Primary topics of interest include Western Americana, history, technical, mining, modern fiction, ephemera, children's, and religion.

Legends Books, Antiques & Old-Fashioned Soda Fountain, 209-532-8120, 131 S. Washington St., Sonora, CA. This is a must-stop for anyone visiting the area. First, there's the 26-foot mahogany and brass bar that has been restored as an ice cream and soda fountain. Very cool, and the folks manning the bar serve up all sorts of tasty goodies. Then there's the underground bookstore. No, not politically underground—*really* underground.

Motorcycle enthusiasts discuss bikes and rides in downtown Jackson.

It's housed in an authentic Mother Lode mine shaft, and features used and rare, out-of-print books.

Mountain Bookshop, mountainbookshop.com, 209-532-6117, 13769-I Mono Way, Sonora, CA. The friendly and knowledgeable staff welcomes you to the largest bookstore in the Mother Lode. Great selection of books, cards, and gifts plus an entire room filled with books, toys, and games for the kids.

Fashion

Mountain Song, www.mountainsongofnevadacity.com, 1-888-604-1165 or 530-265-2523, 104 North Pine St., Nevada City, CA. This is a cheerful boutique, featuring contemporary clothing, handcrafted jewelry, and whimsical gift items. Enjoy a fresh cup at the cappuccino and espresso bar.

The Herb Shop, www.gvherbshop.com, 530-272-8654, 203 W. Main St., Grass Valley, CA. Owner Laura Solano strives to embody spirit and health, with organic herbs from around the world, and a bit of beauty, with great clothing for today's woman. Be sure to treat yourself to her collection of fun gifts.

Turners Wild West, 209-736-4909, 1235 Main St., Angels Camp CA. A western-wear emporium, featuring top name brands of hats, boots, and jeans. Check out the large collection of frog jump and Gold Country souvenirs. Get directions and sage advice from the cowboy settin' on the sidewalk just outside.

Two Rivers Trading Company, 209-795-6253, 1232 Oak Circle, Arnold CA. Check out the unique stock of outdoor and casual wear for men and women. Clothing and accessories are made from environmentally friendly fabrics, including organic cotton, hemp, and merino wool. Voted best men's store in the area.

Gold Mining Supplies

Matelot Gulch Mining Co., 209-532-9693, Main St. at Washington St., Columbia, CA. The store offers mining supplies, minerals, relics, and even kitchen wares. Want to learn how to pan for gold? This is the spot where they specialize in lessons for those "new to the diggins."

Miners Emporium, 30-862-0630, 221 Main Street, Sierra City, CA. A fun and unique store for hobby mining supplies, topo maps, metal detectors, gold nuggets, books, and other neat stuff.

Jewelry

Aimee Taylor Handcrafted, www.aimeetaylorhandcrafted.com, 530-2743737, 163 Mill St., Grass Valley, CA. Jewelry for the soul, is the theme of this beautiful gallery—but it isn't limited to just jewelry. Be sure to check out the wonderful photography, ceramics, and other handmade works of art.

Firefall Jewelers, 209-736-1550, 1255 Main St., Angels Camp, CA. Owners Paul and Noreen Coca have one of the largest selections of unique colored stone pieces in the Gold Country. The master jeweler is ready to assist with all custom design needs, as well as repairs.

Gold Mine Jewelers, www.goldmine-jewelers.net, 209-223-0713, 37 Main St., Jackson, CA. A nice treasure trove of jewelry and specialty items.

OZ! Gallery of Fine Jewelry, www.ozgallery.net, 530-888-9059, 198 Sacramento St., Auburn, CA. OZ! showcases the designs of owner and operator Catherine Rowe, as well as ten other international designers and artists. The gallery specializes in one-of-a-kind and custom-designed pieces. An extensive collection of gemstones and beads can also be found.

Specialty & Eclectic

D.E.A. Bathroom Machineries, www.deabath.com, 209-728-2031, 495 Main St., Murphys, CA. Unlike any plumbing or hardware store you've ever seen, this is an antique plumbing shop featuring original and reproduction claw-foot tubs, high-tank toilets, pedestal sinks, mirrors, restored lighting fixtures, and much more.

Sonora's Secret, 209-588-1400, 98 S. Washington St., Sonora, CA. It's no secret to locals, but Sonora's Secret is a great stop for unique and useful items for the kitchen, bath, and garden. Large supply of cool kitchen gadgets and gizmos, great scents and accessories for the bath, and maybe a gnome for the garden.

The Rusty Bear, www.therustybear.com, 209-795-4303, 2781 Highway 4, Arnold, CA. This shop specializes in unique mountain products, including carved bears, and log and rustic furniture. Some great chain-saw carvings; mostly one-of-a-kind items.

Wierschem's Train Town, 209-223-0250, 139 Main St., Jackson, CA. A fun shop—featuring model railroad supplies, train sets, and models—it doubles as a 1950s-style candy

Yum! Wierschem's Train Town in Jackson offers something for every sweet tooth.

New Melones Lake near Angels Camp, a manmade reservoir, is a popular summer recreation area.

and ice cream parlor, including saltwater taffy, fine chocolates, and many sugar-free selections.

Sports

Ebbett's Pass Sporting Goods, www.ebbettspasssportinggoods.com, 209-795-1686, 925 CA 4, Arnold, CA. Let the adventure begin. This is an old-fashioned sporting goods store, well stocked with everything you'll need for fishing, hunting, skiing, and hiking. Fishing and hunting licenses, along with plenty of good advice.

Glory Hole Sports, 209-736-4333, 2892 Hwy. 49 (at the entrance to New Melones Lake), Angels Camp, CA. The folks at Glory Hole say, "Our mission is to get you fishin'." They feature one of the largest selections of fishing tackle in the Mother Lode. Also, check out their fine line of water toys, wakeboards, and water skis.

Sierra Nevada Adventure Company, 1-888-900-SNAC, 173 S. Washington St., Sonora, CA, and 2293 Hwy 4, Arnold, CA. Outdoor gear store, owned and operated by outdoor lovers. Stocks the latest equipment for skiers, river runners, and hikers alike. Priced so that you can spend more time using your gear than paying for it.

6

INFORMATION

Nuts & Bolts

AMBULANCE/FIRE/POLICE/SHERIFF

Always remember that 911 is the number to report an emergency anywhere in California and Nevada. Should you require an ambulance, need to report a fire, or need to report a situation where police/sheriff's assistance is required, that's the number to call. The person receiving your call is highly trained to redirect your call to the proper authorities. However, for police or sheriff's assistance for a non-emergency situation, refer to the telephone numbers listed below.

Lake Tahoe & Truckee
(Area Code CA 530, NV 775)

TOWN POLICE/SHERIFF

Incline Village	775-832-4110
Meyers	530-544-3464
South Lake Tahoe	530-542-6100
Stateline	775-586-7250
Tahoe City	530-581-6300
Truckee	530-550-2320
U.S. Coast Guard	530-583-8438

Reno, Carson Valley & Virginia City (Area Code 775)

TOWN POLICE/SHERIFF

Carson City	267-3691
Gardnerville	265-7090
Genoa	265-7090
Minden	265-7090
Reno	334-2175
Sparks	353-2231
Univ. of Nevada	784-4013
Virginia City	847-0959

Gold Country North to South
(Area Code 530 north, 209 south)

SIERRA COUNTY

TOWN POLICE/SHERIFF

Downieville	530-289-3700
Sierra City	530-289-3700

Nevada County

TOWN POLICE/SHERIFF

Grass Valley	530-477-4600
Nevada City	530-265-4700
Rough and Ready	530-265-1291

Placer County

TOWN POLICE/SHERIFF

Auburn	530-885-2424
Foresthill	530-889-7846
Loomis	530-889-7846

LEFT: *Antique shopping is a favorite activity for visitors and locals throughout the Gold Country.*

El Dorado County

TOWN POLICE/SHERIFF

Camino	530-621-6600
Coloma	530-621-6600
Diamond Springs	530-621-6600
El Dorado	530-621-6600
Georgetown	530-621-6600
Placerville	530-642-5298

Amador County

TOWN POLICE/SHERIFF

Amador City	209-223-6500
Drytown	209-245-3021
Fiddletown	209-223-6500
Jackson	209-223-6500
Pine Grove	209-223-6500
Pioneer	209-223-6500
Plymouth	209-245-3021
Sutter Creek	209-223-6500
Volcano	209-223-6500

Calaveras County

TOWN POLICE/SHERIFF

Angels Camp	209-736-2567
Arnold	209-795-0473
Copperopolis	209-785-6550
Mokelumne Hill	209-286-1330
Mountain Ranch	209-754-3325
Murphys	209-754-6500
San Andreas	209-754-6500
Valley Springs	209-754-6500

Tuolumne County

TOWN POLICE/SHERIFF

Columbia	209-532-8420
Groveland	209-962-6974
Jamestown	209-533-5831
Sonora	209-532-8143
Tuolumne	209-928-1703

Alpine County

TOWN POLICE/SHERIFF

Bear Valley	209-753-2321
Markleeville	530-694-2231

AREA CODES

Three area codes service this region. Lake Tahoe (California side) and all northern Mother Lode counties use 530. For southern Mother Lode counties, use 209. The area code for all northern Nevada is 775.

BANKS

In this era of electronic teller machines, travelers have easy access to their bank accounts. National and community banks throughout the region offer 24-hour access, as do all gaming houses and even some state parks.

BIBLIOGRAPHY

It can be argued that no other region on earth provides as much historic material and photographic inspiration as Lake Tahoe, Virginia City, and the Mother Lode. Its rich, colorful history and beautiful scenery have inspired countless storytellers, historians, photographers, and cinematographers. Bookstores throughout the region pride themselves on offering a wealth of historical and contemporary material for readers of all ages and tastes. Here are a few suggestions to get you started:

A reproduction of a miner's boardinghouse. The first three burned down, but the spelling of "cotage" has been retained since the 1850s.

Biography and Reminiscence

Anderson, Bill. *Bill's Big Bonanza*. William Anderson, 2003, 150 pp. The true story of one of the most famous ranches in the world. When people started showing up on his property on Lake Tahoe's north shore looking for the fictional Ponderosa Ranch, Anderson quickly threw together a horse stable and called it the Ponderosa Ranch. Tourists loved it and the ranch became a major attraction. Interesting reading of a third-grade dropout living the great American dream.

De Quille, William W. *The Big Bonanza*. A. A. Knopf, 1980 450 pp. Dan De Quille came west in 1857 and traveled to the Comstock upon hearing of the big silver strike. As a miner, he was a failure, but he joined the *Territorial Enterprise* in Virginia City in 1862, and remained with the publication until it folded in 1893. During his first year on the staff, the paper hired Samuel Clemens, who later became Mark Twain. Written in first-person format, the book chronicles the life and times of the author, Twain, and Virginia City during the bonanza years.

Drury, Wells. *An Editor on the Comstock Lode.* University of Nevada Press, 1985, 343 pp. Originally published in 1948, this is a great collection of vignettes about life on the Comstock, highlighting some of the area's most notable individuals.

Frohlich, Robert. *Mountain Dreamers: Visionaries of Sierra Nevada Skiing.* Coldstream Press, 1997, 152 pp. Anyone who has ever strapped on a pair of skis will enjoy this work about the men and women who built the skiing industry in the Sierra Nevada. Most of these people started with a rope tow or two, little money, and very big dreams. Excellent photography as well.

Laurgaard, Rachel K. *Patty Reed's Doll: The Story of the Donner Party.* Tomato Enterprises, 1989, 143 pp. Patty Reed, one of the survivors of the 1846 Donner party, was only 8 years old when she made the trip. She kept a tiny wooden doll hidden in her dress. The book is Patty's story as seen through the eyes of her doll named Dolly. The story gives tremendous insight into the life experiences of pioneer children. Dolly can be seen today at Sutter's Fort State Historic Park in Sacramento, CA.

A rare globe, built in 1880 and valued at more than $100,000, adorns the wall of a Virginia City saloon/restaurant.

Lord, Eliot. *Comstock Mining and Miners.* Howell North Press, 1980, 451 pp. The author was with the US Geological Survey from 1879 to 1883 and was assigned to work and document the Comstock and gather mining statistics in the area. Considered the most definitive study of the Comstock mining history available.

McLaughlin, Mark. *Sierra Stories; True Tales of Tahoe,* Vols 1 and 2. MicMac, 1997-98, 110,121 pp. From Nellie Bly to Mark Twain, these very readable books contain the stories of pioneers who ventured into the Sierra Nevada. Very good reading for all ages.

Waldorf, John. *A Kid On The Comstock.* American West Pub., 1970. During the boom years of the Comstock, it was no place for children, yet the author grew up in the midst of all the action. The son of a miner and school teacher, he arrived there in 1873 and spent the next twelve years as a "menace to parental peace of mind." At age 15, he ran away to make his fortune on the high seas.

Fiction

Clark, Walter Van Tilburg. *The Ox-Bow Incident.* Modern Library Classics, 2004, 288 pp. Set in 1885, this is one of the best examples of frontier life and mob violence in the American West. Originally published in 1940, it tells the story of three innocent drifters hung for a crime they did not commit. This edition contains a great introduction written by Wallace Stegner.

Harte, Bret. *Bret Harte's Gold Rush: The Outcasts of Poker Flat, The Luck of Roaring Camp, Tennessee's Partner & Other Favorites.* Heyday Books, 1996, 178 pp. Along with Mark Twain, Harte is another literary giant who found his roots in the California Gold Country, and this collection contains some of his best gold-rush inspired short stories. Although written more than 150 years ago, these stories have the power to make the reader laugh out loud, and bring a tear to the eye.

Houston, James. *Snow Mountain Passage.* Harvest Books, 2002. This is historical fiction at its best. Told from the perspectives of Patty Reed, just a girl during the crossing, and her father James. Banished from the group, James makes it to the safety of Sutter's Fort before the heavy snow of 1846, but his rescue efforts have to wait out both the weather and political turmoil.

Lasky, Kathryn. *Alice Rose & Sam.* Hyperion, 1999, 208 pp. 12-year-old Alice Rose lives in Virginia City in the 1860s, and hates it. She doesn't give a hoot about silver and, rightly so, believes the ruckus boomtown to be no place for a kid. She witnesses a murder in a dark alley and with the help of a friend and ally, young reporter Sam Clemens, she is able to solve the murder. A lively read for kids.

Twain, Mark. *Roughing It.* University of California Press, 2002, 885 pp. Sometimes with Twain it's hard to tell truth from fiction—and that's just the way he liked it. This is one of his classics, relating his adventures leaving Missouri and traveling to Virginia City, where he fails as a miner, but lands a job as a reporter with the *Territorial Enterprise*. This is where Samuel L. Clemens took the pen name Mark Twain. The saga then moves on to California, and his adventures in the Mother Lode.

Twain, Mark *The Celebrated Jumping Frog of Calaveras County, and Other Sketches,* 1897. Oxford University Press, USA, 1996, 288 pp. This is where Mark Twain's literary career began. Life in the diggings was often difficult, but these stories wonderfully exemplify the sense of fun and frivolity that also existed in the mining camps of California and Nevada.

No riders allowed. A celebration of the Harley-Davidson created out of wicker.

History and Cultural Studies

Brands, H.W. *The Age of Gold: The California Gold Rush and the New American Dream.* Anchor, 2002, 592 pp. This is a well written look at the cultural and economic meaning of the gold rush by one of America's great historians. Brands correctly argues, among other things, that when James Marshall found gold, he unwittingly initiated the modern era of American economic development.

California Council for the Humanities. *Gold Rush: A Literary Exploration.* Heyday Books, 1997, 477 pp. This companion book to the 1998 PBS documentary is a large gathering of firsthand recollections of the gold rush, drawn from memoirs and letters. The first-person narratives give a good sense of what it was like to take part in the Gold Rush adventure. Includes stories from all walks of life.

DiCerto, Joseph J. *The Saga of the Pony Express.* MJF Books, 2005, 244 pp. A well-researched and very readable history of the Pony Express. The author does a commendable job retracing the original route and exploring the personalities of the venture's founders. Fine reading for anyone interested in this short segment of American history.

Goldman, Marion S. *Gold Diggers and Silver Miners; Prostitution and Social Life on the Comstock.* University of Michigan Press, 1981, 248 pp. This is a scholarly, yet readable, examination of those who came to the Comstock to seek their fortune. This book provides a detailed account of prostitution on the Comstock. By considering sexual commerce in a community, she explores general relationships between prostitution and society, shedding light on important sociological issues.

Hardesty, Donald L. *The Archaeology of the Donner Party.* University of Nevada Press, 2005, 168 pp. Hardesty and four colleagues—a historian and three other archaeologists—recreate an original and sometimes surprising new study of the Donner Party and their place in the history of overland migration. Their work is a meticulous investigation of the Sierra sites, analysis of artifacts, and interpretation of the documents of the party, and the memoirs of the survivors.

Hegne, Barbara. *The Unsettled Chinese, Virginia City, Nevada.* Barbara Hegne, 2004. They were enterprising and discriminated against, but the more than one thousand Chinese who lived in Virginia City during the boom years made up a vital part of the cultural and social fabric of the area. This is an interesting look into an area of Comstock that has little documentation, but is an important part of the region's history.

Holiday, J.S. *The World Rushed in: The California Gold Rush Experience.* University of Oklahoma Press, 2002, 568 pp. The author builds upon the copious journals of William Swain, a gold miner, to weave an epic work about the California gold rush. This is a personal, intimate story of one man's search for wealth in the west. The triumphs and tragedies of Swain and his compatriots are captured in vivid, human terms.

The Sun Sun Wo Co. "House of Treasures" in Coulterville reflects the Chinese influence in the Gold Country.

James, Ronald M. *The Roar and The Silence.* University of Nevada Press, 1998, 384 pp. An authentic history of Virginia City and the Comstock. This book brings the Comstock to life, and is a thorough look at the cultural and social makeup of the community, its fraternal groups, and entertainment activities. The author is Nevada's state historic preservation officer.

James, Ronald and C. Elizabeth Raymond *Comstock Women.* University of Nevada Press, 1997, 408 pp. In many ways, Virginia City was nothing more than a ramshackle mining camp, yet it was home to a large number of women and children. This collection of essays by scholars from several disciplines examines the lives of the women who settled in the area and struggled to create a stable community.

Johnson, Susan Lee. *Roaring Camp: The Social World of the California Gold Rush.* W. W. Norton & Company, 2000, 341 pp., index, illus. A award-winning scholarly examination of many of the social issues confronted by those seeking their fortune in the southern mines of the Mother Lode. Including an examination of domestic life in the diggings, and a very interesting reexamination of the "desperado" Joaquin Murieta.

King, Joseph A. *Winter of Entrapment: a New Look at the Donner Party.* K&K, 1998, 257 pp. This is the third edition of one of the best accounts of the tragic Donner party. Of the 89 party members, 41 perished along the trail or in the infamous mountain camps. It explores the strength of character of people faced with unbelievable physical and moral tests. Winner of the Award of Merit from the California Historical Society.

Levy, Jo Ann. *They Saw the Elephant: Women in the California Gold Rush.* University of Oklahoma Press, 1992, 265 pp. All too often, the women who came west during the California gold rush are overlooked. This books rectifies that historical error and offers colorful accounts of these female argonauts—with or without men. She explores the leadership roles of women in many walks of life, including all forms of business enterprise.

McDonald, Douglas. *The Legend of Julia Bulette and the Red Light Ladies of Nevada.* Stanley Paher/Nevada Publishing, 1983. Yes, Julia was a prostitute—but she was also one of the most beloved people in Virginia City during the boom-boom years. She helped organize and operate charities, was a member of the volunteer fire department, and often went out on calls. A massive funeral followed her murder in 1867, and her killer was hanged shortly thereafter.

Roberts, Brian. *American Alchemy: The California Gold Rush and Middle-Class Culture.* The University of North Carolina Press, 2000, 360 pp. California during the gold rush is depicted as a place of shootouts, fights over claims, gambling halls, and prostitutes. However, Roberts argues the story overlooks the fact that whatever the gold seekers abandoned on the road to California, they did not simply turn their backs on middle-class culture.

Secrest, William B. *California Desperadoes* World Dancer Press, 2000, 257 pp. Learn about the ill-starred adventures of Tom Bell, Tiburcio Vasquez, and many other bad boys of the California Gold Rush. Meet stage robbers and highwaymen who will take you on their harrowing, and sometimes hilarious, adventures.

Stillson, Richard T. *Spreading the Word: A History of Information in the California Gold Rush.* A unique analysis of the ways in which those who traveled west during the California gold

RIGHT: *Just what will you find in the Julia C. Bullette Red Light Museum?*

rush obtained, assessed, and used information. Initially there was very little available, but before long newspapers, publishers, and others hastened to cash in on gold fever. Unfortunately, much of the "new" information was unreliable, contradictory, and changed frequently. Stillson examines the connection between media, myth, and reality in the formative years of the nation.

Stone, Irving. *Men to Match My Mountains: The Opening of the Far West, 1840-1900.* Doubleday & Co., 1956, 459 pp. A truly great portrait of the expansion of the American West. Stone weaves several stories depicting how, in a few short decades, the United States grew to dimensions beyond the dreams of the founding fathers.

Nature Guides

Beesley, David. *Crow's Range: An Environmental History of the Sierra Nevada.* University of Nevada Press, 2004, 390 pp. An engaging account of the history, environmental challenges, and political controversies behind the breathtaking scenery of the Sierra Nevada. Examines the effects of the Gold Rush and the roles of regulatory agencies, as well as the impact of tourism and recreational use on the 400-mile mountain range.

The little ones enjoy themselves at the Children's Museum of Northern Nevada in Carson City.

Hill, Mary. *Geology of the Sierra Nevada.* University of California Press, 2006, 468 pp. For more than 30 years, the first edition of this book has served as the definitive guide to the geology of this magnificent mountain range. This edition offers new chapters, sidebars, and incorporates the concept of plate tectonics throughout. She also guides the reader through the eons of geologic time before the land mass that became California existed.

Keater, Glenn, Ph.D. *Sierra Flower Finder.* Nature Study Guide, 1980, 121 pp. This handy guide will help you identify the hundreds of beautiful wildflowers found in the High Sierra region above the foothills. The introductory section explains some of the terms and the distribution, habitat, and life-zone symbols used.

Photography

James, Ronald M. and Susan A. *Castle In The Sky: George Whittell and the Thunderbird Lodge.* Thunderbird Lodge Press, 2002, 80 pp. This collaboration offers a fascinating photo-history of one of Lake Tahoe's most colorful characters. This is the story of how he came to the eastern shore of Lake Tahoe and build his incredible castle. It also chronicles his influence on the environmental legacy of Lake Tahoe.

Pesetski, Larry. *A Journey to Lake Tahoe & Beyond.* Sierra Vista Publications, 118 pp. Pesetski has spent a lifetime shooting beautiful and unique areas in America. This time, he turns his eye to Lake Tahoe and captures some amazing winter and summer shots. Includes a gorgeous section of wildflower close-ups.

Scott, Edward B. *The Saga of Lake Tahoe,* Vols. 1 and 2. Sierra-Tahoe, 1957, 1973, 519, 528 pp. The author is a recognized authority on the Tahoe region, and these volumes contain hundreds of black and white photographs. The works are considered indispensable for the scholar and amateur historian.

Wrisley, Kristin and Charles Moore. *The Mother Lode: A Celebration of California's Gold Country.* Chronicle Books, 1999, 132 pp. Prepared for the 150th anniversary of the California Gold Rush, this publication is filled with lively text and beautiful photographs. Includes more than 150 images.

CLIMATE, WEATHER, WHAT TO WEAR

What to wear depends on just where you are going in this region and the time of year. Let's start with Lake Tahoe.

At lake level, Tahoe receives an average of 125 inches of snow a year, and that zooms up to 300 to 500 inches at alpine skiing elevations. In spite of all the snow, the sun shines 75 percent of the time, or about 274 days a year. During ski season, roughly November through April, daytime temperatures don't get much above 50 degrees and nights drop into the teens. In short, dress warm.

Prime summer months are July and August when temperatures can get into the 80s during the day, and drop into the 30s at night. If you are camping or going out on the town in the evening, take a sweater or jacket. The lake's surface water temperature during the summer usually is in the high 60s.

The spring and fall months at Lake Tahoe are beautiful, usually featuring cool, sunny days and chilly, star-filled nights. Keep in mind than an early or late-season snowstorm can roll in at anytime, so be prepared.

The Carson Valley, Reno, and Virginia City are much lower in elevation than Lake Tahoe, but they are considered high desert. That means that it can get quite cold at night during the winter, and very warm during the summer. Temperatures range from an average high of more than 90 degrees in the summer, to an average low of 20 degrees in the winter. The Sierra Nevada block most precipitation from entering the area, but it still receives about eight inches of rain annually and some snowfall is not uncommon. The winter traveler should also be aware that the entire region is subject to periods of dense fog. Locals call the fog *pogonip*, Paiute for "white death."

Along the western slope of the Sierra Nevada, the Gold Country climate has been described as resembling that of Spain or Italy. As a general rule, the foothills are not subject to the dense, winter tule fog that often shrouds the valley floor for weeks on end. Winters are usually cool and damp, receiving an average of 30 inches of rain plus the occasional snowfall. Temperatures range from in the 20s to the mid-50s. In the higher elevations, the climate is similar to that of Lake Tahoe.

Since virtually all of the rain falls in the winter, summers are hot and dry and it is not uncommon for temperatures to reach triple digits for a week or more. While this is also the peak tourist season, locals will tell you that as far as the weather is concerned, the best time to explore the Mother Lode is during the spring or fall, when the nights are cool and the days are warm.

FISHING & HUNTING REGULATIONS

Both California and Nevada require the appropriate licenses for all fishing and hunting activities in this region. For more information about regulations and fees in California, contact the Department of Fish and Game, License & Revenue Branch at 916-928-5805 or go online at: www.dfg.ca.gov/licensing/. In Nevada, contact the Department of Wildlife at 775-688-1500 or go online at: www.ndow.org/about/contacts/.

HOSPITALS & EMERGENCY CARE SERVICE

The northern Sierra Nevada and western Nevada area is blessed with many top-notch healthcare providers. Most of the facilities listed below provide 24-hour emergency services. Also, keep in mind that if you have a medical emergency, don't hesitate—just call 911.

Lake Tahoe & Truckee

Barton Memorial Hospital, www.bartonhealth.org. 530-541-3420, 2170 South Ave., South Lake Tahoe, CA.

Incline Village Community Hospital, www.tfhd.com. 775-832-3811, 880 Alder Ave., Incline Village, NV.

Lake Tahoe Surgery Center, www.laketahoesurgerycenter.com. 775-588-9188, 212 Elks Point Rd., No. 201, Zephyr Cove, NV.

Tahoe Forest Community Hospital, www.tfhd.com. 530-587-6011, 10121 Pine Ave., Truckee, CA.

LEFT: *Iron doors and a front wall are all that remain of this Gold Rush-era building.*

Reno & Carson Valley

Barton Memorial Hospital, www.bartonhealth.org. 775-782-1519, 1107 Us Highway 395 N. Gardnerville, NV

Carson Tahoe Regional Medical Center, www.carsontahoe.com/ctrmc, 775-882-1361, 1600 Medical Pkwy., Carson City, NV.

Carson Valley Medical Center, www.carsonvalleymedicalcenter.org, 775-782-1500, 1107 US 395 N. Gardnerville, NV.

Carson Valley Medical Center, www.carsonvalleymedicalcenter.org, 775-782-3417, 1649 Lucerne St., Minden, NV.

Eagle Medical Center, www.arcmedcenters.com, 2874 N. Carson St., Carson City, NV.

Evergreen Healthcare, www.evergreenhealthcare.com, 1565 Virginia Ranch Rd., Gardnerville, NV.

Evergreen Mountain View Health, www.evergreenhealthcare.com, 201 Koontz Ln., Carson City, NV.

HCA Truckee Meadows Hospital, 1-800-242-0478, 1240 E. 9th St., Reno, NV.

MedDirect Urgent Care, www.carsontahoe.com/ctrmc, 775-267-6394, 961 Mica Dr # A, Carson City, NV.

Northern Nevada Medical Center, www.northernnvmed.com, 775-331-7000, 2375 E Prater Way, Sparks, NV.

Reno ARC MedCenter, www.arcmedcenters.com, 775-284-5556, 6180 Mae Anne Ave.,Ste. 1 Reno, NV.

Renown South Meadows Medical Center, www.renown.org, 775-982-7000, 10101 Double R Blvd. Reno, NV.

Sparks ARC MedCenter, www.arcmedcenters.com, 775-331-3361, 2205 Glendale Ave., Sparks, NV.

Saint Mary's Regional Medical Center, www.saintmarysreno.com, 775-770-3000, 235 W 6th St. Reno, NV.

Surgical Arts Surgery Center, 775-954-0600, 5411 Kietzke Ln., Reno, NV

University of Nevada, Reno Student Health Center, www.unr.edu/shc/, 775.784.6598, Redfield Building M/S 196, Reno, NV.

Western Nevada Surgical Center, 775-882-4477, 1299 Mountain St., Carson City, NV.

Gold Country (North to South)
SIERRA COUNTY
Loyalton Hospital, www.ephc.org, 530-993-1225, 700 3rd St., Loyalton, CA.

Nevada County
Sierra Nevada Memorial Hospital, www.snmh.org, 530-274-6000, 155 Glasson Way, Grass Valley, CA.

Placer County
Sutter Auburn Faith Hospital, www.sutteramador.org, 530-888-4500, 11815 Education St., Auburn, CA.

El Dorado County
Marshall Medical Center, www.marshallmedical.org, 530-622-1441, 1080 Marshall Way, Placerville, CA.

Amador County
Pioneer–West Point Community Health Center, 209-295-5544, SR 88, Pioneer, CA.

Sutter Amador Hospital, www.sutteramador.org, 209-223-7500, 200 Mission Blvd., Jackson, CA.

Calaveras County
Family Medical Center–Angels Camp, 209-736-0813, 222 S. Main St., Angels Camp, CA.

Family Medical Center–Arnold, 209-795-4193, 2182 SR 4, Arnold, CA.

Family Medical Center–Copperopolis, 209-785-7000, 3505 Spangler Ln Ste 400, Copperopolis, CA.

Immediate Care, 209-772-9538, 1919 Vista Del Lago Dr., Valley Springs, CA.

Mark Twain St. Joseph's Hospital, www.marktwainhospital.org, 209-754-3521, 768 Mountain Ranch Rd., San Andreas, CA.

Mark Twain St. Josephs Hospital, www.marktwainhospital.org, 209-785-7000, 3505 Spangler Ln. Ste 400, Copperopolis, CA.

Mark Twain St. Josephs Hospital Family Medical Centers, www.marktwainhospital.org, 209-772-9538, 1919 Vista Del Lago Dr., Valley Springs, CA.

Tuolumne County
Sonora Regional Medical Center, www.sonoramedicalcenter.org, 209-532-5000, 1000 Greenley Rd., Sonora, CA.

Tuolumne General Hospital, 209-533-7100, 101 Hospital Rd., Sonora, CA.

LOCAL GOVERNMENT & ZIP CODES

Sometimes you just need to talk to the person in charge. It might be a political issue, or some other reason to contact the leadership of a particular community. Here's a list of the main number for each of the communities in this book. If you do have a complaint and get into some sort of brouhaha, just don't tell the person you chew out where you got their number.

Lake Tahoe

Town	Telephone	Zip Code
Incline Village	775-832-4109	89452
Meyers	530-573-3000	96150
South Lake Tahoe	530-542-6004	96150
Stateline	775-586-7215	89449
Tahoe City	530-889-4010	96145
Truckee	530-582-7700	96161

Reno, Carson Valley & Virginia City

Town	Telephone	Zip Code
Carson City	775-887-2100	89701
Gardnerville	775-782-7134	89410
Genoa	775-782-8696	89410
Minden	775-782-5976	89423
Reno	775-334-2433	89501
Sparks	775-353-7783	89431
Virginia City	775-847-0959	89440

Gold Country (North to South)

SIERRA COUNTY

Town	Telephone	Zip Code
Downieville	530-289-3700	95936
Loyalton	530-993-4440	96118
Sierra City	530-289-3700	96125

Nevada County

Town	Telephone	Zip Code
Grass Valley	530-274-4310	95945
Nevada City	530-265-2351	95959
Rough and Ready	530-432-1140	95946

Placer County

Town	Telephone	Zip Code
Auburn	530-823-4211	95603
Loomis	530-652-1840	95650
Foresthill	530-889-4000	95631

El Dorado County

Town	Telephone	Zip Code
Coloma	530-621-5567	95613
Cool	530-621-5567	95614
Diamond Springs	530-621-5567	95619

El Dorado	530-621-5567	95623
Georgetown	530-621-5567	95634
Placerville	530-642-5240	95667

Amador County

TOWN	TELEPHONE	ZIP CODE
Amador City	209-267-0682	95601
Drytown	209-223-6470	95699
Fiddletown	209-296-0918	95629
Jackson	209-223-1646	95642
Pine Grove	209-223-6470	95665
Pioneer	209-223-6470	95666
Plymouth	209-245-6941	95669
Sutter Creek	209-267-5647	95685
Volcano	209-223-6470	95689

Calaveras County

TOWN	TELEPHONE	ZIP CODE
Angels Camp	209-736-2181	95222
Arnold	209-754-6333	95223
Copperopolis	209-754-6333	95228
Mokelumne Hill	209-754-6333	95245
Mountain Ranch	209-754-6333	95246
Murphys	209-736-0139	95247
San Andreas	209-754-6333	95249
Valley Springs	209-754-6333	95252

Tuolumne County

TOWN	TELEPHONE	ZIP CODE
Columbia	209-533-5511	95310
Groveland	209-533-5511	95321
Jamestown	209-533-5511	95327
Sonora	209-532-7725	95370
Twain Harte	209-533-5511	95383

Alpine County

TOWN	TELEPHONE	ZIP CODE
Markleeville	530-694-2235	96120
Kirkwood	530-694-2235	95646

MEDIA

Lake Tahoe

NEWSPAPERS & MAGAZINES

North Lake Tahoe Bonanza, www.tahoebonanza.com, 775-831-4666, 925 Tahoe Blvd., Suite 206, Incline Village, NV.

Sierra Sun, www.sierrasun.com, 530-587-6061, 12315 Deerfield Dr., Truckee, CA.

Tahoe Daily Tribune, www.tahoedailytribune.com, 530-541-3880, 3079 Harrison Avenue, South Lake Tahoe, CA.

Tahoe World, www.tahoe-world.com, 530-583-3487, 395 N. Lake Blvd., Tahoe City, CA.

RADIO

FM

88.7 KUNR   Reno, www.kunr.org, 775-327-5867. Public radio.

90.5 KKTO   Tahoe City, www.csus.edu/npr. 916-480-5900. Public radio.

91.3 KNIS   Carson City, www.pilgrimradio.com, 775-883-5647. Christian.

93.9 KRLT   South Lake Tahoe, www.krltfm.com. 530-541-6681. AC radio.

95.5 KNEV   Reno, 775-789-6700, Top 40.

96.5 KLCA   Tahoe City, www.alice965.com. 775-829-1964. Hot AC radio.

97.3 KZTQ   Gardnerville, www.nvikias.com/radio_fm/kztq.htm, 775-823-1919. News, talk, music.

98.1 KBUL   Reno, www.kbul.com, 775-789-6700. Country.

100.9 KRZQ   Sparks, www.krzqfm.com, 775-333-0123. Alternative.

102.9 KWYL   South Lake Tahoe, www.wild1029.com. Hip hop.

103.7 KODS   Carnelian Bay 775-829-1964. Classic hits.

104.5 KDOT   Reno, www.kdot.com, 775-329-9261. Rock.

105.7 KOZZ   Reno, www.kozzradio.com, 775-329-9261. Classic rock.

106.9 KRNO   Incline Village, sunny1069.com. 775-829-1964. Adult.

107.7 KSRN   Kings Beach, 775-322-9292. Spanish radio.

AM

590 KTHO   South Lake Tahoe, www.airamericaradio.com. 530-542-5800. Talk radio.

1300 KTPL   Carson City, www.kptlradio.com, 775-884-8000, News, oldies.

1490 KOWL   South Lake Tahoe, www.krltfm.com. 530-541-6681. News radio.

TELEVISION

K-MTN-Channel South Lake Tahoe, 530-541-8686. Local.

KOLO-Channel 8, Reno, 775-858-8888, ABC.

KREN-Channel 27, Reno, 775-333-2727. Warner.

KRNV-Channel 4, Reno, 775-322-4444. NBC.

KRXI-Channel 11, Reno, 775-856-1101. FOX.

KTVN-Channel 2, Reno, 775-858-2222. CBS.

Reno, Carson Valley & Virginia City

NEWSPAPERS & MAGAZINES

Nevada Appeal, www.nevadaappeal.com, 775-882-2111 or 1-800-221-8013, 580 Mallory Way, Carson City, NV.

Northern Nevada Business Weekly, www.nnbw.biz, 775-770-1173, 780 Smithridge Dr. Ste. 200, Reno, NV.

Reno Gazette-Journal, news.rgj.com, 1-800-970-7366, 955 Kuenzli St., Reno, NV.

Reno News & Review, www.newsreview.com/reno, 775-324-4440, 708 N Center St., Reno, NV.

The Record-Courier, www.recordcourier.com, 775-782-5121,1503 Highway 395 N., Suite G, Gardnerville, NV.

The Corner Post, 775-782-5121, 1503 US 395 North, Gardnerville, NV.

RADIO

FM

88.7 KUNR   Reno, www.kunr.org, 775-327-5867. Public radio.

91.3 KNIS   Carson City, www.pilgrimradio.com, 775-883-5647. Christian.

93.7 KWNZ   Sun Valley, www.kwnz.com, 775-829-1964. Hip-hop.

94.5 KUUB   Cub Country, Reno, 775-793-2822. Country.

95.5 KNEV   Reno, 775-789-6700, Top 40.

96.5 KLAC   Reno, 775-851-9650. Soft rock.

97.3 KZTQ   Gardnerville, www.nvikias.com/radio_fm/kztq.htm, 775-823-1919, News, talk, music.

98.1 KBUL   Reno, www.kbul.com, 775-789-6700. Country.

99.1 KKFT   Carson City, www.991fmtalk.com, 775-884-8000, Talk.

100.9 KRZQ   Sparks, www.krzqfm.com, 775-333-0123. Alternative.

101.7 KSRN   Reno, 775-324-4819. News talk.

104.5 KDOT   Reno, www.kdot.com, 775-329-9261. Rock.

105.7 KOZZ   Reno, www.kozzradio.com, 775-329-9261. Classic rock.

106.9 KRNO   Sunny 106.9, Reno, sunny1069.com/, 775-829-1964, Easy listening.

AM

1270 KBZZ   The Buzz, Reno, www.kbzz.com, 775-823-1920. Hot talk.

1300 KTPL   Carson City, www.kptlradio.com, 775-884-8000, News, oldies.

1550 KXTO   Reno, 775-828-1550. Spanish language music, talk.

TELEVISION

KAME-Channel 21 Reno, 775-856-2222. UPN.

KENV-Channel 10 Elko, 775-777-8500. NBC.

KNVV-Channel 41 Reno, 775-333-1017, Univision

KOLO-Channel 8 Reno, 775-858-8888, ABC.

KREN-Channel 27 Reno, 775-333-2727. Warner.

KRNV-Channel 4 Reno, 775-322-4444. NBC.

KRXI-Channel 11, Reno, 775-856-1101. FOX.

KTVN-Channel 2 Reno, 775-858-2222. CBS.

Gold Country

NEWSPAPERS & MAGAZINES

Amador Ledger Dispatch, www.ledger-dispatch.com, 209-223-3510, 10776 Argonaut Ln., Jackson, CA.

Auburn Journal, www.auburnjournal.com. 530-885-5656, 1030 High St., Auburn, CA.

Calaveras Enterprise, www.calaverasenterprise.com, 209-754-3861, 15 Main St., San Andreas, CA.

Foresthill Messenger, 530-367-3966, 5830 Sunset Dr. No. 50, Foresthill, CA.

Georgetown Gazette, 530-333-4481, 2775 Miners Flat, Georgetown, CA.

Gold Country Times, www.goldcountrytimes.com, 209-267-9886, P.O. Box 897, Sutter Creek, CA.

Mountain Democrat, www.mtdemocrat.com. 530-622-1255, 1360 Broadway, Placerville, CA

Mountain Messenger, 530-289-3262, 313 Main St., Downieville, CA.

Sacramento Bee, www.sacbee.com, 916-321-1000, 2100 Q Street, Sacramento, CA.

Sierra Booster, 530-993-4379, 411 2nd St., Loyalton, CA.

Sierra Mountain Times, www.sierramountaintimes.com, 209-586-3675, 18711 Tiffeni Dr Ste K, Twain Harte, CA.

The Foothill Trader, 530-272-4919, 11890 Maltman Dr., Grass Valley, CA.

The Record, www.recordnet.com, San Andreas Bureau 209-754-9534, 39 Main St., San Andreas, CA.

The Union, www.theunion.com, 530-273-9561, 464 Sutton Way, Grass Valley, CA.

The Union Democrat, www.uniondemocrat.com, 209-532-7151, 84 S. Washington St., Sonora, CA.

The Valley Springs News, www.valleyspringsnews.com, 209-772-2234, 10 Nove Way Ste. A, Valley Springs, CA.

Yosemite Highway Herald, www.yosemitehwyherald.com, 209-962-7425, 18800 Main St., Groveland, CA.

Radio (North to South)

Sierra County
FM

89.5 KVMR   Nevada City, www.kvmr.org, 530-265-9073. Music, talk.

94.1 KNCO   Grass Valley, www.mystarradio.com, 530-272-3424. 80s, 90s music.

95.9 KNLF   Chico, www.afr.net, 530-283-4145. Family radio.

97.7 KHHZ   Oroville, 530-345-0021. Spanish language radio.

99.3 KLVS   Grass Valley, www.klove.com, 707-528-9236. Christian.

103.3 KCEE   Grass Valley, www.kcee.fm. Talk radio.

AM

830 KNCO   Sacramento, www.knco.com, 530-272-3424. News, talk radio.

1370 KPCO   Quincy, 530-283-1370. Nostalgia radio.

Nevada County
FM

89.5 KVMR   Nevada City, www.kvmr.org, 530-265-9073. Music, talk.

92.1 KREL   Placerville, www.realcountry921.com. Country.

93.7 KHWD   Roseville, www.howard937.com. Alternative radio.

94.1 KNCO   Grass Valley, www.mystarradio.com, 530-272-3424. 80s, 90s music.

95.1 KFOK   Georgetown, www.kfok.org. Variety radio.

97.7 KHHZ   Oroville, 530-345-0021. Spanish language radio.

99.3 KLVS   Grass Valley, www.klove.com, 707-528-9236. Christian.

101.1 KHYL   Auburn, www.v101fm.com, 916-929-5325. Rhythmic oldies.

101.9 KCCL   Shingle Springs, www.kool1019.fm. 916-418-1555. Oldies.

103.3 KCEE   Grass Valley, www.kcee.fm. Talk radio.

103.9 KXCL   Yuba City, www.flash1039.com, 530-673-1600. 80s Rock.

AM

710 KFIA   Carmichael, www.kfia.com, 916-924-0710. Religious radio.

830 KNCO   Sacramento, www.knco.com, 530-272-3424. News, talk radio.

950 KAHI   Auburn, www.kahi.com, 530-885-5636. Oldies radio.

1110 KLIB   Roseville, 916-456-3288. International radio.

1410 KMYC   Marysville, 530-742-5555. Talk radio.

1450 KOBO   Yuba City, 415-978-5378. Ethnic radio.

1530 KFBK   Sacramento, www.kfbk.com, 916-576-2205. News, talk radio.

1600 KUBA   Yuba City, www.kuba1600.com, 530-673-1600. Nostalgia.

Placer County

FM

89.3 KQEI   North Highlands, www.kqed.org. Public radio.

89.5 KVMR   Nevada City, www.kvmr.org, 530-265-9073. Music, talk.

90.9 KXPR   Sacramento, www.csus.edu/npr. 916-480-5900. Classical.

91.5 KYDS   Sacramento, www.sacramento.org/voice, 916-971-7453. Public radio.

92.1 KREL   Placerville, www.realcountry921.com. Country.

92.5 KGBY   Sacramento, www.y92.com, 916-929-5325. Adult contemporary.

93.7 KHWD   Roseville, www.howard937.com. Alternative radio.

94.1 KNCO   Grass Valley, www.mystarradio.com, 530-272-3424. 80s, 90s music.

94.7 KSSJ   Fair Oaks, www.kssj.com, 916-334-7777. Smooth jazz.

95.1 KFOK   Georgetown, www.kfok.org. Variety radio.

96.1 KYMX   Sacramento, www.kymx.com, 916-923-6829. Adult contemporary.

96.9 KSEG   Sacramento, www.eagle969.com, 916-334-7777. Classic rock.

98.5 KRXQ   Sacramento, www.krxq.net, 916-334-7777. Rock.

99.3 KLVS   Grass Valley, www.klove.com, 707-528-9236. Christian.

100.5 KZZO   Sacramento, www.radiozone.com, 916-923-6800. Hot AC radio.

101.1 KHYL   Auburn, www.v101fm.com, 916-929-5325. Rhythmic oldies.

101.9 KCCL   Shingle Springs, www.kool1019.fm. 916-418-1555. Oldies.

103.3 KCEE   Grass Valley, www.kcee.fm. Talk radio.

103.5 KBMB   Sacramento, 916-440-9500. Hip hop.

103.9 KXCL   Yuba City, www.flash1039.com, 530-673-1600. 80s Rock.

104.3 KRRE   Davis, 916-646-4000. Spanish radio.

105.1 KNCI   Sacramento, www.kncifm.com, 916-338-9200. Country.

106.5 KWOD   Sacramento, www.kwod.net, 916-448-5000. Alternative radio.

107.9 KDND   Sacramento www.endonline.com, 916-334-7777. Top 40.

AM

650 KSTE   Rancho Cordova, www.talk650kste.com, 916-576-2113. Talk, news.

710 KFIA   Carmichael, www.kfia.com, 916-924-0710. Religious radio.

830 KNCO   Sacramento, www.knco.com, 530-272-3424. News, talk radio.

950 KAHI   Auburn, www.kahi.com, 530-885-5636. Oldies radio.

1110 KLIB   Roseville, 916-456-3288. International radio.

1140 KHTK   Sacramento, www.khtkam.com, 916-338-9200. Sports radio.

1210 KEBR   Rocklin, www.familyradio.com, 916-641-8191. Gospel.

1240 KSQR   Sacramento, www.airamericaradio.com, 916-641-1043. Talk radio.

1320 KCTC   Sacramento, 916-334-7777, Nostalgia.

1380 KTKZ   Sacramento, www.ktkz.com, 916-924-0710. Talk radio.

1450 KOBO   Yuba City, 415-978-5378. Ethnic radio.

1470 KIID   Sacramento, www.radiodisney.com, 916-780-1470. Children's radio.

1530 KFBK   Sacramento, www.kfbk.com, 916-576-2205. News, talk radio.

1600 KUBA   Yuba City, www.kuba1600.com, 530-673-1600. Nostalgia.

1620 KSMH   Auburn, www.ihradio.org/stations/ksmh, 530-584-5700. Religious.

El Dorado County

FM

89.3 KQEI   North Highlands, www.kqed.org. Public radio.

89.5 KVMR   Nevada City, www.kvmr.org, 530-265-9073. Music, talk.

90.9 KXPR   Sacramento, www.csus.edu/npr. 916-480-5900. Classical.

91.5 KYDS   Sacramento, www.sacramento.org/voice, 916-971-7453. Public radio.

92.1 KREL   Placerville, www.realcountry921.com. Country.

92.5 KGBY   Sacramento, www.y92.com, 916-929-5325. Adult contemporary.

93.7 KHWD   Roseville, www.howard937.com. Alternative radio.

94.1 KNCO   Grass Valley, www.mystarradio.com, 530-272-3424. 80s, 90s music.

94.3 KOSL   Jackson, www.sol943.com. Spanish radio.

94.7 KSSJ   Fair Oaks, www.kssj.com, 916-334-7777. Smooth jazz.

95.1 KFOK   Georgetown, www.kfok.org. Variety radio.

95.9 KBYN   Arnold, 209-883-8760. Spanish radio.

96.9 KSEG   Sacramento, www.eagle969.com, 916-334-7777. Classic rock.

98.5 KRXQ   Sacramento, www.krxq.net, 916-334-7777. Rock.

99.3 KLVS   Grass Valley, www.klove.com, 707-528-9236. Christian.

100.5 KZZO   Sacramento, www.radiozone.com, 916-923-6800. Hot AC radio.

101.1 KHYL   Auburn, www.v101fm.com, 916-929-5325. Rhythmic oldies.

101.9 KCCL   Shingle Springs, www.kool1019.fm. 916-418-1555. Oldies.

103.3 KCEE   Grass Valley, www.kcee.fm. Talk radio.

103.5 KBMB   Sacramento, 916-440-9500. Hip hop.

103.7 KWLK   Valley Springs, www.calvarychapel.com. Religious.

105.1 KNCI   Sacramento, www.kncifm.com, 916-338-9200. Country.

106.5 KWOD   Sacramento, www.kwod.net, 916-448-5000. Alternative radio.

107.9 KDND   Sacramento www.endonline.com, 916-334-7777. Top 40.

AM

650 KSTE   Rancho Cordova, www.talk650kste.com, 916-576-2113. Talk, news.

710 KFIA   Carmichael, www.kfia.com, 916-924-0710. Religious radio.

830 KNCO   Sacramento, www.knco.com, 530-272-3424. News, talk radio.

950 KAHI   Auburn, www.kahi.com, 530-885-5636. Oldies radio.

1110 KLIB   Roseville, 916-456-3288. International radio.

1140 KHTK   Sacramento, www.khtkam.com, 916-338-9200. Sports radio.

1210 KEBR   Rocklin, www.familyradio.com, 916-641-8191. Gospel.

1240 KSQR   Sacramento, www.airamericaradio.com, 916-641-1043. Talk radio.

1470 KIID   Sacramento, www.radiodisney.com, 916-780-1470. Children's radio.

1530 KFBK   Sacramento, www.kfbk.com, 916-576-2205. News, talk radio.

1620 KSMH   Auburn, www.ihradio.org/stations/ksmh, 530-584-5700. Religious radio.

Amador County

FM

90.1 KYCC   Stockton, www.kycc.org, 209-477-3690. Christian college.

91.5 KYDS   Sacramento, www.sacramento.org/voice, 916-971-7453. Public radio.

91.7 KXSR   Groveland, www.csus.edu/npr, 916-480-5900. Classical.

92.1 KREL   Placerville, www.realcountry921.com. Country.

92.7 KZSQ   Sonora, www.kzsqfm.com, 209-533-1450. Adult contemporary.

93.5 KKBN   Twain Harte, www.kkbnfm.com, 209-533-1450. Country.

93.7 KHWD   Roseville, www.howard937.com. Alternative radio.

94.3 KOSL   Jackson, www.sol943.com. Spanish radio.

94.7 KSSJ   Fair Oaks, www.kssj.com, 916-334-7777. Smooth jazz.

95.1 KFOK   Georgetown, www.kfok.org. Variety radio.

95.9 KBYN   Arnold, 209-883-8760. Spanish radio.

97.7 KWIN   Lodi, www.kwin.com, 209-476-1230. Top 40 radio.

98.5 KRXQ   Sacramento, www.krxq.net, 916-334-7777. Rock.

99.3 KJOY   Stockton, www.993kjoy.com, 209-476-1230. Adult contemporary.

100.1 KQOD   Stockton, www.megajamminoldies.com, 209-551-1306. Oldies.

100.5 KZZO   Sacramento, www.radiozone.com, 916-923-6800. Hot AC radio.

101.1 KHYL   Auburn, www.v101fm.com, 916-929-5325. Rhythmic oldies.

101.9 KCCL   Shingle Springs, www.kool1019.fm. 916-418-1555. Oldies.

103.7 KWLK   Valley Springs, www.calvarychapel.com. Religious.

105.1 KNCI   Sacramento, www.kncifm.com, 916-338-9200. Country.

105.5 KRVR   Copperopolis, www.krvr.com, 209-544-1055. Smooth jazz.

106.1 KCFA   Arnold, 916-686-2255. Spanish language radio.

106.5 KWOD   Sacramento, www.kwod.net, 916-448-5000. Alternative radio.

AM

650 KSTE   Rancho Cordova, www.talk650kste.com, 916-576-2113. Talk, news.

770 KCBC   Riverbank, 209-847-7700. Religious radio.

950 KAHI   Auburn, www.kahi.com, 530-885-5636. Oldies radio.

1110 KLIB   Roseville, 916-456-3288. International radio.

1140 KHTK   Sacramento, www.khtkam.com, 916-338-9200. Sports radio.

1210 KEBR   Rocklin, www.familyradio.com, 916-641-8191. Gospel.

1230 **KWG**   Stockton, www.ihradio.org, 209-462-8307. Religious.

1420 **KSTN**   Stockton, www.kstn.net, 209-948-5786. Oldies.

1450 **KVML**   Sonora, www.kvmlam.com, 209-533-1450. Talk radio.

1570 **KCVR**   Lodi, 209-474-0154. Spanish radio.

Calaveras County

FM

90.1 **KYCC**   Stockton, www.kycc.org, 209-477-3690. Christian college.

91.5 **KYDS**   Sacramento, www.sacramento.org/voice, 916-971-7453. Public radio.

91.7 **KXSR**   Groveland, www.csus.edu/npr, 916-480-5900. Classical.

92.1 **KREL**   Placerville, www.realcountry921.com. Country.

92.7 **KZSQ**   Sonora, www.kzsqfm.com, 209-533-1450. Adult contemporary.

93.5 **KKBN**   Twain Harte, www.kkbnfm.com, 209-533-1450. Country.

94.3 **KOSL**   Jackson, www.sol943.com. Spanish radio.

95.1 **KHOP**   Oakdale, www.khop.com, 209-766-5000. Top-40 radio.

95.9 **KBYN**   Arnold, 209-883-8760. Spanish radio.

97.7 **KWIN**   Lodi, www.kwin.com, 209-476-1230. Top 40 radio.

98.5 **KRXQ**   Sacramento, www.krxq.net, 916-334-7777. Rock.

99.3 **KJOY**   Stockton, www.993kjoy.com, 209-476-1230. Adult contemporary.

100.1 **KQOD**   Stockton, www.megajamminoldies.com, 209-551-1306. Oldies.

100.5 **KZZO**   Sacramento, www.radiozone.com, 916-923-6800. Hot AC radio.

102.3 **KJSN**   Modesto, www.sunny102fm.com, 209-551-1306. Adult contemporary.

103.7 **KWLK**   Valley Springs, www.calvarychapel.com. Religious.

105.1 **KNCI**   Sacramento, www.kncifm.com, 916-338-9200. Country.

105.5 **KRVR**   Copperopolis, www.krvr.com, 209-544-1055. Smooth jazz.

106.1 **KCFA**   Arnold, 916-686-2255. Spanish language radio.

106.5 **KWOD**   Sacramento, www.kwod.net, 916-448-5000. Alternative radio.

AM

650 **KSTE**   Rancho Cordova, www.talk650kste.com, 916-576-2113. Talk, news.

770 **KCBC**   Riverbank, 209-847-7700. Religious radio.

860 **KTBR**   Modesto, 559-526-8600. News, talk radio.

970 **KESP**   Modesto, www.espnradio970.com, 209-766-5000. Sports.

1110 **KLIB**   Roseville, 916-456-3288. International radio.

1140 KHTK   Sacramento, www.khtkam.com, 916-338-9200. Sports radio.

1210 KEBR   Rocklin, www.familyradio.com, 916-641-8191. Gospel.

1230 KWG   Stockton, www.ihradio.org, 209-462-8307. Religious.

1280 KUYL   Stockton, www.lighthouse1280.com, 209-551-1306. Talk.

1360 KFIV   Modesto, www.kfiv1360.com, 209-551-1306. Talk radio.

1420 KSTN   Stockton, www.kstn.net, 209-948-5786. Oldies.

1450 KVML   Sonora, www.kvmlam.com, 209-533-1450. Talk radio.

1570 KCVR   Lodi, 209-474-0154. Spanish radio.

Tuolumne County

FM

88.3 KLVN   Livingston, www.klove.com, 707-528-9236. Christian contemporary.

88.7 KMPO   Modesto, www.radiobilingue.org, 559-455-5777. Spanish radio.

89.9 KEFR   Le Grand, www.familyradio.com, 209-389-4659. Religious.

91.7 KXSR   Groveland, www.csus.edu/npr, 916-480-5900. Classical.

92.7 KZSQ   Sonora, www.kzsqfm.com, 209-533-1450. Adult contemporary.

93.5 KKBN   Twain Harte, www.kkbnfm.com, 209-533-1450. Country.

94.1 KBKY   Merced, www.foxsportsmerced.com. Sports radio.

94.3 KOSL   Jackson, www.sol943.com. Spanish radio.

95.1 KHOP   Oakdale, www.khop.com, 209-766-5000. Top-40 radio.

95.9 KBYN   Arnold, 209-883-8760. Spanish radio.

96.3 KUBB   Mariposa, www.kubb.com, 209-383-7900. Country.

97.5 KABX   Merced, 209-723-2191. Oldies radio.

98.3 KWNN   Turlock www.kwin.com, 209-476-1230. Top-40 radio.

99.1 KTUO   Sonora,. K-12 radio.

99.9 KCIV   Mount Bullion, www.bottradionetwork.com, 209-524-8999. Religious radio.

101.5 KAMB   Merced, www.celebrationradio.com, 209-723-1015. Christian.

102.3 KJSN   Modesto, www.sunny102fm.com, 209-551-1306. Adult contemporary.

103.7 KWLK   Valley Springs, www.calvarychapel.com. Religious.

103.9 KDJK   Mariposa, www.104thehawk.com, 209-572-0104. Classic rock.

104.7 KHTN   Merced, 209-383-7900. Top-40 radio.

105.5 KRVR   Copperopolis, www.krvr.com, 209-544-1055. Smooth jazz.

106.1 KCFA   Arnold, 916-686-2255. Spanish language radio.

106.3 KHPO   Merced, www.hippo1063.com. Classic hits.

AM

770 KCBC   Riverbank, 209-847-7700. Religious radio.

860 KTBR   Modesto, 559-526-8600. News, talk radio.

970 KESP   Modesto, www.espnradio970.com, 209-766-5000. Sports.

1360 KFIV   Modesto, www.kfiv1360.com, 209-551-1306. Talk radio.

1390 KLOC   Turlock, 209-521-5562. Nostalgia radio.

1450 KVML   Sonora, www.kvmlam.com, 209-533-1450. Talk radio.

TELEVISION

The Sierra Nevada foothills, including the Gold Country, are served by a number of cable and satellite television companies. Additionally, there are a number of independent stations serving specific areas. Virtually all hotels, motels, and B&Bs provide either cable or satellite television access. Check local listings for your favorite programs.

REAL ESTATE

Very often a visit to Lake Tahoe and the northern High Sierra evokes a desire to actually live in the region. Putting the year-round scenery and outdoor adventure in your own backyard is a natural response. However, if you are looking at buying property in the Tahoe Basin or the Sierra foothills, be prepared for some serious sticker shock. The vast majority of the region is federal property, and the private parcels that are available are not inexpensive.

However, on the east side of the Sierra Nevada, the situation is a little different. Housing and land prices are much more affordable in the Reno and Carson Valley areas. As a matter of fact, in the past few years, Carson Valley has become a haven for retirees.

If the possibility of relocating to this region is something you want to explore, the guide below is a good place to start. These Web sites offer a wealth of demographic and price information. And if you get serious about purchasing a home or property, be sure to hire a local realtor, one who is familiar with housing values, available services, and local building codes.

State Associations

California Association of Realtors, www.car.org, 213-739-8200, 525 S. Virgil Ave., Los Angeles, CA.

Nevada Association of Realtors, www.nvar.org, 1-800-748-5526, 760 Margrave Drive, Suite 200, Reno, NV.

Local Associations

Amador County Association of Realtors, www.amadorrealtors.com, 209 223-3874, 557 South Highway 49, Suite 6, Jackson, CA.

El Dorado County Association of Realtors, www.edcar.org, 530-676-0161, or 916-933-3223, 4096 Mother Lode Drive, Shingle Springs, CA.

Calaveras County Association of Realtors, www.calaverasrealtors.com, 209-736-4600, 1270 Suzanne Drive Suite B, Angels Camp, CA.

Nevada County Board of Realtors, www.ncbor.com, 530-272-2627, 336 Crown Point Circle, Grass Valley, CA.

Placer County Association of Realtors, www.pcaor.com, 916-624-8271, 4750 Grove St., Rocklin, CA.

South Tahoe Association of Realtors, www.staor.org, 530-541-7007, 2307 James Ave., South Lake Tahoe, CA.

Sierra Nevada Association of Realtors, www.sierranvar.com, 775-885-7200, 300 S. Curry St., Carson City, NV.

Tahoe Sierra Board of Realtors, www.tahoemls.com, 530-583-0275, 1810 Squaw Valley Rd., Olympic Valley, CA.

Tuolumne County Association of Realtors, www.tcrealtors.org, 209-532-3432, 14195 Tuolumne Rd., Sonora, CA.

TOURIST INFORMATION

All of the communities throughout this region have associations eager to share information beyond the scope of this book. By all means, contact these bureaus and they will happily send you piles of glossy brochures and pamphlets filled with gorgeous photos and heaps of information extolling the bounty to be found in their area. Of course, this information should be read with a critical eye. After all, these folks are professionals in the art of selling you on their area.

Lake Tahoe

Incline Village Crystal Bay Visitors Bureau, www.gotahoenorth.com, 775-832-1606 or 1-800-GoTahoe, 969 Tahoe Blvd., Incline Village, NV.

Lake Tahoe South Shore Chamber of Commerce, www.tahoechamber.org, 775-588-1728, 169 Highway 50, 3rd Floor, Stateline, NV.

Lake Tahoe Visitors Authority, www.bluelaketahoe.com, 1-800-AT-TAHOE or 530-544-5050, 1156 Ski Run Blvd., South Lake Tahoe, CA.

North Lake Tahoe Chamber of Commerce, www.northlaketahoechamber.com, 530-581-6900, PO Box 884, Tahoe City, CA.

North Lake Tahoe Resort Association, www.gotahoenorth.com, 1-888-434-1262 or 530-583-3494, P.O. Box 1757, Tahoe City, CA.

South Lake Tahoe Chamber of Commerce, www.tahoeinfo.com, 530-541-5255, 3066 Lake Tahoe Blvd., South Lake Tahoe, CA.

Tahoe City Visitors Information Center, www.gotahoenorth.com, 530-581-6900, 380 North Lake Blvd., Tahoe City, CA.

Truckee Donner Chamber of Commerce, www.truckee.com, 530-587-2757, 10065 Donner Pass Rd., Truckee, CA.

Reno, Carson Valley & Virginia City

Carson City Chamber of Commerce, www.carsoncitychamber.com, 775-882-1565, 1900 Carson St., Carson City, NV.

Carson City Convention & Visitors' Bureau, www.carson-city.org, 1-800-NEVADA-1 or 775-687-7410, 1900 Carson St., Suite 200, Carson City, NV.

Carson Valley Chamber of Commerce & Visitors Authority, www.carsonvalleynv.org, 1-800-727-7677 or 775-782-8144, 1512 US Highway 395 N., Suite 1, Gardnerville, NV.

Reno-Sparks Chamber of Commerce, www.reno-sparkschamber.org, 775-337-3030, 1 E First Street, 16th Floor, Reno, NV.

Reno-Sparks Convention & Visitors Authority, www.renolaketahoe.com, 1-800-367-7366 or 775-827-7366, 300 N. Center St., Reno, NV.

Sparks Chamber of Commerce, www.sparkschamber.org, 775-358-1976, 831 Victorian Ave., Sparks, NV.

Virginia City Chamber of Commerce, www.vcnevada.com, 775-847-0311, V & T Railroad Car, 131 South C St., Virginia City, NV.

Virginia City Convention & Tourism Authority, www.virginiacity-nv.org, 775-847-7500, P.O. Box 920, Virginia City, NV.

Gold Country (North to South)

Sierra County

Sierra County Chamber of Commerce, www.sierracountychamber.net, 1-800-200-4949, P.O. Box 436, Sierra City, CA.

Nevada County

Grass Valley/Nevada County Chamber of Commerce, www.grassvalleychamber.com, 1-800-655-4667 or 530-273-4667, 248 Mill St., Grass Valley, CA.

Nevada City Chamber of Commerce, www.nevadacitychamber.com, 1-800-655-6569 or 530-265-2692, 132 Main St., Nevada City, CA.

Rough & Ready Chamber of Commerce, 530-272-4320, P.O. Box 801, Rough And Ready, CA.

Placer County

Auburn Chamber of Commerce, www.auburnchamber.net, 530-885-5616, 601 Lincoln Way, Auburn, CA.

Foresthill Divide Chamber of Commerce, www.foresthillchamber.org, 530-367-2474, 24600 Main Street, #A, Foresthill, CA.

Placer County Visitor & Tourist Info Center, www.visitplacer.com, 530-887-2111, 13411 Lincoln Way, Newcastle, CA.

El Dorado County

Coloma-Lotus Chamber of Commerce, www.colomalotus.com, P.O. Box 608, Coloma, CA.

El Dorado County Chamber of Commerce, www.eldoradocounty.org, 530-621-5885, 542 Main St., Placerville, CA.

El Dorado County Visitors Authority, www.visit-eldorado.com, 1-800-457-6279 or 530-621-5885, 542 Main St., Placerville, CA.

Amador County

Amador County Chamber of Commerce and Visitors Bureau, www.amadorcounty chamber.com, 571 South Highway 49, Jackson, CA.

Calaveras County

Calaveras County Chamber of Commerce, www.calaveras.org, 209-736-2580, 1211 So. Main St., Angels Camp, CA.

Calaveras Visitors Bureau, www.visitcalaveras.org, 209-736-0049, 1192 South Main St., Angels Camp, CA.

Tuolumne County

Tuolumne County Chamber of Commerce, www.tcchamber.com, 1-877-532-4212 or 209-532-4212, 222 South Shepherd St., Sonora, CA.

Tuolumne County Visitors Bureau, www.tcvb.com, 1-800-446-1333 or 209-533-4420, 542 W. Stockton Rd., Sonora, CA.

U.S. Forest Service

Tahoe National Forest, www.fs.fed.us/r5/tahoe/aboutus, 530-265-4531, 631 Coyote St., Nevada City, CA.

Eldorado National Forest, www.fs.fed.us/r5/eldorado, 530-622-5061, 100 Forni Rd., Placerville, CA.

Stanislaus National Forest, www.fs.fed.us/r5/stanislaus/about, 209-532-3671, 19777 Greenley Rd., Sonora, CA.

General Index

Lodging by Price

Lake Tahoe

$49 and up
Tahoe Biltmore Resort & Casino, 43

$59 and up
Horizon Casino Resort, 52
Lakeside Inn and Casino, 52

$69 and up
Fireside Lodge Bed & Breakfast, 47
Harrah's Lake Tahoe, 50
Harveys Resort & Casino, 50, 52
Montbleu Resort Casino & Spa, 52

$85 and up
The Block, 48
Donner Lake Village Resort, 56
River Ranch Lodge, 54
Tahoma Meadows Bed & Breakfast Cottages, 43

$109 and up
Cal-Neva Resort Hotel and Casino, 41, 43
Inn by the Lake, 47–48
Red Wolf Inn at Squaw Valley, 49
Village at Squaw Valley USA, 50

$125 and up
Brockway Springs, 44
Gabrielli House Bed & Breakfast, 44
Inn at Heavenly Bed & Breakfast, 47
Olympic Village Inn at Squaw Valley, 48–49
Ridge Tahoe, 52–53
Rockwood Lodge Bed & Breakfast Inn, 43
Tahoe Lakeshore Lodge & Spa, 48

$139 and up
Cedar House Sport Hotel, 55
Fantasy Inn & Wedding Chapel, 45, 47
Squaw Valley Lodge, 50

$158 and up
The Cottage Inn of Lake Tahoe, 54

$165 and up
Chaney House A Lakefront Guesthouse, 53
The Plumpjack Squaw Valley Inn, 49

$179 and up
Embassy Suites Lake Tahoe Hotel and Ski Resort, 45
Resort at Squaw Creek, 49

$200 and up
Black Bear Inn Bed and Breakfast, 44–45
Hyatt Regency Lake Tahoe, 44
The Shore House at Lake Tahoe, 54–55

Reno, Virginia City, and Carson Valley

$30 and up
Bordertown Casino and RV Resort, 111
Fitzgeralds Casino & Hotel, 112

$45 and up
Atlantis Casino Resort Spa, 109–10
The Gold Hill Hotel, 118

$50 and up
Carson Nugget, 104–5
Circus Circus Reno Hotel & Casino, 111

$59 and up
Carson Valley Inn Hotel Casino RV Resort, 109
Eldorado Hotel Casino, Reno, 111–12
Grand Sierra Resort and Casino, 112
John Ascuaga's Nugget Casino Resort, 113
Peppermill Hotel Casino, 113–14
The Plaza Hotel and Conference Center, 105–6
Silver Legacy Resort Casino, 114

$80 and up
Edith Palmer's Country Inn, 116–17
Gold Dust West, 105

$99 and up
Boomtown Casino Hotel, 110–11
Deer Run Ranch Bed & Breakfast, 105
Genoa House 1872 Inn, 107
Siena Hotel Spa Casino, 114–15
Walker River Resort, 116
Wildflower Village Bed & Breakfast, 115

$115 and up
Bliss Bungalow . . . An Inn, 103–4

$125 and up
Cottonwood Creek Farm Bed & Breakfast, 106–7
Seven Mile Canyon Guest Ranch, 117

$135 and up
Chollar Mansion, 116

$140 and up
David Walley's Resort, Hot Springs & Spa, 109
Wild Rose Inn Bed & Breakfast, 108

Gold Country

$55 and up
The Leger Historic Hotel, 177

$60 and up
St. George Hotel, 186

Dining by Price

Inexpensive: Up to $15
Moderate: $15 to $30
Expensive: $30 to $50
Very Expensive: $50 and up

Lake Tahoe

Inexpensive to Moderate

Moderate

Moderate to Expensive

Expensive

Reno, Virginia City, and Carson Valley

Inexpensive

Inexpensive to Moderate

Moderate

Moderate to Expensive

Expensive

Gold Country

Inexpensive

Inexpensive to Moderate

Moderate

Moderate to Expensive

Expensive

Very Expensive

Dining by Cuisine